Copyright 2025 by RE O'Malley

NEIGHBORHOOD
Stories from Boston's Chinatown

1988 to 2001

THE STREETS

CHINATOWN IS THE STARTING POINT — a neighborhood where Chinese immigrants live and work surrounded by people who share the same language and culture.

For decades, Boston's Chinatown has helped Chinese immigrants ease the transition to an American life that often feels distant and impenetrable.

In the 1870s Chinese immigrants migrated to Boston from the western United States to escape discrimination and limited opportunities.

Chinatown's original settlement was just a few blocks from the Chinatown gate — a proud reminder of the distinctive traditions and beliefs Chinese immigrants carry with them to Boston.

An elaborately designed gate or paifang marks the entrance to a Chinese city's most important precinct — to a city within a city.

Stretching from Washington Street to Hudson Street, from Marginal Road to Boylston Street near downtown Boston, Chinatown today is a mix of businesses and residences, of 19th century row houses and high-rise apartment buildings.

On most days the neighborhood's streets are bustling. Workers push dollies loaded with flapping fish along restaurant row.

Graffiti-covered trucks from New York City haul restaurant and market supplies to shops and restaurants. Workers wait for vans to carry them to restaurant jobs in the suburbs.

Restaurants, bakeries, and shops line the ground floor of ageing brick buildings. Fish swim in giant storefront aquariums, roast duck hang from racks in shop windows, moon cakes glow in glass cases.

The heart of the neighborhood's commercial district is Harrison Avenue, Beach Street, Hudson Street, and Kneeland Street.

The sidewalks are often blackened and slippery with discarded grease from restaurant fryers. The city installed new sidewalks in the 1990s but in no time they were once again caked with grease.

In a small park next to the Chinatown gate, street people gather to drink and carouse as Chinese residents watch from nearby benches.

The residents seldom complain about the homeless people from outside the neighborhood who take over the park, or ask the city to take action against them.

Locked inside their private worlds, talking quietly in Chinese to their companions, they seem unfazed by the commotion that surrounds them.

Nineteenth century row houses line sections of Tyler Street and other nearby streets.

Some residents live in these older buildings but most residents live in high-rise apartment buildings south of Kneeland Street.

In the early part of the 20th century Chinatown's southern district was a thriving Syrian neighborhood, but by the turn of the century only a handful of Syrians still lived and owned property there.

Chinatown residents share the neighborhood with the New England Medical Center and Tufts University's medical schools.

Chinatown has often been in conflict with the institutions — while the Chinatown community seeks available neighborhood land to expand housing, open space, and community services, the institutions want the same land to expand their facilities.

In the 1990s a truce is called between the competing factions. Both develop master plans for the neighborhood and reach agreements on how the remaining land will be used.

The city, which controls much of the available land, is usually the broker in these discussions.

Along Washington Street, Chinatown meets the remnants of the Combat Zone, the city's adult entertainment zone.

When urban renewal in the 1960s led to the razing of Scollay Square and the West End, the adult entertainment district was relocated to the edge of Chinatown.

On weekend nights, streetwalkers lure customers at the corner of Beach Street and Harrison Avenue.

Car engines rev, women lean into the windows of idling cars, the street has the air of a carnival but with sinister undertones.

The edge of Chinatown is a haven for low-level street crime. Drug dealers prowl nearby Essex Street.

Women on their way to Chinatown often complain about being taunted by men in front of the Naked i lounge.

The corner of Washington and Essex streets has a gritty, threatening tone.

The police initiate weekend sting operations to arrest Johns and prostitutes, while the Chinese community organizes demonstrations against adult businesses.

Neighborhood activists ask property owners to refuse to rent or sell buildings

to X-rated businesses.

At least one Chinese property owner sells a building to a porn entrepreneur despite community opposition.

Rising real estate values and development pressures gradually force adult entertainment out of the district.

In the late 1990s, construction begins on the mixed-use Millennium Place high-rise complex on Washington Street.

Buildings housing the x-rated Naked i and PilgrimTheater are razed as a first step toward redevelopment.

Morning on Beach Street

THE CORNER OF BEACH STREET and Harrison Avenue is the busiest intersection in Chinatown.

On summer mornings, restaurant workers stand on the sidewalk clutching coffee cups, smoking cigarettes, talking quietly.

On winter mornings they crowd inside the steamy Maxum Café, solemnly peering through the storefront windows at passersby moving along Beach Street.

The workers are originally from China, Taiwan, and Hong Kong. Most are men but women are also among them now.

They speak Toisanese or Fujianese, Cantonese or Mandarin. Many have come from Chinese villages and have little education. Some were teachers and engineers in China but lack the language skills to do the same work here.

The Chinatown economy offers the opportunity to take home a decent wage each week, but there's a price to be paid for it.

The Double Rich Café is bustling this morning. Restaurant workers converge on the counter to order coffee, tea, and Chinese pastries — crispy buns, roast pork buns, ham and egg buns.

The workers shout out their orders at the same time. Customers impatiently push to the front of the line to be waited on, waving dollar bills to get the counter woman's attention. They seldom patiently wait in line.

In Chinatown it doesn't matter if you wait in line or not because everyone is pushing just like you to get to the front.

In Chinatown, no one pays much attention to the pushing. No one seems to mind.

The workers make their purchases and squeeze into booths to wait for company vans to take them to their jobs in suburban Chinese restaurants.

When the morning rush is over, Wai Li, a cashier at the cafe, settles into a booth to take a break.

She says she came to the United States from Guangzhou, China, in 1989, marrying a man who had been living in the U.S. since 1968.
Like many immigrant Chinese men, her husband is a cook in a Chinese restaurant.
A friend introduced her to her husband and they were married in China in the 1980s.

"My husband's brother and sister and mother are in Boston," she says, "my mother and father are here too. They live with me in our house [in Charlestown]. Six people live in the house now.
My husband's father lives with my husband's sister. I have an older brother in Guangzhou and a brother in Hong Kong who are waiting in line to come here.

Why did I come here – I came here because you have freedom here.

I have two children – a boy and a girl. My daughter was born here, but my son was born in China.
When I first came to the U.S. I didn't work because I didn't have anybody to help me take care of the children.
Working here is not very hard, not very easy. I work eight hours a day, but I only work hard for three hours.

My life in America is good – freedom! freedom! – there's no freedom in China...here there's freedom.
All American citizens can register to vote but in China you can't register to vote.

No...I don't vote (she smiles...hides her face in shame).

I'm a citizen, but I don't vote...I don't know enough English....there are a lot of words I don't know.
I want to learn more English so I can find an American job, a job with a good vacation.
In Chinatown you get no vacation...just Christmas...July 4th...no other days off... no holidays.

I want to work in the Post Office. I'd like a government job. There are no layoffs in a government job.

But I need to study English and computers to get a job in the post office.

It's hard to get to the class in Chinatown. Quincy School has an English class at night but the bus is gone by 7:35. If you miss the bus you have to wait an hour for the next one.

Last year I went to a training program downtown. My English was not very good but the teacher helped me and showed me how to use the computer.

I studied one year in the training program. Some students study only six months, but I needed one year. A long time!

My children are 12 and 10 now — trouble, trouble!

Sometimes when I go home from the job, I don't want to watch TV, I don't want listen to the tape or read a newspaper or an English book, I'm very tired, I'm very lazy.

I'm happy with my daughter at school, but I'm not happy with my son.

My daughter likes to study, but my son doesn't like school, he likes to play with computers and games.

I can't help him study because my English grammar is not very good.

At home we speak Chinese but my son and daughter speak English with each other.

They speak very fast. Sometimes I don't know what they are saying — lulalulala!

In Chinatown, I only speak Chinese. Some American people come in here, so I have the chance to speak English a little bit.

I don't have American friends because my English is not very good. Only the English teacher is my friend.

But my children have different friends — not just Chinese friends.

I go back to China to visit but I don't ever want to go back there to live. I just go there to play now."

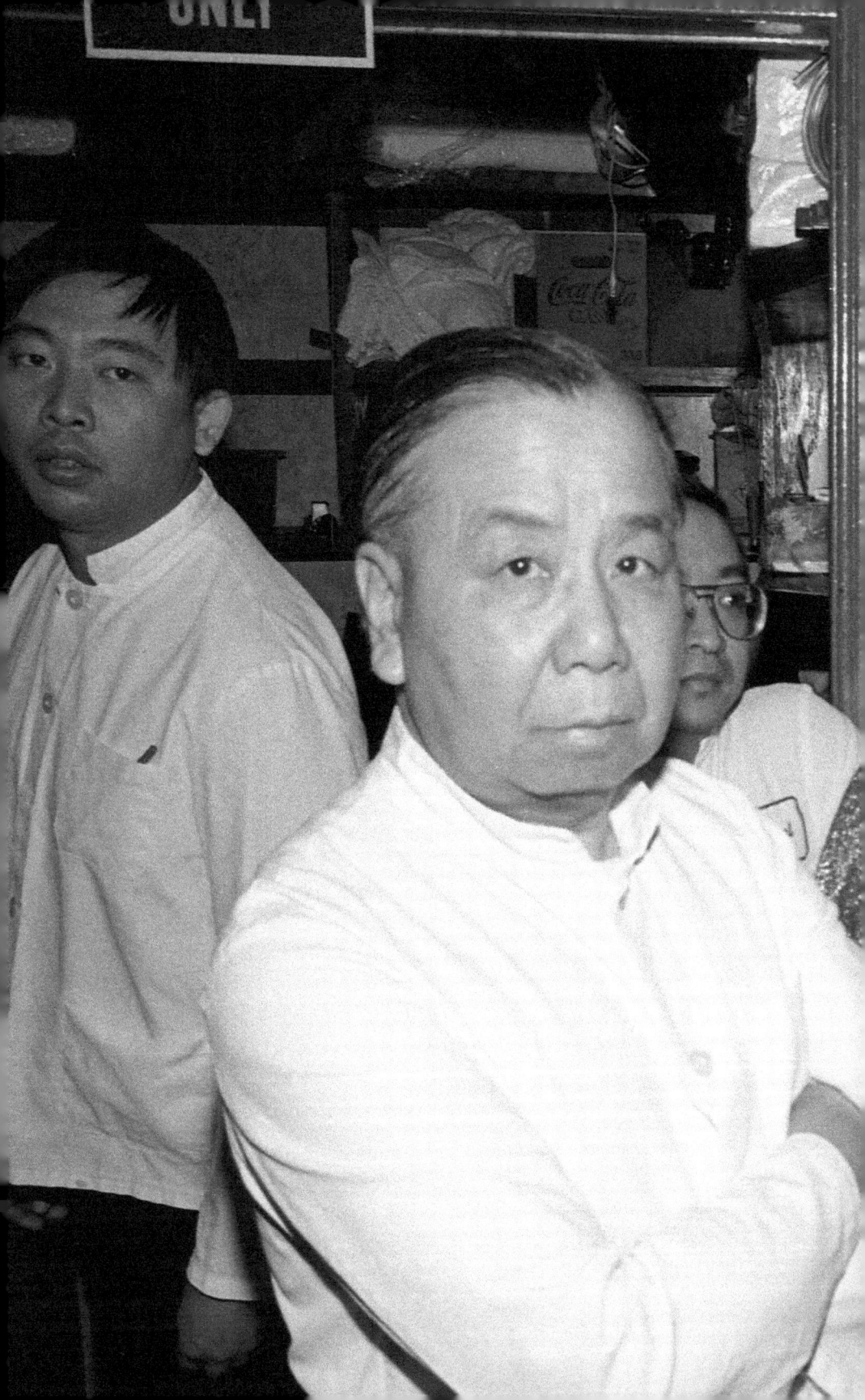

ptable
THIS WORKING LIFE

'I Just Followed the Routine'

HE HAS THE SCULPTED, deeply lined face of a longtime restaurant worker. For about 25 years he worked as a cook in Chinatown restaurants.

He's retired now and spends much of his time volunteering at the Chinese Progressive Association — a short walk from the Chinatown senior housing complex where he lives.

"I was born in China and came to the U.S. in 1972. I was 40 years old and had been living in Hong Kong. I had gone to Hong Kong in 1949 and was working as a machinist on a ship.

I was married in Guangzhou in 1951, but my wife died from throat cancer in 1962.

I have a daughter who lives in China and another who lives in Hong Kong, but they didn't want to come here. They were married and were already settled into their lives.

I worked on the boat for 15 years. I traveled around the world. But working on the ship was really hard. The waves made me feel uncomfortable all the time. The boat was not stable.

And if we had a bad captain, life could be even more difficult. Because of this I didn't really like working on the boat.

In 1972, six of us — three sailors and three machinists — jumped ship in San Francisco. We were tired of moving around and decided to settle down.

When I arrived in San Francisco, the government wasn't so strict about immigration. I applied for a social security card and I got it in one week. In 1986, I applied for amnesty and became documented.

When I came to Boston, I found work in a restaurant. I worked in Chinese restaurants for almost 25 years. I don't remember which restaurants because I worked for so many. I retired in 1991 when I was 65 years old. I had a kidney stone operation and stopped working after that.

I lived on Harvard Street in Chinatown. I usually went home at 1 o'clock in the morning and went to work the next afternoon at 2 o'clock. I had to wash the dishes, peel the shrimp, cut the pork. After that I would cook. I spent the whole day in the kitchen.

It was a hard life working in a restaurant because we didn't have a break. We had to keep working all the way through. If I finished cooking one order I would have to cook another.

The kitchen is hot and sticky. We work with knives, so it's also very dangerous.

After work I would just go home and sleep. When I woke up I would go to the restaurant and do the same thing again.

The work was hard but the pay was not that good. When I came to Boston in 1972, the salary was about $500 a month, and when I left the job in 1991 it was like $1,300 a month.

If I had been able to speak English I could have been a waiter. Being a waiter is better than working in the kitchen.

I didn't think I could get a better job in this country because I couldn't speak English. There were times when I thought about going to learn English, but I didn't have the time because I was spending all of my time working and sleeping.

Working in Chinese restaurants I didn't really need to speak English. I only stayed in Chinatown.

My only entertainment was seeing Chinese movies but I can't even do that now because there's no longer a Chinese movie theater.

I didn't go shopping outside of Chinatown because Chinatown had everything I needed.

I didn't drive but sometimes I would take the T to go outside of Chinatown to buy something. I'd only go with my friends. I would never go by myself.

I didn't really have any interest in finding out what Americans were like. I really didn't care.

But I think America is better than other countries. It's richer and easier to get a job here.

The best thing about America is the way the government treats elderly people. They treat them very well. I live in the elderly apartment now.

Before I came here I thought it would be really easy to find a job. I thought I could quickly make a lot of money. Until I got here I didn't know that working in the restaurant could be so hard.

When I first came here I thought about returning, but I decided I was too old to ever go home again.

I think if I had spent my life in China or Hong Kong, I would in some way have had more freedom. If I didn't want to work in the restaurant, I could have tried to do something else. I could have gone wherever I wanted to go because I would have known the language.

In China I could have been more involved in the life around me. I would have been able to speak up and argue with people. I could have let people know what I thought and what I wanted. But here nobody listens.

I feel the government treats people well here, but maybe I would have been happier if I had stayed in China.

But I really didn't think much about it. I just followed the routine. I went to bed. I went to work. That was it. I didn't want to think. I knew that thinking about it would be useless. Thinking about it wasn't going to change anything.

I work to eat and I eat to work — that's the meaning of my life.

These days I wake up in the morning. I either eat breakfast at home or go out to Chinatown to get something. After I eat my breakfast, I walk over to Boston Common to talk with my friends. At noontime I go back to my apartment to eat because they serve lunch there.

In the afternoon I come to CPA (the Chinese Progressive Association) to read newspapers or see if I can do something. Sometimes I help CPA send out mail.

When I was sick in 1991 I came to CPA for help. I knew the services here were free.

After I went to the hospital for treatment, I received many documents I didn't understand and CPA translated them for me.

Later in the day I return to the park. In the afternoon there will be older ladies there who can talk. We get together to talk about our past about nothing very real. We talk about our history. What else can we talk about?

I don't have any girlfriends. If I had wanted to remarry I could have done that a long time ago. I didn't have to wait until now to do it.

After I leave the Common I go home to cook dinner and then go to bed.

I am old now. I cannot do anything. I live on a retirement plan and SSI (Supplemental Security Income). The retirement money comes on the third of the month and SSI comes on the first.

I don't know what will happen tomorrow. I don't even know what will happen after I go to bed. I am old, and that's just the way it is."

'So Many Troubles'

SHE WORKS IN A SUBURBAN Chinese restaurant. Five days a week she makes a trip into Chinatown from her home in East Boston to catch the restaurant van that will take her to her job outside the city.

When she isn't working, she is a student in an office-skills training workshop in Chinatown.

She arrived in the U.S. a year ago (in the late 1990s) and is still struggling to adapt to her new country.

"In China I studied economics and worked as an accountant for 12 years. I am 49 years old and came here with my husband.

He was an automotive engineer in China but he works part-time in an auto repair company here.

My son is 20 and a university student in China. Every week I call him. He lives at the school during the week, but every weekend he stays at my mother's home.

We came here so our son could come to America. After my son takes his TOEFL test, we will help him look for a university here.

I started working last November. I work five days a week from 11 a.m. to 10 p.m. I am off on Wednesdays and Sundays.

I board the company van near Tai Tung Village. The workers on the bus often talk to me about how they don't like America or how they have so much trouble with their jobs and families — so many troubles.

Sometimes the workers are sick but they hide their illness. The workers who come from Fujian have no hope. They feel as though they haven't a future, haven't anything.

But some of the workers are happy. There are two waiters in my restaurant who are very happy. They always talk with the American customers.

At the restaurant I make salads for the salad bar. I receive $1,200 a month and am paid in both checks and cash — half and half. I don't care if I am paid by check or in cash. I don't get tips.

Working in a restaurant is hard. There's not much lifting, but we work too many hours. I'm always standing. If I were making $1,500 a month, I would be happy, but I'm paid only $1,200 because I have two days off. Other people have only one day off and get paid between $1,400 and $1,500.

The customers are mostly Americans, but a few Chinese people come in too. The restaurant makes Chinese food but it's not like the food in China. Some of the cooks here don't know the correct method, so the food is not very good.

We say the food looks dirty, as if it had been sitting there for a few days. In Chinese, we say it looks like gan dou, like dried beans in water.

I think the restaurant owner is a good person because he loves my country and helps other people. He gives some people free food and helps some students learn English and study hard.

He came from Taiwan, but he doesn't like Taiwan's government. He hopes Taiwan and Beijing will someday be united.

I think most of the restaurant workers are happy to be here because America is a more developed country than China. They like the medical care and the insurance and the technology. They can make more money here than they could in China.

I think Americans are friendly and willing to help other people, but American culture and Chinese culture are different.

Before I left China my idea of America was different from what it is now.

I thought America would be a very clean country, but when I got off the plane I saw many dirty streets. I thought, 'Oh my God, America is dirty.'

Before I left Beijing I didn't know there were so many foreigners living here. I don't think I like having so many kinds of people living together.

Many people living here have customs that are different from those of the Americans.

I have been here already about a year and three months. I think I will need to live here longer — maybe three or four years — to get used to it.

I very much miss my country because my mother, my younger sister, and my brother live in China.

In China, I had a very good job in a hotel accounting department, and it wasn't hard work.

If I get a green card or become a U.S. citizen I can look for a good job. A student visa allows me to stay here for three years, though I can get two more years if I study computer science.

My husband doesn't want to get a green card. Many times he says, 'Let's go back to China!' He doesn't like it here. He designed cars in China, but here he fixes cars.

After my son comes here maybe we will go back to China. I want him to come here to study science at a higher level. After that, he can maybe go back to China."

Long Shifts, Sweltering Kitchens, Steady Pay

WHEN CHINESE IMMIGRANTS ARRIVE in Boston, many have no choice but to find jobs in the area's booming Chinese restaurant industry.

The immigrant economy is both a savior and a bane to Chinese immigrants — a savior because it offers them jobs in America, a bane because working conditions in some of the restaurants are less than ideal.

Working in a Chinese restaurant provides a safe haven for non-English speaking immigrants who often find the mainstream world complex and threatening.

Even if they want to, most immigrants find it impossible to get good-paying jobs in the mainstream economy if they don't speak English.

The most vulnerable workers are those who are illegal and can't go to the authorities to seek redress when they're dissatisfied with their bosses.

They have no standing in American life and must take what they can get here.

The illegal workers also put added pressures on the legal workers, who could easily be replaced by undocumented workers if they demand too much from their bosses.

Guided by its own rules, the Chinese restaurant industry developed an array of financial practices designed to squeeze the maximum amount of profit out of its businesses.

Like many small business owners in America, the Chinese entrepreneur isn't eager to pay taxes if he can finagle his way around them.

He's also in no hurry to provide workers with benefits such as health insurance or workers' compensation.

A worker in a Chinese restaurant almost never receives health insurance, relying instead on free health care or health insurance through a wife's mainstream job.

The workers themselves are also in no hurry to pay taxes. Those who came from China aren't accustomed to having the government take such a large chunk of money out of their paychecks.

Many immigrants also find it more difficult to put their finances on a more stable footing if they are forced to pay additional taxes and report their full income when applying for affordable housing and other income-eligible benefits.

In the past the mainstream world turned a blind eye to many of these practices, in part because it was difficult to penetrate Chinatown and its business practices.

Mainstream officials only bother to venture into Chinatown if they think activities there are affecting the non-Chinese population; otherwise they simply ignore the Chinese community.

It isn't easy for the Chinese Progressive Association to take a public stand and pressure the Chinese business community to uphold basic labor standards in the late 1990s.

Subtle pressure is exerted in Chinatown to keep community secrets within the community.

In fact, a few years after the Progressive Association takes a public stand on the issue, it reverts to a less aggressive approach after members of the business community cautioned that it was unwise to air the community's "dirty laundry" in public.

At the time, though, the Progressive Association launches an effort to focus on working conditions in Chinese restaurants and other businesses where Chinese are employed.

Besides restaurants, many new immigrants find work in garment shops, hotels, institutional food services, and factories.

Immigrants sometimes complain about racial discrimination and unfair treatment in some non-Chinese businesses, but they often must contend with an array of illegal practices in some Chinese-owned businesses.

Workers in many Chinese-run businesses, for example, are not paid overtime rates for hours worked in excess of 40 hours, says Lydia Lowe, director of the Progressive Association's Workers Center.

Many Chinese restaurant workers also end up working six 10-hour days per week. "I think there are a lot of standard practices in the restaurants that are illegal," says Lowe.

While state law exempts restaurants from overtime regulations, federal law requires compliance, she says.

The CPA has investigated instances in which restaurant owners have failed to pay workers on time or withheld wages when their businesses ran into financial troubles.

Restaurants are required by law to pay workers within five days of the end of the work period, she says.

"There are a lot of times when the owner will say, 'I'm short of money. I can't pay you this month,'" says Lowe. "We've seen cases where this has dragged on for months."

In the late 1990s, a group of unpaid Chinatown workers sought back wages from the Grand China Restaurant, which ran into financial troubles and closed.
When the Grand China began to falter, several partners bailed out of the business, leaving David Wong to struggle alone to keep the restaurant afloat.
Wong, who owns the Washington Street building in which the restaurant was located, was forced to close the restaurant, which was rumored to be the largest in the city.

While Wong said his financial troubles made it impossible for him to pay his workers and suppliers, the payments were also apparently delayed because the three partners couldn't agree on who was responsible for the wages.

Even though Wong's partners withdraw from the business, their names remain on the company's legal documents, according to the Progressive Association.

Wong eventually brings in a new partner and reopens the restaurant as the Emperor's Garden. Although the Grand China workers agree to work for the Emperor's Garden, they continue to seek their back wages.
About 20 Grand China workers eventually file a complaint with the state Attorney General's office over the unpaid wages.

Immigrant workers are also affected by the practice of paying wages under the table. Most Chinese restaurants pay workers a portion of their pay by check and the rest in cash. The owners follow this practice to reduce their declared income and taxes.
In the past, many workers preferred to be paid in cash so they wouldn't have to pay taxes.
But an increasing number of workers now are seeing the benefits of being paid by check.

Workers paid under the table may not receive full Social Security benefits when they retire and may also fail to qualify for full unemployment and health insurance if they are laid off, says Lowe.
They may also lack proof of income if they need to apply for Workers' Compensation.

Under-the-table workers may also find it difficult to sponsor a family member who wants to immigrate to the U.S.

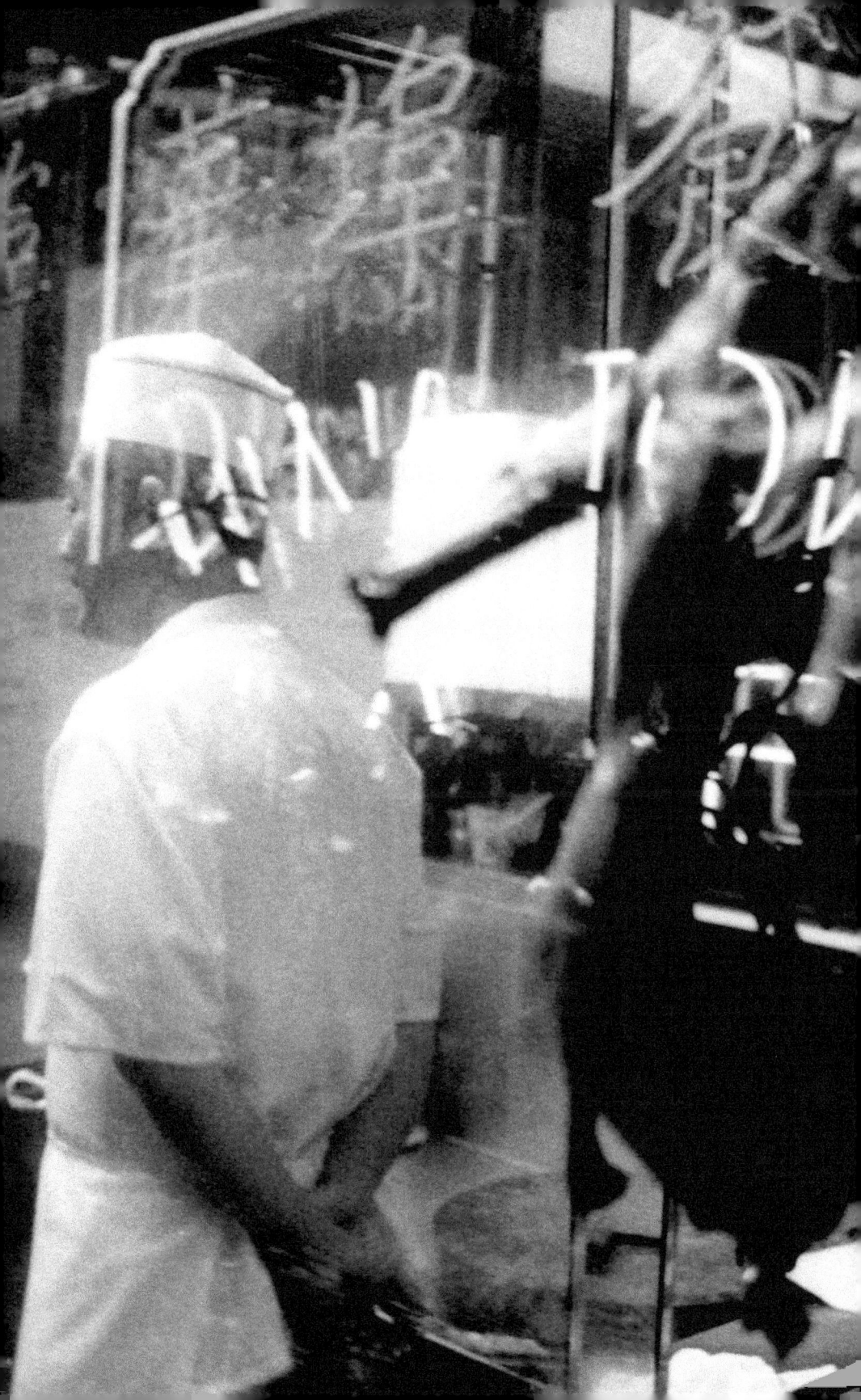

In the 1990s, the government increased the income requirement of citizens sponsoring relatives to immigrate to the U.S.

Lack of work documentation and failure to pay taxes may also make it more difficult to qualify for citizenship and business or education loans.

Other social benefits are also at stake. Non-citizen legal immigrants can only receive Supplemental Security Income (SSI) and Food Stamps if they have worked a minimum of 40 quarters, or 10 years, in the U.S.

Workers can't get full credit for their time worked if they have been working under the table.

Many older Chinese who have immigrated to the U.S. late in life rely on SSI for survival.

In addition to these practical reasons for being paid by check, there are also moral arguments, says Lowe.

Paying taxes represents a willingness to contribute to the larger social good, not just one's personal welfare.

Those who avoid paying taxes often take advantage of government services purchased with tax dollars, including education, affordable housing, trash removal, and police and fire protection.

Those who refuse to pay end up placing a heavier tax burden on those who have taxes deducted from their paychecks.

Not paying taxes may also reinforce "American stereotypes that Chinatown is a dangerous den of illegal activity and that Chinese people are sneaky and not to be trusted," wrote Lowe in an article on the under-the-table issue.

"I don't think that [paying taxes] is high in the Chinese people's consciousness," she says. For some Americans, paying taxes is considered a civic duty, but "for some reason that doesn't seem to be a big thing to Chinese."

Lowe and others say that many Chinese immigrants have a poor understanding of the law and were not accustomed to paying taxes in China.

Many come to the U.S. with the idea that America is a place to make money, not pay taxes, says one immigrant from Mainland China.

"These are the issues we want the whole community to support," says Lowe. "We're not trying to cause a lot of trouble for Chinese restaurants but we think there has to be some kind of standards."

Striking Back at the System

XIANG IS AN IMMIGRANT WORKER who struck back at the Chinese restaurant system.

In 1996, he is hurt on the job while working at a large Chinese restaurant in Quincy.

He soon finds out that his boss is more concerned about his restaurant's bottom line than about his well-being.

Xiang is fired from his job as a cook two months after sustaining a back injury that makes it impossible for him to continue working.

He tells his story one day in 1998 in the office of the Chinese Progressive Association in Chinatown.

Xiang says his boss often asked him to move heavy bags of rice and beef because he was taller and stronger than many of his coworkers.

But on July 7, 1996, his back snapped while he was lifting a bag of beef. Although he was unable to continue working, his boss didn't offer to take him to the hospital to have a doctor check out his injury.

Xiang's employer told him he would pay for his medical costs, though it turns out the employer wasn't doing it out of the goodness of his heart.

He says the employer's real motivation was to keep the injury off his insurance records so he could avoid paying higher premiums in the future.

Xiang initially went to a local medical center to seek treatment for his injury. X-rays showed irregularities in his backbone. Although Workers' Compensation should have covered his medical costs, Xiang initially ended up paying the bills himself.

After staying home for about three weeks, Xiang's boss told him he could return to work part-time at full-time wages.

Xiang offered to work part-time and be paid only for the hours he worked, but his boss insisted on paying him for a full day's work. To Xiang, this seemed too good to be true, but his boss insisted.

He thought his boss was just being "a nice guy," but he wasn't, says the 43-year-old worker. "It was a kind of trap."

After returning to work, Xiang's boss told him he should see a doctor affiliated with the restaurant's insurance company. "The doctor said: 'You're okay; you haven't any problem, you can work,'" Xiang recalls.

But Xiang was still in pain and unable to do strenuous work. Then, three weeks after he was called back to work, he was abruptly fired.

The boss said he could no longer do the job. He also told him he was ineligible for Workers' Compensation because the insurance company's doctor said there was nothing wrong with him.

But Xiang's story doesn't end there. With the help of the Progressive Association, Xiang finds a lawyer to fight what he believes is a blatant injustice. In time, Workers' Compensation awards him a lump-sum payment to cover the cost of his doctors' bills and lost salary.

After he is fired from the Quincy Chinese restaurant, Xiang enters a job-training program and studies English. He is unemployed for a year but eventually finds jobs as a sushi chef at a local supermarket and hotel.

"I feel the American restaurant's conditions are better than the Chinese restaurant's," says Xiang, who was a herbal medicine salesman in Guangzhou, China, before coming to the U.S. in the early 1990s.

In the American restaurants, he says, the work is less strenuous and the workday is limited to eight hours.

When Xiang worked in the Chinese restaurant, he generally worked 10 hours a day on weekdays, 11 1/2 hours on weekends, and up to 17 hours a day on Christmas, New Year's, and Mother's Day.

When Xiang worked in the Chinese restaurant, he was paid $1,500 a month, with most of his payments paid in cash. Occasionally, he says, he received a check for a few hundred dollars. "The Chinese all work this way," he says.

In the American restaurant where he is working in the late 1990s, Xiang is earning $11 an hour and being paid by check.

Receiving wages in cash may be more attractive to workers in the short term because it allows them to avoid paying taxes, says Xiang, but in the long run, payment by check is better because it allows them to receive full Social Security and unemployment insurance benefits.

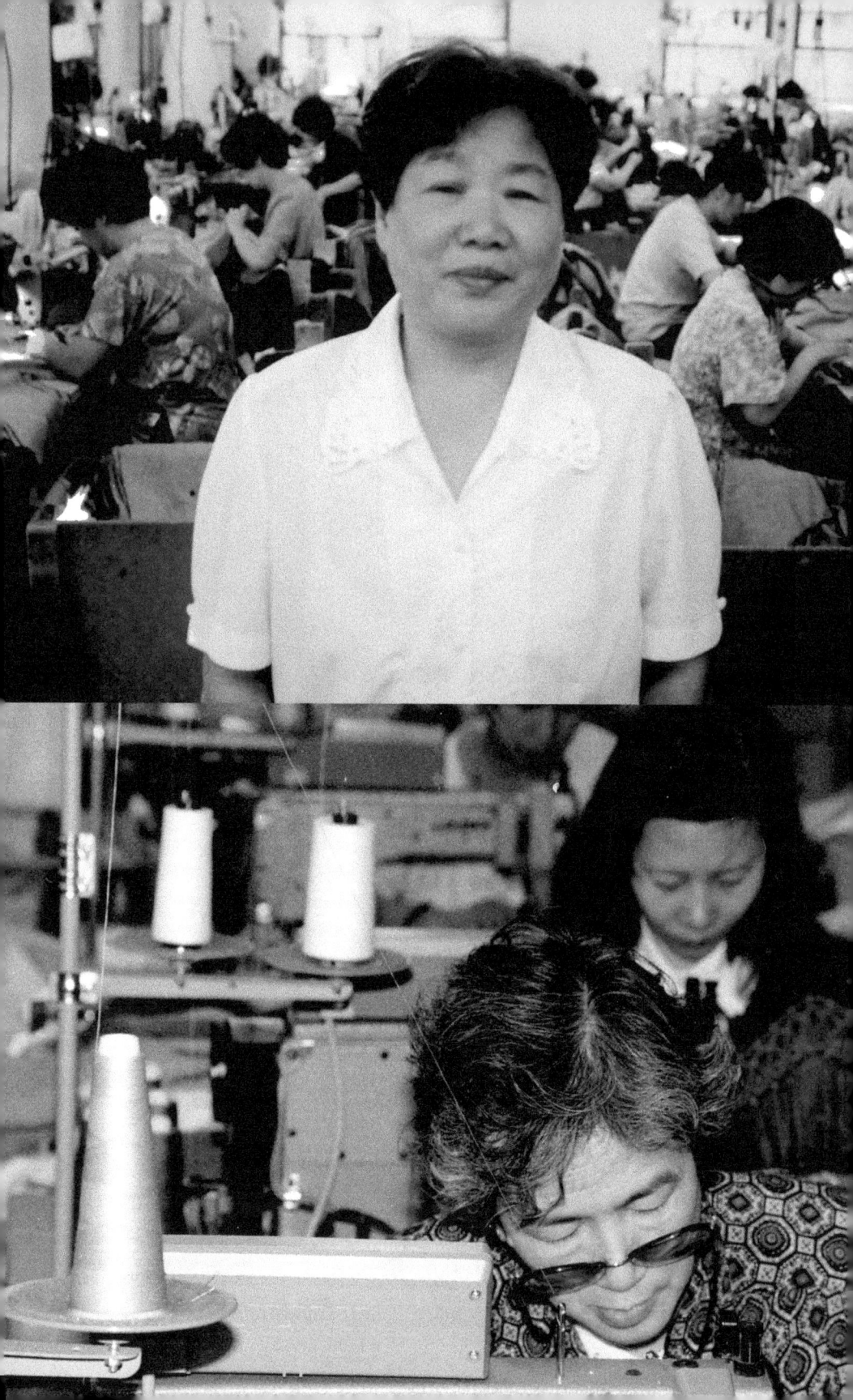

Stiching for a Living

IT USED TO BE ONE OF THE CHINESE community's biggest employers but by the late 1990s it was struggling to survive.

The garment industry years ago was centered in many of the large brick buildings dotting the neighborhood, including several buildings at the intersection of Beach Street and Harrison Avenue.

But the flight of garment manufacturers to the South and eventually to countries like China where labor is less costly led to a major decline in the industry in Boston.

Today's immigrant garment workers are divided between those who work for union shops and those who work non-union.

Helen Jue is assistant manager in the Chinatown office of the Union of Needletrades, Industrial and Textile Employees AFL-CIO.

She had been working in the garment industry as a stitcher, floor worker, and union agent for more than 30 years.

As in many Chinese immigrant families, her husband worked in the restaurant industry while she worked in the garment industry.

"I was born in China, not far from Canton (Guangzhou). In 1949 I went from China to Toronto, Canada, and in 1958 I came to Boston.

After I married my husband we lived on Oak Street in Chinatown. Eleven years later, we bought a house and moved to Brighton, and 11 years after that we moved to Newton. My husband was half-owner of a restaurant.

Six months after I was married, I went with my landlady to learn how to stitch right here on Stuart Street, though about a year and a half later I had to quit the job when my first child was born.

I didn't work again until my youngest son went to kindergarten. I started over at Kneeland Skirt in 1967. I would go to work in the morning and leave at 2 o'clock in the afternoon.

In the beginning I made skirts and later I made jackets. I made the whole garment. I did plain stitching on a single-needle machine.

I liked the work. I had friends who worked there, and we had fun together. The boss never bothered us. We had to keep our mind on our work but we knew what to do, so we could talk to each other while we worked.

Most of the people I worked with were Chinese, but there were also Italians, Spanish, all kinds of people. I talked to everybody.

When I worked for Kneeland Skirt, the boss there asked me if I wanted to be a floor lady.

I said, 'Okay, I can help you out temporarily.' But I ended up helping him out six or seven years. Eventually I didn't want that job anymore, so I quit and found a different job.

When my youngest son was 14 years old, the union sent somebody out to look for me. It was 1981 and the union needed a Chinese agent.

Why did they pick me? They said because I always helped out the union people — the agents — when they came into the shop to talk with the workers.

Most of our [Chinese] people have a little problem with the language, so when the union people came up I would have to translate for them.

They never had a Chinese agent working here before they hired me.

I was interviewed three times, and each time he said, 'Your children are old enough. You can work a steady job now. You go home and think about it.'

Two weeks later they called me in again, but I still didn't want the job. I didn't want to work long hours.

One week later the agent called me again. 'Our boss wants to see you,' he said.

So I went upstairs to the eighth floor. He said, 'Look, I know you don't want the job, but we need help. We got lots of Chinese in the garment shop. Don't you want to help your people?'

That's when he got me. So I said, 'Well, all right, if you put it that way. Because our people — the Chinese people — need help, and I'm going to try.'

That was 1981 — early March. So I said, 'But if I don't like it, don't make me stay.' He said, 'I promise you.' So I tried even though I had never worked as a business agent before.

In the first four weeks, I can tell you, I wanted to quit, because I had never gone to work so early. That boss required us to be there at quarter to nine. When I was stitching I went to the shop at 9:30 or 10 o'clock and left at 2:00 o'clock or 2:30, but now it was 9 to 5.

I told him, 'I don't like it.' And somebody working for the union — his name was Sam and he was very nice — said, 'Helen, try again.' I said, 'I don't want this job anymore.' He said, 'You can try. Come on, when anybody starts a new job it's hard.'

So I tried it and I tried it and later I came to like it because I like to help people.

I realized that a lot of Chinese people out there needed help.

Every week I make sure I go to every shop to talk to the people. I talk to everybody, including the boss. If they need help I help them. I say, 'How are you? Is everything okay?'

If someone says, 'Helen, I need your help with my Blue Cross,' I say, 'Fine, what do you want to know?'

If they say, "Can you explain to me what's covered?' I do my best to help

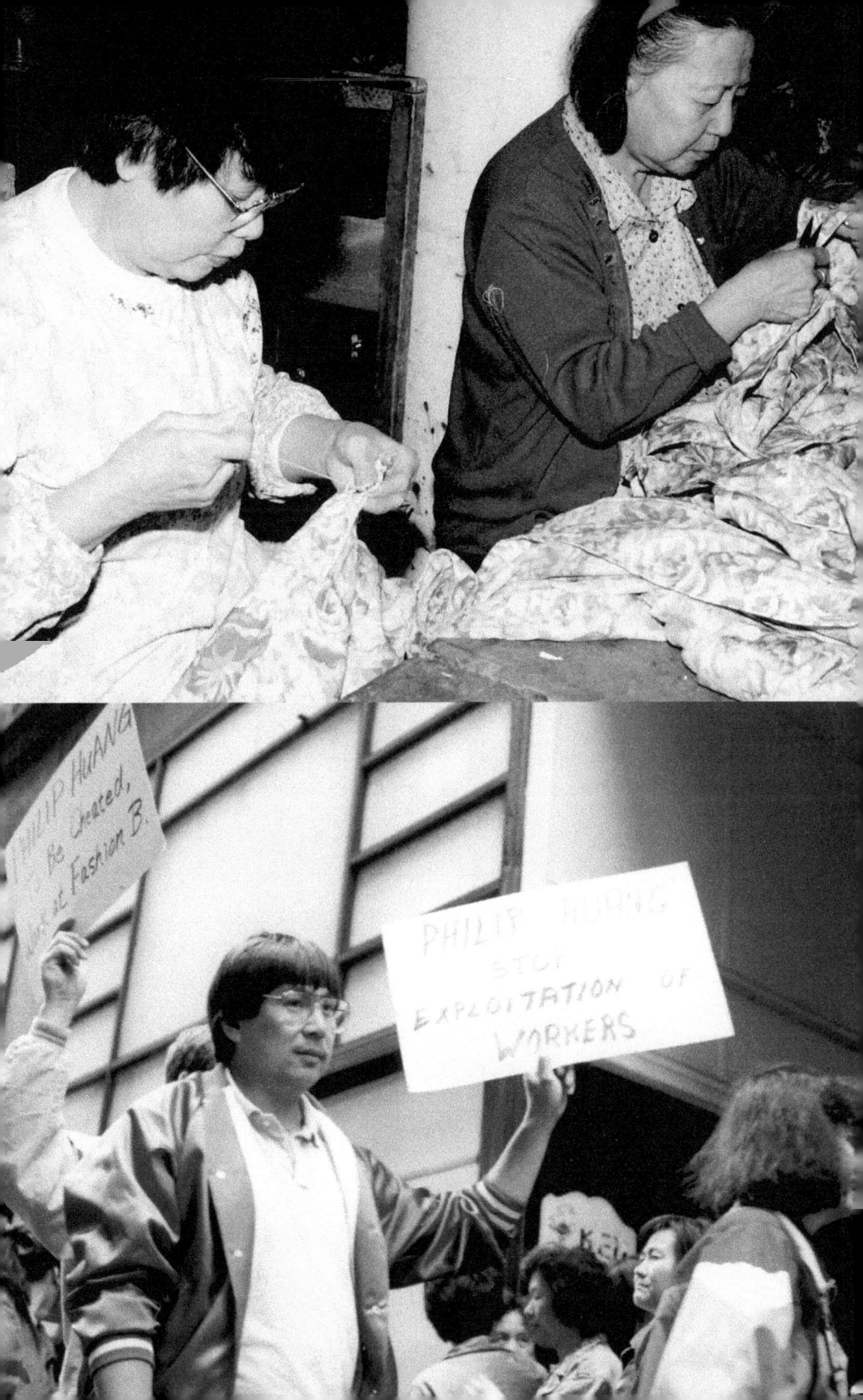

them.

If anyone comes to the office with a question I will try to help them. Mostly the Chinese workers look for me. If there's something they don't know about the union — like why they have to pay this bill — they ask me.

Today I went to East Boston because I needed to talk to the boss at one of my shops. Normally, if somebody is unhappy with the boss they will call me and I'll go over there.

I talked to the people and I talked to the boss. There was a problem over the price the workers were being paid for each garment. I wanted to make sure the price was right for the stitchers.

That's my job. I'm friendly with everybody. I talk to them nicely. I don't scream, but if I need to scream I scream.

In the last couple of weeks, I had to go to every shop to translate the new health insurance plan for the Chinese stitchers. I make sure they understand. I've been doing this for over 16 years.

The garment industry has changed a lot over the years. When I started with the union, most of the shops were in this area — on Essex Street, Harrison Avenue, and Kneeland Street.

New England Medical Center bought some of those buildings and the garment shops had to move out.

When I started, the union had 72 shops. Right now we've got about 18. At that time, garments were manufactured in this country, but now it's cheaper to make clothing outside the U.S., though they're not really selling it cheaper in this country. They charge the same price but they make it overseas very, very cheap.

When I started working there were maybe 3,000 or 4,000 garment workers, but now we got about 1,000. Some workers have gone to non-union shops or found different kinds of jobs.

Some of the garment workers found jobs in food service when the shops closed. When I first came here, there were not that many restaurants in Chinatown. Now there are more.

Some new people come looking for garment jobs, but not a lot. Right now it's bad because there are a lot of non-union shops — sweat shops — out there. Some of the non-union shops are in Chinatown. The non-union shops don't pay more and they have no benefits. We have benefits.

I think I know why they want to work in the non-union shops. Some young immigrants come here and they don't have that much money.

They know they can get free health care out there if they say they are low-income. The husband is working in a restaurant, and they claim they are low-income. If they are sick they can go to the hospital and get free care. That's what I hear.

The union shop pays more money. We have an increase every year, but I heard that the non-union shops pay them under the table. They pay cash.

Near here there are at least a half dozen non-union shops...there's one on Kingston Street.

I think we tried to unionize the shops but it's very hard. The owners don't want to come in the union because they have to pay the people benefits.

In the non-union shops, they get no health care and they work long hours. In our union shop, they only work seven to eight hours.

These non-union people work all day; they come in at 6 o'clock in the morning and go home at 11 o'clock at night. They work long, long hours — that's why we call them sweatshops.

Our union benefits are very good. We have new insurance called HMO Blue. You only pay $10 when you go to see the doctor. Some people have heard about the plan and they're coming back.

The union spends lots of money on benefits. We have vacation pay and benefits for people who are too sick to go to work. A worker who retires at 65 after 20 years of work gets $2,000 a month. You also get 12 paid holidays and life insurance. If a person suddenly dies the family gets $12,000.

We had one new union shop open last year on the fifth floor of this building, but we have also lost a couple of big shops. A big shop of mine closed because it couldn't compete with overseas shops. They didn't have that much work so they had to close. But there are still some new union members coming in.

Some of the new immigrants don't understand anything about the union. Some learn about the union shops from friends and come in looking for work.

If I know new immigrants who are looking for a job I'll ask them if they want to look for a garment stitcher job. I'll tell them about the union benefits.

'If the boss wants to fire you,' I say, 'They cannot just fire you; they've got to give you a second chance. The union wants to make sure you get a second chance. That's my job.'

My life hasn't been a bad life. I lost my son who died of cancer, which was a really sad time. Except for that everything else has been good...my family is good.

I'm going to retire soon. My daughter is married and I have grandchildren. I take care of a baby two or three times a week. They'll have to train somebody to take my place.

Maybe I'll retire in a couple of years. Warren (Pepicelli) says no, I can't retire; he says, 'Maybe in 10 years.'

When I walk out there at 3 or 4 o'clock a lot of people know me. They say hello to me. It's all those years I've been here."

ON THEIR OWN

If You Lose, You Lose Everything

STRIKING OUT ON YOUR OWN can be perilous. Chinatown's would-be entrepreneurs never know how their risky ventures will turn out.

They put much of their savings in jeopardy when they take that leap into the unknown.

If they lose they often lose everything — all their hard work, all their savings can evaporate instantly if they don't move cautiously.

That's what Alan Yen believed when he opened his restaurant in Chinatown in the mid-1990s.

For years Yen had been working for the China Pearl Restaurant in Chinatown, saving for the day when he could set out on his own.

That day came when he opened Cindy's Planet in a section of Chinatown generally reserved for residences.

Yen opened his small restaurant on the quiet end of Tyler Street, across from the 19th century brick row house where he lives with his wife and two children.

For months he labored in his spare time to renovate the space and open the restaurant. To passersby the venture seemed questionable, a little like Don Quixote tilting at a windmill.

Why would anyone want to open a restaurant in such an out-of-the way corner of Chinatown?

"I came here with my mother from Hong Kong in 1980. It was wintertime, so cold when I stepped out of the airport.

The first few weeks it was very uncomfortable because I didn't speak English well. I could only go into McDonald's and buy a hamburger.

I was stuck in Chinatown for a few months, living in Tai Tung Village, and I was getting bored. I was 18.

When I came here my sister told me to work for a laundry but I avoided that. I tried to find a school, and they sent me to Charlestown High School. There was a fight there between whites and blacks, so I quit after a month and transferred to Brookline High School.

Charlestown High felt like a jail. There was a police officer standing on every single stairway. I was so afraid, so uncomfortable. You had to get a pass to go to the bathroom.

Brookline High School was more like the kind of school I like. There was no bilingual education over there, so it forced me to speak English and learn it.

Every day I spoke for six hours. I had to talk to my teachers and my classmates. It took me about six years to learn English. When you're in bilingual education you think and translate the sentence all the time.

I was in high school for six years. I was the oldest one in the high school. When I graduated in 1987 I was almost 25 years old.

I stopped school for one year because I didn't have any money. My family had a problem and my mother went back to Hong Kong.

I was living with my sister, but my sister got married and had a family. It was very uncomfortable living with another family. I moved out and rented an apartment.

I got a part-time job in a Chinese restaurant in Weymouth. I started in the kitchen. I washed the dishes. I chopped onions. I cleaned up.

The chef liked me and taught me how to cook. The pay was like $300 a month, but they let you eat twice a day. It was full-time but they let you learn over there. They didn't really hire you.

After a half year I learned something and they sent me down to the Chop Sticks Restaurant on Cape Cod. I worked there for $700. They had a mini van that picked me up.

I worked there for a half year and then went back to the old restaurant. The manager sent me out to the dining room to learn how to be a waiter.

I made a little money and I saved up. I quit the job after about a year because I was still studying.

I didn't really want to go to school. I don't know why. I hate to read. I get tired every time I have to pick up a book.

But I forced myself to finish school and get a degree. At least I have a high school degree.

By 1987, I thought about going to college, but I didn't have the money. I joined the army, but ended up not going. My counselor said I shouldn't go. She talked to me a lot. She said if you have a little money you can finance going to school, but don't go into the reserves.

I went to Bunker Hill Community College and got a two-year degree in graphic design. I like drawing. My drawing is pretty good. I have good hand-skill. I studied graphic design for two years and got all A+'s, but in English I got C's and B's.

My thinking is better than my reading. But I always feel that I have a good future. I don't know why.

After Bunker Hill, I worked a full-time job in the China Pearl Restaurant in Chinatown. I met my wife Cindy there. Everything was pretty good. My life was better. I worked there for like six years.

I went from being a waiter to being captain of the waiters. Once you work in the dining room, you don't want to go back to the kitchen.

A year and a half ago the economy wasn't good and I wasn't making any money...like $20 or $30 a day. I was living across the street from here (on Tyler Street), and every time I walked by here I saw this closed store. For like two years. No one wanted it.

In my mind I said, 'This store is not bad at all because it faces the hospital and all the neighbors are at the back.'

So I thought about opening up a store, like a little restaurant, an ice-cream place maybe.

I talked to the landlord. I didn't have that much money. I used all my savings to open this store.

To tell you the truth, when I opened up this restaurant I didn't know what to do. I was so scared.

I renovated this restaurant for about half a year. I did half the work and two other people did the rest. I didn't have money to hire a big construction company. I got all the licenses myself.

I was lucky and got the store open, but I still had a problem: I didn't have a cook. I cannot cook the real Chinatown thing, so I thought: 'Why not do barbecue? That way you don't have to cook all the time.'

At home I cook pretty good. Pork chops here are my bestseller. I cook pork chops at home all the time and my wife and kids like them. So I moved the pork chops to the restaurant.

All the people — American people and Chinese people — accept them. I know I'm in first place in Chinatown where barbecue is the main thing.

In Boston we're the first one to make Chinese ice cream. I learned how to make it and improve it. I spend a lot of time thinking about it.

We carry mango, red bean, coconut, and taro ice cream. There's one store that sells red bean and mango ice cream, but it's made with mango base and color. We don't use mango base and color. We make only natural ice cream. We run out of ice cream all the time.

The other restaurant people think I'm crazy because no one ever opened a restaurant at this end of Tyler Street. They think there's no business here.

They call it a junk store, but we're doing pretty good right now. The hospital people like it. We cook it fresh.

I have two kids now: one boy and one girl. I live with them and my wife in a 450-square-foot space across the street. It's really crowded when you have two kids running around and you have a lot of toys. It's very crazy.

But it's close to my work. That's the main thing. I like Chinatown. Tyler Street isn't bad at all.

I've lived in a real nice space, like in Chestnut Hill, where I paid $1,000 in rent a month. I lived there for like three years.

But I thought, 'Why spend $1,000 in rent? Why don't you spend it on something else?'

What I first noticed about Chinatown was that it was real dirty and old and no one cared about it.

But it has changed a lot. They've opened up a lot of new stores, a lot of new restaurants. They also have travelers coming in here.

Before they used to say Chinatown had a lot of prostitutes, but Washington Street has been cleaned up a lot. We complained a lot to 911 about the prostitutes at night and now I don't see them that much.

I put everything I know into this store. This store is my future. I came to the U.S. when I was 18 years old and now I'm a 36-year-old man. Whatever I have learned in those 18 years I put into this store.

Work and sleep, work and sleep every day. I stay here for 13 hours a day. I don't charge much so I don't make that much profit.

If I'm making money after two years our store will stay open and I will open another restaurant. I want to go into a franchise, push out this restaurant's name.

My name, Cindy's Planet, is really different from other names in Chinatown. Little kids remember Cindy's Planet. We chose my wife's name, 'Cindy,' because my wife and I opened this restaurant.

One thing, though, if I open another restaurant, I will choose an upper-class place like Newbury Street or Brookline so we can do better. One day I hope you can find Cindy's Planet all over Boston."

Hanging by a Thread

FIVE YEARS LATER CINDY'S PLANET is still open and thriving. On a 90 degree summer day in 2001, the shop was busy, with parents and children from the Tyler Street neighborhood coming and going, buying cold drinks and ice cream to ease the summer heat.

But a few blocks away in the recently opened Chinatown mall in the Leather District, a young woman is as worried about her new business as Yen was about his a few year's earlier.

An immigrant from China's Guanxi Province, she is trying to make it on her own in Boston but her dream is hanging by a thread.

Sitting alone in her recently opened hair salon on Lincoln Street, she tells how she gave up a job as a hairstylist in a trendy Newbury Street salon to open this shop in Chinatown.

She is anxious about the future. Business hasn't been good. She opened her salon in this new Chinatown Mall, but there's not enough foot traffic from Chinatown.

Every month the rent bill comes calling and she worries she won't have enough customers to cover her costs. She's been advertising in a Chinese newspaper, but it still hasn't brought enough customers to the shop.

In a way, she says, she didn't know what she was getting herself into. The owner of the mall persuaded her that everything would work out fine, but so far it hasn't.

She seems frustrated and wants to blame somebody but she's not sure whom to blame.

You have to be careful when you open your own business, she says, you never know who to trust in a new country.

Like many new immigrants, she lacks confidence working with the local culture to help her solve her problems.

Instead, she turns to other Chinese for help.

But you can't rely on them either, she says, because some Chinese will cheat you if you don't keep an eye on them.

They don't always play by the rules or do what they say they'll do, she says.

She claims the Chinese contractor who renovated her salon tricked her. He said he would get a building permit for her but he never got it. She needed the building permit to open her shop and had to obtain one and pay for it herself.

He didn't get the building permit because he doesn't have a license, she says.

He did a beautiful job remodeling the shop, she says, but he didn't play by the rules and do what he said he'd do.

He probably knew she wouldn't complain to the authorities or even know how to file a complaint.

"He lied to me," she says. "He said he would get the permit. Some people here are pretty bad. You can't trust them."

You Always Need a Friend

RICHARD KONG SMILES A LOT, even when things don't go his way.

He opened the new Chinatown Mall on Lincoln Street in 2001, but it hasn't been a smooth ride so far.

Kong had a hard time convincing people to rent space in the nearby Leather District — a three block neighborhood squeezed between Chinatown and South Station.

In recent years, Chinese businesses have been slowly moving into the area.

But the Leather District has one major drawback: it's separated from Chinatown by the busy Surface Artery, which some customers may find inconvenient to cross.

Kong, who owns the building where the mall and his Mei Tung Supermarket and Double Rich Bakery are located, seems unfazed by the delay in renting out space in the mall.

His market earns enough profit to cover the cost of his mortgage, he says, so he really doesn't have to worry.

And the mall restaurant he recently opened is finally starting to take off.

Look, he says, most of the tables are occupied.

Kong says successful malls have been developed in Chinatowns in New York and Toronto, so why shouldn't the same kind of business be possible in Boston?

Kong says the mall will provide ambitious immigrants with space to open their own businesses in Chinatown, where markets, restaurants, and shops cater to Asian customers from across New England.

"It's very hard to get space right now in Chinatown," he says.

Kong grew up in Toisan County in China's Guangdong Province and lived for four years in Hong Kong before arriving in America in 1967. He was the last member of his family to immigrate to the U.S.

Hard work, good luck, and chance encounters with friendly people have been the key to his success in America, he says.

"My brothers, my mother, my sisters — all the family was here when I got here. I have seven brothers and sisters, and I'm the last — the youngest one.
When I came here I went to Bentley College for a year and a half to study accounting. I was working full time and going to school full time.

I worked at my sister's restaurant — the Hong Kong Restaurant in Harvard Square. My sister opened that restaurant about 50 years ago.
I was a waiter and worked at the front desk. I worked there for about a year and a half, then finally went off on my own to work for a Chinese restaurant in North Andover.

When I first came here I had to pay back my sister — you know, the lawyer's fee and air ticket. It's understandable. She was working hard so I had to pay it off. Once I paid her off I moved out — but I had to pay her first.

I worked in that restaurant for about two months, then went back to Hong Kong to get married in 1969. I didn't know my wife before I went back there. Like everybody else, friends and relatives introduced me to her.
I got married and came back here. I quit school and worked as a maitre de in the China Blossom Restaurant in North Andover.

I planned to become a real estate broker and got a real estate broker's license. But opening a restaurant was easier than doing real estate.
With real estate you need to have capital. My idea was to do the real estate and the restaurant business at the same time.

When I was working in the restaurant I met an American friend who was a vice president at Arlington Trust.
I was talking to him one day and said: "Can you give me a loan to open a restaurant?" And he said, "Yeah, I'll do it."
I rented a space for the restaurant on the Lawrence-Lowell line. I only had $4,000 at that time, but my friend gave me a loan of almost $50,000, which I used to remodel the space and buy the equipment.

I opened the restaurant in 1971 or '72. I actually didn't know how to do it,

but I was young and just tried. I asked different people. I talked with friends and people I knew.

It was a good size restaurant. It had 200 seats and a bar with about 50 seats. In two years I paid off the mortgage and business was going well.

I did the right things, so we were busy. I watched the kitchen and watched the outside. The food was normal, it was good.

The reputation is very important and your personality is also very important. You have to socialize with people, treat the people right when they come into the restaurant.

You have to cooperate with the kitchen because that's what a restaurant is about.

When I was young and had a restaurant business, I thought, 'Jeez, everybody has a restaurant business, maybe I should get into something else.'

So I kept looking for different stuff. I made some money from the restaurant and I'm thinking there are a lot of restaurants in Chinatown but nobody supplies the restaurants with canned goods, rice, sugar, flour, whatever.

I wanted to do that but it takes a lot of money. The restaurants were getting their supplies from Samuel Kerr, a Jewish company that supplied all of New England.

One day I got started in the wholesale business. I was the first Chinese to open a wholesale business for Chinatown and the Chinese restaurants.

When you do business you got to have a friend to help you out, just like when I started the restaurant. Wherever you go, you got to have friends. You never know how it will happen. It's just chance.

So I knew a friend and we used to hang out a lot. He was an American friend, an engineer.

In the restaurant, I used a lot of oil, a lot of fat for deep-frying. One day he brought me four or five cases of oil in the trunk of his car.

I said, 'Jeez, where did you get the oil?' He said, 'My company.' I said, 'What do you do?'

He said, 'I oversee them making the oil, making the lard.' I said, 'Jeez, I never knew that.' He said, 'Yeah, I'll give it to you.'

So he gave me about five or six. So I asked him, 'How much does it cost?' He said, 'I don't know. I'll find out.'

I wanted to know the difference between what the oil was worth and what I was paying for it.

So I found out that the wholesaler I was buying from was making eight or nine dollars on each case — on the lard alone. They were selling it to me for $20, but it only cost them about $12.

I was surprised he got it for only $12. 'Jeez, that kind of profit!' I said. 'Can you go to talk to your manager. I want to buy from him and meet him.'

So he lined up a date for me to meet him and talk to him. He said, 'Yeah, I can sell it to you.'

I used the van and bought 20 or 50 cases. I sold it to Kowloon and another big restaurant. They would give me cash right away.

So the other wholesaler was making $8 dollars, but I'm making $5. I can make a lot of money.

So I started out with the oil. I didn't have a place to store it. I would just go and pick it up in Somerville, then deliver it right away, every day. I did that for two or three months.

Then I bought a truck and hired a driver. A half year later I was doing sugar, rice, everything, every day, every month. I'd add a new face here and there so that in a couple of years I got big and rented a basement store — 4,000 square feet on South Street (at the edge of Chinatown). That was about 1976, so I started out wholesale a long time ago — 25 years ago.

So I kept getting bigger and bigger. I bought nine trucks — including one trailer — for my wholesale business. I moved to a bigger space in the meat market on Mass Avenue, then I moved to Chelsea. I have my own place over there now.

After I did it for five or six years my Universal Foods Specialties became the biggest wholesaler. I was even bigger than Samuel Kerr.

I think about 80 percent of my business came from Chinese and 20 percent from American restaurants. I was able to beat them price wise. Actually the America restaurants use about the same thing.

Now my wife is managing the business and my daughters are working there too. I have three salesmen. I have trucks and trailers. I import from China, Hong Kong, Singapore, and Taiwan. I usually import at least 50 containers a year.

When you're big enough the suppliers come looking for you. They have a person from China who's looking for you, so you don't even have to be in China.

At the same time I was operating the wholesale business I still owned restaurants. I sold the first restaurant and opened a second restaurant, which I operated for seven years.

Then I sold that one and opened the Hong Kong Restaurant on Route 1 in

Foxboro, near Route 495.

That's a big restaurant, with about 500 seats. It's still there, but I sold it to my friends.

Then there was a recession. Black Monday — when the stock market dropped. In one year, I lost $600,000 from the wholesale business because a lot of Chinese restaurants closed.

They had been doing so well that I let them owe me for 60 days or 90 days, but they couldn't keep up with it and then zoom they closed up. Some people owe me $60,000, $30,000, $20,000.

After the stock market dropped, business at some of the restaurants dropped 20 percent. But I was so strong I could still afford to lose money. A lot of companies at that time were closing.

I was just careful. But the Chinese way is that when you have money, you save it. I think it's a tradition in my family — from my mother — to save.

But that's what most Chinese people do. I don't gamble. I don't smoke. I don't even like coffee.

After the recession I downsized the restaurants and shrank the wholesale business by almost 60 percent. I only controlled about 40 percent of the restaurants. I dropped some customers because their credit wasn't so good.

At that time new wholesale businesses opened, so competition was hot. It was too hot, but I still reached my goals. It's friendly competition.

They know I'm a person who is very open when I do business. If you do business I'm not the enemy.

We're still friendly. He is my friend. We always sell to each other. It's just part of the game.

After the recession I knew people weren't eating in the restaurants as much as before. I thought that if they don't eat in the restaurants they're going to eat at home. I thought, "Jeez, why not open a supermarket in Chinatown."

That's why I opened the Mei Tung Supermarket. I've been open here for over 12 years now — since about '89.

Before I moved in a furniture store and the First National Bank were here. During the recession they all closed up. That's why I grabbed this place cheap. I made a very good deal with the real estate company.

When I moved in here I signed a lease that gave me an option to buy this building, and almost seven years ago I bought the building.

I used only $70,000 to open this market. It was very easy to open because I knew the suppliers. They all gave me credit.

I stocked maybe a quarter million dollars in food. I didn't have to pay one penny for it because the wholesalers supplied me with their products. I only put $70,000 into the equipment.

When I first opened the market, business was only so so. But after one, two, three years, almost every year my business was increasing and I was generally making money. Even now I'm still making money.

After I bought the building I opened this bakery and built this mall. Mei Tung makes enough money to cover the mortgage.

I went all over the place to see malls like this. I thought: Why don't I make a space like that in Boston. Nobody has a space like that.

If I tried to rent out the space that was here before I wouldn't make that much money on the rent. I said to myself, 'Why don't you make a mall. If I can't rent it out to other people I'll just open it myself.'

So I planned this first mall in Chinatown. So far, it's lucky. I think it's on the up side. I have rented out all the stores.

I opened my own restaurant in the mall about a month ago and it seems to be doing very well.

Actually running a restaurant is my experience — I know how to handle a restaurant. I have a few partners, but I'm the manager — the chairman.

I don't care what the people say about me, but if I'm successful in business, in my career, in my life — part of it is because I worked hard.

To be successful you have got to control yourself and have good planning. That's how you'll hit the top.

Working hard means you have to look after the business. Even if your business is good you still have to watch it. You see a lot of people who go away or give the business to someone else to watch for a while when the business is good.

I don't think you can do this in Chinatown. I saw so many people who lost control when business was good.

It's hard to find good managers in Chinatown. If you have that kind of ability you also have the ability to open a business of your own. So it's very hard to get a good person to serve as a manager.

It's hard for new immigrants. In Chinatown, my market is the first step for many of them. They come in here to ask for a market job or they go to find a job as a dishwasher in a restaurant.

These jobs don't pay much because you don't need experience to do them. They just have to do them.

Many will work here maybe a month or two months or a year and then try to expand — go out and find another job to move up.

When people come here from China, many live in their relatives' house and get whatever job they can find. They don't care how much it pays.

They come into the market without any experience. They can work here as long as they're willing to work. Then after a couple of years they maybe try to be a cook to get more pay.

Percentage-wise the newcomers do well. Some of them are very smart. They know how to control themselves. They don't get into gambling. They don't get into other bad habits.

If both the husband and the wife are working they're still making a good living. They save their money.

It's kind of hard for them but I still think they have a better life here than they would have in China.

There was one guy who worked for me in the market maybe eight years ago. Both the husband and wife worked. They saved $20,000, $30,000 and bought a house.

Right now they're worth a half million dollars because they bought a three-family house. The down payment was only about $30,000.

They rent out two apartments and live in one apartment. One rental is for profit and the other is to pay the mortgage.

The Chinese people are a little bit different. Whenever they go into any country it's very easy for them to put themselves on the ground — to step out on the ground.

That's the tradition of the Chinese people. You work hard. Seems they're different from other immigrants but I can't tell you why.

When I finish over here with the mall I'll probably try to have a real estate business. I still own other properties.

I work hard but I still enjoy myself by traveling around — that's part of my happiness. I spend money. I consider myself satisfied with what I've done here. I never expected to do so well.

Top of the Table

ON A WARM SPRING NIGHT IN 1998, Madeline Wong and her husband William Wong sit with other members of their big Boston-area restaurant family at a table at Anthony's Pier 4 Restaurant.

It's a special night for the Wongs and for the Chinese restaurant industry.

For the first time ever, Chinese restaurant owners have been named Restaurateurs of the Year by the Massachusetts Restaurant Association and the Northeast Foodservice and Lodging Association.

The restaurant is the Kowloon in Saugus, which was founded by the Wongs in 1960.

Although Madeline wonders why it has taken the organization so long to honor a Chinese restaurant, she doesn't make a big issue out of the oversight.

Her husband William, who spent much of his early life in China, is quiet and low-key. He owns property in Chinatown and is known for his generosity toward his workers and friends.

The American-born Madeline is personable and energetic. Many people — including the owner of Legal Seafoods — come by the table to chat with her. She always has a smile on her face.

Madeline was a major player in building the family's successful restaurant business but she also had a second life as the first Chinese American woman to successfully sell insurance in New England.

Her career as a saleswoman for John Hancock Insurance has been phenomenally successful and went hand-in hand with her success in the restaurant industry.

Madeline says she grew her insurance business in Boston's Chinatown after first helping her husband establish the Kowloon Restaurant north of Boston.

"I was born in Providence and graduated from Central High School. The Chinese population in Providence wasn't that great at the time, but we had a lot of American friends.

My father was a partner with my brother-in-law in the Ming Garden Restaurant in Providence.

There was a small Chinatown a couple blocks from Central High School on Summer Street. It had maybe three or four buildings and a grocery store, but it wasn't much.

After I graduated from high school I went to work as a cashier for my brother-in-law and my father at the Ming Garden. That was in 1945, more than half a century ago.

I wanted to go to college but my mother did not believe in a college education for the girls.

She said, most of the daughters will be married, they will have husbands who support them, it's the man who needs the education, not the woman.

My mother thought a woman would stay at home and take care of the family and not go into business.

My older brother, who is now the executive vice president of a stock firm in California, is the one who went to college. He went to Harvard and wasn't interested in the restaurant business.

A few years after I graduated from high school I met my husband. A mutual friend of our families who worked for my father-in-law at the time brought my husband to visit us at our home in Providence.

My father and my husband's father had worked together many years ago in Boston. I guess his father knew that my father had a daughter, and my father knew that my husband's father had a son.

So that was our introduction. But I thought I was still too young to get married and didn't want to take anyone seriously at that time. We knew each other for about three years before we were married. That was 1948, so we've been married 49 years now.

After we were married we moved to Boston and had an apartment on Commonwealth Avenue. His father had opened a successful restaurant called the Mai Fong a block away from Symphony Hall in Boston. It was a very successful business.

We both had grown up knowing how to take care of restaurants because his father and my father were in the restaurant business.

My husband worked for his dad for quite a few years before I had the opportunity in 1958 to buy my mother's share in a restaurant.

My mother and dad had sold their share in the Ming Garden in Providence and had gone into business with another brother-in-law who had opened the Mandarin House at 948 Broadway in Saugus.

After working for my father-in-law for a few years, we had a chance to buy shares in the Mandarin House.

By about 1960 we owned all the shares of the Mandarin House and could do whatever we wanted to improve the business. We changed the name to Kowloon because the Mandarin House at that time wasn't doing too much business.

We wanted to improve it by working long hours and putting everything we earned back into the restaurant.

There's a lot of pressure in the restaurant business, and it's very difficult to make it a success unless you are there to watch over things all the time.

In 1960 we were not making money. My husband was the only chef and I was the only waitress and cashier at lunchtime. It was a two-person operation.

We worked by ourselves for two or three years at lunchtime and were able to save some money to remodel the restaurant and add a lounge. We had only about $2,000 to our name.

After we opened the lounge it was awfully slow. We advertised, but it didn't take off. My husband had to put in long hours.

But he took care of his customers really well, so they came back and introduced other people to the Kowloon Restaurant. That's how it started, by word of mouth and good service and good food.

After a few years it was quite successful and people were waiting for tables, so we added another 100 seats. And then it got even busier and we added another small party room.

The business was increasing every year and the people used to wait one or two hours for a table on weekends. This was about 15 years ago. And they still wait for tables now, but not for that long — maybe an hour at the most.

About four years after we were married I got into the insurance business. My husband was still working for his father and I thought I would like to work part-time.

When we had our first restaurant I was selling insurance, working at the restaurant, and taking care of the house at the same time.

In 1952, I applied for a job as an agent at New York Life, but I was turned down because I was a woman.

At that time they were not hiring any woman agents. They can't do that now (she laughs), but at that time they could. They had hired some woman agents but they did not have much luck.

After I was turned down by New York Life I went to Sun Life, because they have offices in Hong Kong and I wanted to work with the Chinese people.

I decided I wanted to go into the insurance business when my husband bought a couple of policies from a Sun Life agent from Chicago who came to Boston once a year to sell to Chinese people.

I thought that was ridiculous. Shouldn't we have an agent here to call for services instead of calling Chicago or the Sun Life Company? I wanted to be an agent right in town where people could reach me easily.

But I was turned down by Sun Life too because of that agent from Chicago. But if at first you don't succeed, try, try again. This time I went to John

Hancock. I met a very nice person who gave me an aptitude test. I passed it with flying colors, and they hired me.

I would always ask for referrals when I got a client. And since nobody knew me I also canvassed businessmen. I went to different restaurants. Chinatown was not as busy as it is today, but I knew Ruby Foo and a lot of other restaurant owners. My father-in-law knew most of the people because he had one of the busiest restaurants in Boston at that time.

I used to go into Chinatown and I knew everyone. I would eat in different places just to introduce myself. I would tell them I was a new agent in town and just wanted to let them know there was a Chinese agent in town who could help them out.

It was very difficult. Everyone said, 'Oh we bought from the agent in Chicago, you're too late.'

And that sort of discouraged me. I thought, well, it's just like a tree branching out. There will be more babies coming, more people getting married, more people coming over. That's what I tried to focus on: the newcomers and the new babies.

But I was also quite discouraged because that agent from Chicago practically had a monopoly on selling to the Chinese here. At that time there were only about 6,000 Chinese in the New England states. That's not a big number.

I also used to go to Providence and Connecticut to make my rounds and introduce myself. I would let people know I was in Boston and tell them to give me a call.

Sometimes people would call me up, which made me feel good. After making a few calls and not getting any sales, you'd finally get one on the third or fourth try, which would make up for all the time you'd spent on the previous ones.

But you can't expect to sell to everyone you meet. You just need a lot of patience — and I do not have that much. But you have to make yourself be patient if you want to be successful in this business.

I remember one time I was very insulted when someone said, 'No, you're too late' and then returned my card. How do you think I felt? So I said, 'No, keep it just in case you need it.'

And I said it with a smile, naturally. And so she kept it. And you can't believe this but a few years later she called me up and said she wanted insurance for her five kids.

I was going to give up because she gave me my card back. I still have her daughter and her son as my clients.

So over time it just grows and grows. The clients buy it for their husbands, wives, and children. Before you know it you have four generations of business. And that's quite good, because the four generations are still living.

And because I sold insurance I didn't have to depend on my husband's income to support the family at that time. I was in insurance for eight years and was making substantial income. In fact, I think I was making more than he was at that time.

I was very young at the time and made friends very easily. I had people who would introduce me to new workers and new employees.

I always made myself known to the bosses of restaurants and laundries. They knew I was trying to be successful and make a go of it.

I guess most of my clients and friends helped me a lot along the way and I'm very thankful for that. A friend would refer me to a person who owned a laundry, then I would go there and introduce myself.

I would say, 'Such and such a person referred me to you...I thought you might be interested in insurance...I'll show you a plan to protect your family.'

And if he already had a policy he would introduce me to his employees.

There's really no technique to selling insurance. You just have to find out the needs of the customer. You try to see if they have a family. The question is, if anything should happen to them, who is going to support the family?

At the same time you say you hope nothing will happen to them. I try to show them different plans that would be suitable for them. The idea is that whether they live or die someone is going to gain.

But some Chinese did not believe in insurance because there weren't any agents at the time to explain it to them. They all thought: death, death — insurance deals with death. And they try not use the word death around New Year's because they're superstitious.

So I do not go out to sell life insurance around New Year's because you always have to talk about living and dying one way or another. You had to be careful how you worded it. You don't say you're going to die. You show them both sides.

I would tell them that we hope we can live to old age and be able to live off this retirement policy.

If you live long enough you will build up a pretty good estate for you and your family. If something should happen to you, the amount of your insurance will go to your family and help them out.

I would generally go out once or twice a week because I had to take care of the children. I only had two when I started but I eventually had four more to make a family of six.

I tried to arrange all my appointments on the day I had a baby-sitter and did not have to work in the restaurant.

I tried to make the convention and my Million Dollar Round Table every year. To make it we had to sell over a million dollars a year, which was a lot of money at that time.

Now I've been a member for 30 years. But my biggest year was 1982 when I made Top of the Table. That requires double the production of the Million Dollar Round Table.

I'm the only woman in John Hancock to make that. That was one of my goals, because I don't think any Asian in Boston had ever made it. I think at that time I just wanted to be the leading John Hancock agent for the whole country.

But you know how people are. They would say, 'Oh, you're the leading woman agent, but you can't beat us men.'

And I would say, 'I'm going to show you one of these days.' They used to kid me about it. They would say, 'So she's the leading woman agent, so what.'

But that was something, being the leading woman agent. Anyway, I showed them in 1982 when I made Top of the Table. I think I was the only one who made Top of the Table that year. I sold the most insurance in the country for John Hancock and beat all of the men.

That was my glory year. I went to the convention and they gave me a big plaque. That was very prestigious for me and my office and my agency. I really worked very hard.

I'm the only woman who is in the Hall of Fame for making the convention for more than 25 years. My picture is at the home office with the other Hall of Fame people.

Now I want to enjoy life. My four sons are taking care of the business. Oh, yes, people still call me up, but I don't have a quota now, so there's no pressure. I can sell as much as I want or not sell anything at all.

I still enjoy it because it gives me a reason to make house calls and visit and socialize with my friends.

If you do not enjoy your work you should take another job. I never wanted an office job. I enjoy meeting people. I enjoy talking to them. I really don't mind if they do not buy from me.

You cannot sell to everyone you meet. But percentage wise – you do well, you can make up to $250,000 a year, the sky is the limit in this business.

I think the key to my success was hard work and being in the right place at

the right time.

And, you know, I tried to help people out — I'm always trying to do whatever I can to make a better life for my clients."

You Step on Solid Ground

HE SITS AT A TABLE AT THE CHINA Pearl Restaurant. It's the summer of 1989, and Billy Chin has just sold the China Pearl to Ricky Moy and Frank Wong.

As usual, he is eager to talk. He has the natural flair of a successful businessman or politician. He knows how to smile and press the flesh to make his point.

For 30 years, Billy was the owner of the China Pearl, turning it into the restaurant powerhouse that it is today.

The China Pearl gave him a stage for a career that also included dabbling in community politics and feting Boston mayors.

In the old days, he says, he knew exactly where he was going when he stepped into Chinatown.

But now he's not so sure — sometimes he has to stop himself from slipping into the China Pearl out of habit.

It's a little unsettling, he says, not to have a headquarters in Chinatown. He's someone who likes to have a headquarters — a place where people can find him.

Still, he says, he doesn't have to worry much about being homeless in Chinatown. He can still go over to his younger brother Frank's Cathay Corner shop on Beach Street.

In Chinatown, Billy and Frank Chin are often discussed in the same breath.

Billy can typically be found at the center of a Chinatown political fight, stirring things up if necessary to reach his goal.

It could be a battle fought by the English-speaking generation that controls the Chinatown Neighborhood Council or the kind of dispute that regularly sends tremors through the Toisanese-speaking Chinese Consolidated Benevolent Association, where Chin once served as president.

Many Chinatown businessmen focus largely on business but Billy and Frank give Chinatown a place in the broader Boston community.

Many people in Chinatown have influence in either the American-born or Asia-born cliques in the community, but the Chin brothers have influence in both domains, navigating that imaginary line between here and there, past and present, Asia and America.

It could be because their early years were spent in both the U.S. and China.

Billy was born at 32 Oxford Street in the heart of Chinatown but was sent back to China as a youth for 14 years.
Like many people in the Chinatown community, he started out in restaurants at an early age. In those days, restaurants and laundries were the lifeblood of the Chinese community.
Starting in high school, he and his brother worked in Chinese restaurants, serving as waiters at the House of Wong on Hudson Street and drying silverware at the Cathay House.
In the early 1950s, America was again at war and Billy joined the army, serving as an army interpreter in Korea during the Korean War.

After the war, he returned to Boston to attend a two-year business school, then worked for State Street Bank for two and a half years.
In 1959, he made the leap and opened the China Pearl in a space that was once the home of the Hong Loy Doo Restaurant — better known around town as the Number 9 Restaurant.
"We opened a few months and almost went out of business," he says.
But they stuck out the hard times and soon business was improving. The rest is history.

Chin's memories of the restaurant trade go back to the 1940s, to well-know establishments such as the Ruby Foo Restaurant and the Cathay House.
In those days, people got dressed up when they came to Chinatown, he says. Life was more formal then. The men wore suits and ties. People lined up along the street to get seated in the most fashionable Chinese restaurants. You gave the maitre de "a few bucks tip" just to get a seat.

Over the years, he watched the food style and decor of Chinese restaurants go through numerous changes.
In the early days, Chinese and American dishes were served at the restaurants. American food was included on the menu because many customers weren't familiar with Chinese food.

During the Second World War, many American GIs visited Hawaii and people started to go on vacation there.
Sometime during the 1950s, Hawaiian and Polynesian motifs suddenly became popular at Chinese restaurants across the country.

In Boston's Chinatown, the trend started with Bob Lee's place on Tyler Street. Billy says Lee visited Los Angeles and came back to Boston with new ideas for his own restaurant.

After his return, Lee opened Bob Lee's Islander on Tyler Street, where Hawaiian style influenced both the food and the decor.

Bright colored flowers, waterfalls, and Hawaiian music were all popular Polynesian motifs, says Chin.

But like every phase, the Polynesian-style would run its course and be replaced by something new.

In the 1970s, Szechwan-style food became popular, and in the 1980s Thai food made inroads.

In the 1990s, Hong-Kong-style establishments — with fish tanks in the windows and more austere decorations — became fashionable.

In the earliest days of the Chinese restaurant industry, most of the customers were Caucasians. Eating out wasn't common among Chinese, who tended to view restaurant dining as an extravagance.

They preferred to save their money, spend it on their families in other ways, or put it into a business, Chin says.

But as Chinese became more established and secure in the U.S., more people began to eat out, he says.

They were more willing to spend money. "The lifestyle and thinking is changing," he says. "They [the Chinese] want to enjoy it a little bit. They come out and eat more."

In the second half of the century more new immigrants began to arrive in Boston. "The population of [Chinatown] has increased," says Chin. "The buying power is good because everyone has a job."

Chinese restaurants also started to open in suburban towns across the region so Caucasians no longer had to go to Chinatown to eat Chinese food.

Today the majority of customers eating in Chinatown restaurants are Asian.

Other changes also had an effect on the Chinese food industry. Vietnamese-owned businesses began to sprout up in Chinatown as refugees from the Vietnam War made their way into the local Asian community.

Many of these Vietnamese were ethnic Chinese who had been persecuted and forced to leave Vietnam at the end of the Vietnam War.

While restaurants are Chin's platform and livelihood, it's his relationships with people that drive him.

He loves to be in the thick of things, offering his opinion, maybe pulling a few strings to make a project happen.

Twice in the 1950s and 1980s he served as president of the Chinese Consolidated Benevolent Association, which put him at the center of Chinatown social life.

If somebody was getting married in the neighborhood, the CCBA president would probably show up at the wedding, he says.

In those days, the CCBA "represented the people more than today," he says, adding that back then people in Chinatown tended to be more "community oriented."

Chin attributes his political success in the Chinese community to his reliability and trustworthiness.

You have to be straight with people, he says, you have to be there when they need you. "You step on the solid ground," he says. "You don't do a phony deal."

Billy's success has also been shaped by his knack for making friends in high places. Over the years, he has been on speaking terms with some of the state's most powerful politicians.

He served in the army with William Bulger, the former president of the State Senate, and if Senator Edward Kennedy made an appearance in Chinatown, he was almost certain to single out Billy for special attention.

Billy has also been on speaking terms with many Boston mayors, from Kevin White to Raymond Flynn to Thomas Menino.

Chin recalls the day he went over to City Hall to ask Mayor White for help with building the Chinatown gate. The materials were in storage but no one was stepping forward to get the job done.

White asked Chin: How many votes can you give me? Chin replied: 200 votes. Now, adds Chin, "we can't carry five votes."

Chin says he and his brother have been successful in Chinatown because they know how to make things happen. "You have to create it," he says. "You can't just go around and act like a big shot. You have to follow up your words with action."

He says he once used his influence with Senator Kennedy to get Tufts University and the New England Medical Center to begin more constructive bargaining with Chinatown over use of the neighborhood's limited available land.

He sought the help of State Senator William Bulger to keep a Chinatown housing development moving forward.

"You see there's politics," says Chin. "It's the 200 votes in the pocket but you do it for the community."

Billy says, sure, he has made some money in Chinatown, but he also tries to give something back to the community.

Over the years he has approached people for contributions to various causes. In the 1980s he was involved in a drive to raise money to build South Cove Manor, a nursing home for Chinese in Chinatown.

At times, he says, people may have been taken aback by his persistence and aggressive approach to raising money for the home, but he says he believed in what he was doing and in the end he got results.

The nursing home was built and became an integral part of the Chinese community. "Part of the blood is community," he says. "First thing is you have to sacrifice...you have to help people...you do it from your heart."

Although his critics like to say that Billy's community activities disguise a calculated effort to stake out good business deals for him and his friends, Billy counters that his critics are just being jealous — jealous of the Chin brothers' success in Chinatown and in the city.

Billy isn't shy about admitting that community involvement and business go hand in hand.

"When I started the China Pearl, everyone trusted me from the start," he says. Once you're considered trustworthy in Chinatown, he adds, "every time you go out to open a new place they trust you."

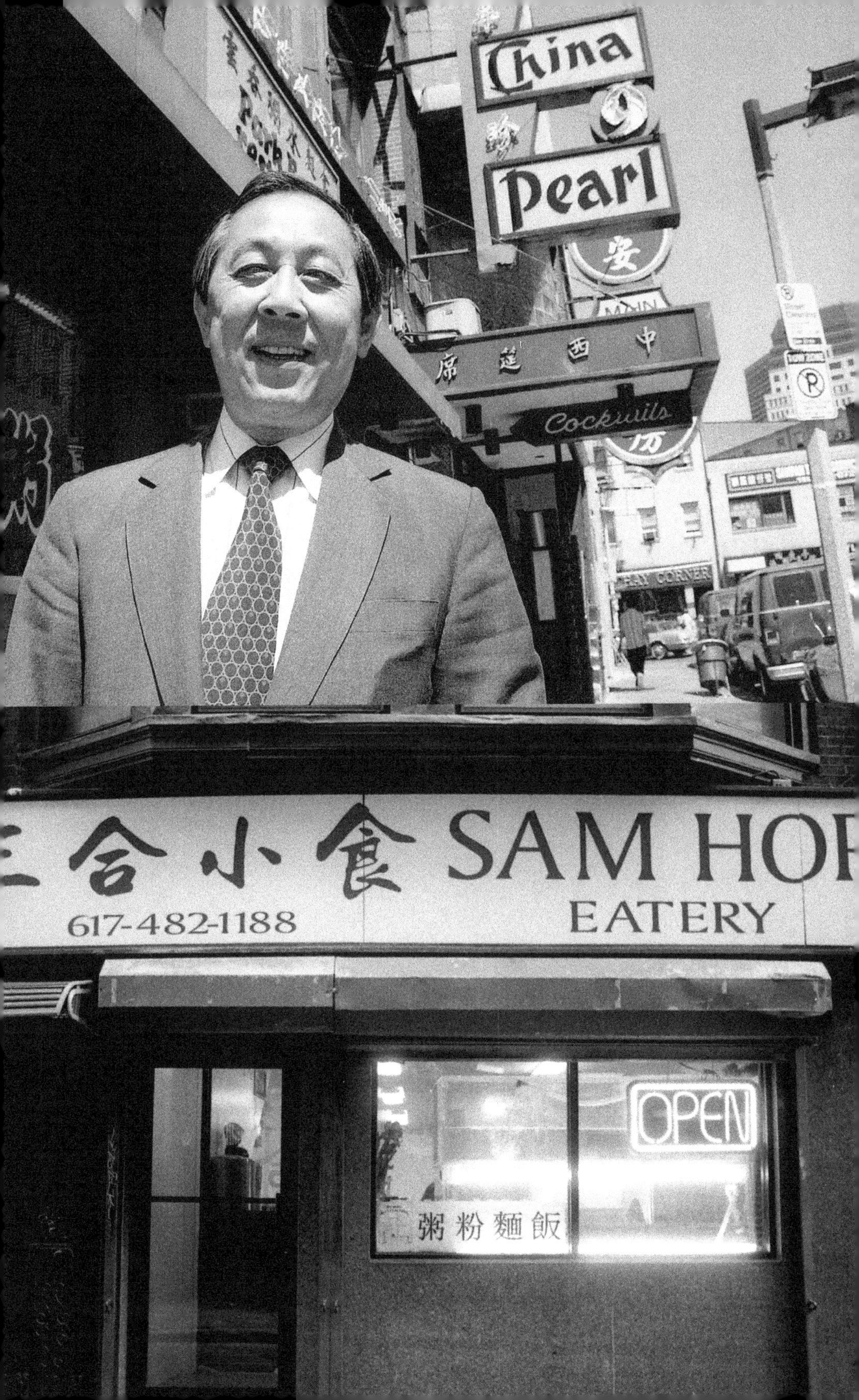
China
Pearl
中西筵席
合小食
SAM
EATERY
617-482-1188
OPEN
粥粉麵飯

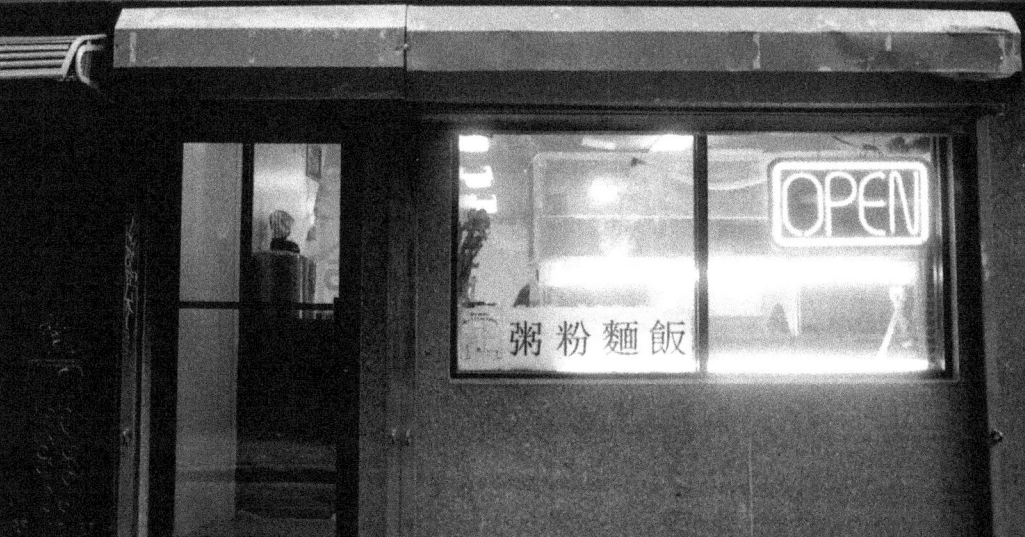

HOME IS CHINATOWN

Not Just Toisanese

THIRTY YEARS AGO SHE COULD WALK into a neighborhood store and be greeted by people who spoke her family's Toisanese dialect.

"They would take one look at us and know who we were," says Stephanie Fan, who moved away from Chinatown in 1972 but continues to work there. "You did feel you were part of a small neighborhood."

When she walks into a Chinatown shop today, people often don't know her name and are as likely to speak Cantonese or Mandarin as Toisanese.

The neighborhood is no longer the tightly knit Toisanese enclave it was when she was growing up there, she says.

Fan says Chinatown began to lose its Toisanese flavor in the early 1970s when new Cantonese-speaking immigrants started to arrive from Hong Kong and other Asian countries — the beneficiaries of the 1965 U.S. immigration law that lifted restrictions on Asian immigration and promoted family reunification.

Before the 1970s, says Chinatown resident Ralph Yee, the community was essentially a Toisanese enclave, though a small number of Mandarin-speaking northern Chinese began arriving in the 1940s.

In the late 1970s, refugees who had escaped from Vietnam in small boats also arrived in Boston. These refugees were mostly ethnic Chinese who opened restaurants and shops on lower Beach Street and Washington Street in the Combat Zone.

Among them were the Chaozhou who had roots in the northwest section of China's Guangdong Province. The Chaozhou owned the 88 Supermarket, the Pacific Supermarket, and other Chinatown businesses.

Other events also had an impact on Chinatown, including the start of full diplomatic relations with China in 1979 that led to an influx of Mandarin-speaking university students from Mainland China during the 1980s and 1990s.

Mandarin-speakers were also arriving from an increasingly wealthy Taiwan, where families could now afford to send their children to American universities to study.

In the 1990s, Chinatown's population again began to change as more people from China's Fujian Province — some of whom were illegal began to show up on the neighborhood's streets.

Over the last 40 years the area's Asian population has been growing steadily. The Boston Asian population went from 5,200 in 1960 to 7,900 in 1970, 15,000 in 1980, and 30,388 in 1990. The number of Asians living in Massachusetts has grown even more dramatically, rising from 52,615 in 1980 to 143,392 in 1990.

Fifty years ago, immigrant Chinese tended to live in Chinatown, but in recent years new Chinese communities have sprouted up in outlying areas.

Although Chinatown continues to attract new immigrants, a shortage of housing has led many Chinese to settle in outlying cities such as Malden and Quincy.

More educated professional tend to gravitate to wealthier suburbs such as Lexington and Newton.

New housing has been built in Chinatown in recent years but not enough to satisfy the demand. Recent immigrants, families, and the elderly make up the bulk of today's Chinatown population.

While many Chinese immigrants have been moving to suburban communities, those who live in Chinatown tend to stay longer. "I think Chinatown has become a less transitional community," says Bak Fun Wong, a Chinatown educator who lives near the neighborhood.

In the past, the elderly and new immigrants made up the bulk of the Chinatown population, but there are more families in the neighborhood now, says Wong.

"We have a more stable Chinatown in terms of residents and a more family-oriented Chinatown," he says.

But Wong believes Chinatown shouldn't be just for first-generation Chinese or low-income immigrants. It's not good to have the poor in one area and the wealthy in another, he says.

A Chinatown with more mixed-income housing would attract more second-generation Asians.

Wong says the college-educated second generation moves to the suburbs in part because Chinatown tends to offer only low-income housing. "That's one thing we all have to look into," he says.

The Asian community is getting big, but you can see the discrepancy between the rich and the poor," he says. "Chinatown has made some progress, but it's still being stereotyped as a ghetto."

Summer Days at Tai Tung Village

BETTY WONG SITS with her two young sons on a bench in the courtyard of Chinatown's Tai Tung Village. It's a warm summer day in 1994 and the courtyard is quiet.

At least three times a week Wong and her children make the trip from suburban Newton to Tai Tung Village.

Wong comes to Chinatown to visit her husband's parents, who have lived in this Chinatown housing complex for almost a quarter century.

Her husband has a business nearby, so it's easy for him to drop in on his Asia-born parents during the workweek.

Life at Tai Tung Village revolves around family. Parents and grandparents share the same space in the courtyard with children and grandchildren.

Adults from the suburbs regularly make trips to the city to visit their elderly parents.

The trees and bushes are well kept. The building and yard are spotless. The elevators are always working.

Wong says she always feels safe at Tai Tung Village.

She takes her children into town with her because she wants them to know more about Chinese culture.

She brings them to the neighborhood to have their hair cut or to attend community events.

She says she wants her son to "know his roots."

On a shaded bench in the courtyard, 80-year-old Soo Lee takes in the summer morning, a bag of groceries from nearby Ming's Market resting on the bench beside him.

Lee wears a baseball cap and looks much younger than his 80 years. He came to Boston from Hong Kong in 1941 and has lived in Tai Tung Village since 1978.

Before his retirement, he was a cook for many years at the former Cathay House Restaurant in Chinatown.

Lee likes the convenience of living in Chinatown: people speak Chinese and share a common culture, shops and restaurants are close by.

"Everything is taken care of here," he says. "I get up early and walk to Boston Common for exercise."

You're still so young, says an acquaintance passing through the courtyard.
Lee nods and smiles, happy to receive the compliment.

In a storefront martial arts club, a group of older women talk and play mah jongg at a card table.
A breeze flows through the open doorway, cooling the cavernous club.
Swords, drums, and lion heads lie scattered around the room.

The women don't want to have their picture taken because they don't want anyone to see them playing mah jongg.
They don't want people to think they are gambling.

When Fannie Kwan walks through the Tai Tung courtyard, she keeps bumping into someone she knows.
Just about everybody at Tai Tung Village seems to know her. As manager of the complex, Kwan is responsible for keeping the complex in good working order.

Kwan grew up in a small town in rural Mississippi where her grandfather owned a cotton farm and a grocery store.
The town had just three Chinese families and they were all related, she says.
Kwan has been managing Tai Tung since 1978 and at one time lived in the building.
Overseeing the development has allowed her to see the Chinatown community grow and change.

"The community has become more modern," she says. "The attitude of more recent immigrants is different from the earlier generations."
"We were brought up differently, more disciplined...but they (the young people) don't have the same feeling ... they take everything for granted.
The new generation has more job options than their predecessors, she says. They're not as confined to restaurants and the insulated world of Chinatown.

They also face less prejudice than earlier generations. Chinese today feel comfortable moving to the suburbs if they want.
They don't feel pressured to limit themselves to Chinatown as they did in an earlier era.

"Our grandfathers came here mainly to make a living and sent their money back to China," she says.
Many hadn't planned to stay in America forever. Immigration laws were biased against Chinese and often made them feel unwanted here.

But this new generation will stay and make America their permanent home, she says.

Kwan has witnessed many changes in Chinatown over the years, but she says some things about the community remain constant.

Hard work is still the mainstay of Chinatown life, she says. In many Chinatown families, both parents work "to provide the best for their children."

Kwan says the people who live in Tai Tung Village generally get along well with each other, though some tenants have been complaining that more problems exist now than in the past.

There are some noisy people in the development and some of them are not Chinese.

Some people in Chinatown privately complain about the non-Chinese residents who moved into the complex during the 1990s.

Like other groups in Boston, many Chinese are reluctant to have people outside their racial and ethnic group move into their neighborhood.

More than 80 percent of Tai Tung tenants are Chinese, but whites, Hispanics, and African Americans also live there now.

"Some non-Chinese have lived here a long time, over a decade, and they don't want to move," says Kwan. "It's a peaceful community."

Kwan says that when disagreements arise, she tries to sit down with the people and talk through their differences.

"I try to work with people," she says. "Every story has two sides. You have to listen to what's going on."

Most Tai Tung tenants are families or couples whose children have grown up. Many residents have lived in the 214-unit complex since the 1970s and many are still employed in restaurants.

A percentage of the apartments are government subsidized. Under the federal Section 8 housing program, the government pays a portion of the monthly rent of low-income tenants.

Sometimes tenants start out paying the subsidized rate but switch to market rate when their incomes rise.

It's unclear, however, if everyone plays by these rules. Restaurant workers get paid under the table and many restaurant workers live in Tai Tung Village.

Michael Wong, chairman of the Tai Tung Tenants Association, has lived in Tai Tung for 20 years.

He started out paying a subsidized rate for his apartment but now pays market rate because his income has risen.

He continues to live here because his business, the Lun Fat Produce Company, is just across the street.

Between 800 and 900 people live in the 25-year-old housing complex, and many have at one time or another worked in restaurants, he says.

Most of the people who live here know each other. In the evening "the old folks come down and sit," he says.

Young and old share the same space in the courtyard. The American-born children speak English, but their parents and grandparents speak Toisanese.

Tai Tung Village, says Wong, is a successful development. "People get along well with each other here."

On an upper floor of Tai Tung Village, Fut Gee Moy sits with his mother in the living room of her one-bedroom apartment. His mother has lived in the building since the day it opened in 1973.

Moy lives with his wife in an apartment upstairs, and his son, a student at Cornell University, lives with them when he's not away at school.

Before he immigrated to the U.S. from Mainland China in the early 1980s, Moy was a teacher in China.

But like many immigrants who arrive in the U.S. with limited command of English, he had no choice but to become a restaurant worker.

In a nearby apartment, Chun Yuen Mak and Kan Ho Mak sit with their son, daughter-in-law and granddaughter in the living room of their apartment.

The granddaughter says her family lives in North Quincy but makes the trip into the city to visit her grandparents almost every day.

The apartment's sunny living room has a spectacular view of the expressway and the South End.

Family photographs are displayed on a shelf and a small ancestral shrine is attached to the wall above the kitchen table.

A retired restaurant worker, Mak has few complaints about Tai Tung Village.

It's safe and well-managed, he says, but it would be nice if his subsidized $290 monthly rent dropped a bit now that the Chinese Consolidated Benevolent Association has purchased the building.

Cultures Collide at Castle Square

RACE AND ETHNIC BACKGROUND are issues in Chinatown, though people seldom talk about them openly.

When the Asian American Civic Association — the community's primary social service organization — started to provide education services for Somali refugees in the 1990s, some leaders at the Chinese Consolidated Benevolent Association complained about the agency providing services for people who were not Chinese.

And when the Vietnamese started to open businesses in Chinatown after a wave of boat people arrived in the city following the Vietnam War, some Chinese complained about them too, even though most of the migrants were ethnic Chinese.

When an increasing number of Fujianese Chinese started to appear in the neighborhood — many of them illegal — in the 1990s, there were similar complaints from the dominant Toisanese Chinese, the original settlers of Boston's Chinatown.

The residents of Chinatown's Tai Tung Village, Mass Pike Towers, and Oak Terrace housing complexes remain predominately Chinese, though nearby Castle Square, on the other side of the Mass Turnpike in the South End, has a mix of Asian, African-American, Latino, and white tenants.

For years, Castle Square prided itself on its racial diversity and the ability of its tenants to live peacefully together.

But in 1997, that reputation was challenged when tensions developed between the development's Chinese and African American and Latino tenants over issues that struck at the heart of cultural conflict in a diverse American city like Boston.

It's a typical afternoon at the Castle Square Learning Center. Children sit at tables quietly working on their homework.

The room resembles a classroom, with drawings and writings in Chinese and English attached to the wall.

It's a controlled, peaceful learning environment where children arrive after the formal school day to continue learning.

The scene, however, may not be as innocent as it seems. Castle Square is a multiracial housing complex, but all of the adults and students taking part in this after-school program are Asian.

Not far away, in a Castle Square community space at 480 Tremont St., several other after-school programs are also in progress.

In Winn Management's computer learning center, teenagers sit at computers under the guidance of Leibiana Feliz. In another room, teenagers watch a large-screen TV and prepare for a group discussion. In a third room, an older student is helping several younger children with their homework.

In these rooms something also seems amiss: all of the students and adults taking part in these programs are either African American or Hispanic.

The result is obvious: Chinese do not appear to be learning with African Americans and Hispanics at this 500-unit complex on the edge of Chinatown where residents are 55 percent Asian American, 27 percent African American, 13 percent Hispanic, and 5 percent Caucasian.

In recent months, a group of African American and Hispanic tenants charged that Harry Kwan, co-president of the Castle Square Tenants Association (CSTO), has tried to segregate children in its programs by race and discriminated against non-Asian children.

The group has leveled similar charges of racial bias against Paul Lau, the association's executive director.

Eight tenants — including one Asian — recently wrote a letter outlining their charges against the leaders. The group is also asking that Kwan be removed from his position as CSTO co-president.

"There have been complaints to Winn Management from the children of Castle Square against Harry Kwan," states the letter. "They state incidents of mistreatment, prejudice, profanity, and unfairness. They are complaints from Afro-American and Hispanic children. These are serious issues that were brought to Harry and Paul's attention with no resolution."

The letter goes on to complain that Kwan "chooses to separate children by racial background" and helps Chinese children in the Learning Center without offering similar help to non-Chinese students.

They also charge that he has encouraged Chinese and non-Chinese to sit apart at a membership meeting. They say the Tenant Management Committee has had difficulty communicating with Kwan and that he tends to make decisions independently.

The letter charges that Lau "has shown racial bias in dealing with staff and residents" and "has openly stated that Afro-American and Hispanic children do not want to learn."

The letter also complains that Lau speaks Chinese "without consideration for non-Chinese staff." The letter notes that "the entire staff is able to speak English."

Both Kwan and Lau deny the charges, arguing that conflicts at Castle Square

have more to do with different approaches to learning and governing than to racial bias.

Moreover, they say, Chinese tenants never complained in the past when African Americans controlled the CSTO board and created programs more to the liking of their own community than to the Chinese.

Kwan argues that Asians have historically been victims of discrimination in the U.S. and generally haven't spoken out when others discriminated against them.

"Nobody speaks loud in our Chinese community," he says. "I want to speak loud."

Kwan believes that CSTO board politics is at the root of the controversy and that Winn Management Co. is also partly to blame for the conflict — a charge that Winn denies.

"This has been an internal issue among two factions of the tenants group," says Stephanie Lewis, a Winn regional vice-president.

Hired to attract more Asians to CSTO programs, Lau points out that Asians never brought charges of racial bias against the organizers of past programs for leaving out Asians.

Few Asian teenagers, for example, participated in an earlier Youth Enrichment: Drug Elimination and Awareness Program for which CSTO had received a large grant.

Pictures on the wall at 480 Tremont St. suggest that most participants in that program were African American and Hispanic.

Any racial divisions that may exist among the 1,300 residents of Castle Square is "a reflection of the macro-society," says Lau. "We are reflecting that trend. We are not creating it. We are just a mirror of the broader society."

"What I don't want to see is the minority groups fighting with one another," he says.

Lau believes that much of the current controversy began after a new board was elected in 1995. Six of the nine members of that board were Asian American, including two co-presidents and two vice-presidents.

Asians did not dominate the previous board, where co-president Deborah Backus, an African American, played a dominent role. The other co-president was Ann Moy, who is Chinese.

"This is the first time we have six Asians serving on the board," says Lau.

The gender mix of the board also changed. Females tended to dominate the previous board but males were in the majority after the election.

Age also came into play. Members of the new board were aged 60 to 80, compared with 30 to 45 for the old board.

In the last election, Asians worked hard to gain control of the board. About 169 people (about one-third of the eligible voters) cast votes in the election, and the majority were Chinese. "They have been doing the door-to door organizing," says Lau.

Seeking political power through elections is a natural part of the democratic process, says Lau, who believes Asians shouldn't be faulted for trying to get their own candidates elected.

After he was elected co-president of the board, Kwan developed his controversial after-school program.

While Kwan had been a member of the previous board, his actions were more constrained because Asians didn't dominate the board back then.

A teacher in Hong Kong for 20 years, Kwan uses a traditional Chinese classroom style to teach children enrolled in his program.

Obedience and discipline are required of the children. Kwan believes that "if there is no discipline there is no education," says Lau.

But this kind of learning style may not sit well with non-Chinese children, who are accustomed to a less-autocratic, American approach to education.

At first, Kwan's program was held in the CSTO space and served both Asian and non-Asian children.

Eventually, though, he decided that the existing space wasn't appropriate for what he was trying to do with the younger children.

Teenagers were coming and going while the program was in session and there was a fair amount of cursing going on in the area. In the end a struggle developed over how the space should be used.

When new space became available at 476 Tremont St., Kwan moved his program over there. Over time, the non-Asians dropped out of the program, apparently because they believed it was too strict.

One board member says this was when they started to hear complaints that Kwan favored Asian children.

In October, about eight non-Asian children were still enrolled in the program, but they also dropped out after the recent controversy erupted.

Kwan and Lau say the program is 100 percent Asian now because the adults pressured the non-Asian children to drop out.

Kwan, meanwhile, argues that he is providing the kind of program that Chinese parents want for their children.

Chinese parents are "serious about their kids' education," he says. "They don't like their kids fooling around and watching TV after school."

He says Chinese children growing up in immigrant households also need after-school help with English so they can catch up with their non-immigrant peers.

Kwan's critics, meanwhile, complain that much of the time in the after-school program is spent teaching children Chinese — which may not be of interest to many non-Chinese children.
"Chinese parents want to keep their culture for their kids," counters Kwan, who wasn't clear about what non-Chinese children should do during the Chinese lessons — whether they should learn Chinese, study on their own, or leave.

Kwan says his program is widely advertised and open to everyone at Castle Square. Non-Asian parents, he argues, simply choose not to send their children to it.
Lau contends that children and parents support programs they find interesting and worthwhile.
Chinese families tend to favor a disciplined approach to learning, while African Americans and Hispanics may prefer a less-rigid program.
"We cannot say good-bye all of a sudden [to our cultural values] because that is the way we were brought up," says Kwan.

Lau notes that Chinese make up more than half of Castle Square residents and shouldn't be blamed for developing programs appropriate for their population.
"I think they have equal access to services and programs, " says Lau, referring to African-American and Hispanic residents. "It's hard to break down the barriers, but we are aiming at getting there."

Long-time resident and board member Neice Snow was one of eight concerned residents who wrote the letter complaining about Kwan and Lau.
"The program is skewed toward Asian Americans," says Snow, who is African American.
"If you have a multicultural development and you want to serve the whole community, you have to serve every ethnic group."
Snow says some African American and Hispanic children complained they were not being allowed to enter the room while Kwan's after-school program was in progress.
She says a program that is suitable for Chinese children may not be appropriate for non-Chinese students.

Before Kwan became involved, the program was more relaxed, she says, offering a mixture of study and games. "He has turned it into a classroom setting," she adds.

She believes children started dropping out of the program because they thought it "was very strict and serious" and had an obvious Chinese-language focus. It was "not a friendly environment" for non-Chinese, she says.

Snow feels Kwan has generally been unwilling to compromise. "He just didn't want to work with anyone," she says. "He wanted to do everything himself."

While she says she understands Kwan's ideas about education are rooted in his Chinese background, she points out that "we at Castle Square have always been multicultural." Board members "are elected by many different races of people," she says.

As the board's co-president, Kwan should be looking out for the interests of all groups, not just those of his own, she argues.

Kwan is "trying to work with the Chinese community," but he is "not interested in working with other groups," she adds.

Snow believes Kwan wants to segregate children by race, noting that he once refused to allow Chinese children to take part in a pizza party with non-Chinese children from another program.

"Why separate the children?" she asks. "What we're saying is, approach it in a different way."

Snow says racial segregation is a problem affecting other Castle Square programs as well.

There are currently separate Girl Scout programs for African Americans and Asians, and the elderly program is also skewed toward Asians.

Castle Square tenants recently voted to clarify CSTO's bylaws so they could avoid similar conflicts in the future. They also voted to hire a mediator to help them resolve the current dispute.

"It's like we're stepping back instead of moving forward," says Snow. "But he (Kwan) doesn't see it that way."

At Castle Square, the races have always gotten along well, and the kids continue to get along well, says Snow. "It's not a problem with us living together," she says. "It's the leader that is leading toward segregation."

Although Chinese, African Americans, and Hispanics haven't had major difficulties living together over the years, relations among the groups have sometimes been distant, especially among the adults, says one Chinese parent. "Chinese — they don't talk to black people," she says.

Cultural differences often come into play at Castle Square, she says. African-American and Hispanic young people, for example, tend to be bigger, more aggressive, and more outgoing than Chinese kids, who tend to keep to themselves.

Chinese parents also tend to keep their children inside at night and generally under their control, while non-Chinese parents tend to be more liberal in this regard. "Chinese people are mostly quiet," she says.

African-American kids have also been known to use racial slurs against Chinese or make fun of them by imitating the Chinese language, she says.

But for Castle Square to work as a multicultural environment, people need to respect each other and be friendly with each other, she says, adding that she tries to say hello to her African-American neighbors.

She says that when Kwan knocked on her door and asked her to vote for him, he emphasized that it was important for Asians to get control of the board.

But she says she rejected his argument and eventually voted against him because she believes Chinese and other groups shouldn't be focusing only on the needs of their own group.

"As a rule, in their heart, they (Chinese) think they (African Americans) are different, but they don't hate them and they try to get along with them," says 80-year-old George Leung, CSTO co-president and a long-time Castle Square resident.

Thomas Ku, a high school student who volunteers at the Chinese after-school program, says the division at the Learning Center tends to work both ways.

While Asians may seek to associate with members of their own group, "blacks do not want to be with Asians," he says.

Ku says the dispute over the Learning Center programs shouldn't be construed as a case of the Chinese discriminating against African Americans and Hispanics.

At Castle Square, he says, he has heard racial slurs from both African Americans and Asians.

"I don't think that's race discrimination," he says. "They (African Americans and Hispanics) just think the program isn't interesting."

African Americans, he adds, like programs that include field trips and other kinds of learning experiences, while Chinese take a more traditional classroom approach.

Ku says he doesn't know if there was a calculated effort to segregate racial groups at Castle Square or if it just turned out that way.

But he believes that an integrated approach is the best one because America is a diverse society.

Ku says English should be used in Castle Square programs because Chinese

is a "foreign" language to non-Chinese.

Castle Square resident Hiraida Hiraldo says people stereotype each other. They have ideas about each other without knowing each other well.

If a black or Hispanic youth is "dressed with a hood or black jeans, they might think he's going to do something," says the 13-year-old.

On the other hand, African Americans and Hispanics are guilty of the same behavior. They stereotype Chinese young people as being quiet but smart, she says.

Hiraldo says the silence of Chinese youths is often interpreted as unfriendliness. "They don't talk to us," she says. "Some of them do, but they don't talk to us."

Hiraldo believes that people of different races generally get along well with each other at Castle Square and says she was upset by recent newspaper articles suggesting that discrimination is a big problem at Castle Square. "It makes Castle Square look bad," she says.

"I think it would be better if everybody is in one group," says 15-year-old Miguel Ferrer, a 15-year-old who attends a computer program at Castle Square.

Diana Davis, an African-American women who organized one of Castle Square's Girl Scout programs, says kids attend programs based on the needs of the children and the parents.

The adults who start programs naturally tend to attract and recruit people from their own racial group, she says.

Davis believes that many African-American and Hispanic children do not want to attend a strict after-school program like the one being offered by Kwan.

"A lot of black and Hispanic kids don't want to buckle down after school," she says. "Kids go where they feel comfortable."

Davis points out that the Chinese never complained when African Americans dominated the tenants organization, so why should African Americans and Hispanics complain about the Chinese now?

"Nobody complained when there were all blacks running it," she says.

One Chinatown leader suggests Kwan may be insensitive to the realities of a multicultural American life.

In the past, Chinese could isolate themselves in Chinatown and follow their own code of behavior without worrying about anyone questioning it, he says, but times have changed and adjustments must be made now.

Another Chinese resident at Castle Square says that ethnocentric attitudes held by some Chinese may be contributing to the problem and that Chinese are sometimes insensitive to the concerns of other groups.

At the same time, some African Americans and Hispanics stereotype Chinese. They see them as different from themselves and don't hesitate to let them know it.

Snow believes that stereotypes and misunderstandings on all sides is precisely why racial groups shouldn't be segregated at Castle Square.

"You've got to work on those sensitive issues, she says. "Don't ignore it and run from it! Open up to it!"

The Gun and Knife Are Easy to Have

WHEN SHE LEFT VIETNAM one night in the late 1970s, Susan had no idea where her journey would lead her.

Like many of the Vietnamese who live or work in Boston's Chinatown, she is of Chinese ancestry.

The mother of two children and a resident of Castle Square, she told her story one summer afternoon in the late 1990s.

"I left Vietnam with my family. I was on a boat for six days and I got very sick. At that time it was very difficult in Vietnam.

The communists had come. We didn't have work. We didn't have food. We had nothing.

In my life I passed a lot of difficulty but I'm still alive. It's fate. Sometimes I have a problem and someone comes to help me.

I was in a refugee camp in Indonesia for more than two years. I almost died when I was there...I almost died!

On the day I got the news I could leave the camp and come to Boston I was so happy.

All the time we were in the camp we were just thinking, 'When can we get to America?'

We didn't have work. We didn't have money. The only thing we thought was: 'When can we leave the camp?'

Everything was so different when I came here. So quiet! In Vietnam there were so many people — so many businesses on the street. There were a lot of people walking outside all the time. In Vietnam there weren't many cars. There were many bicycles and motorcycles.

Sometimes I prefer here to Vietnam. You have more benefits here. Sometimes in Vietnam — even if you are right — people with power will say you are wrong.

Only the top people can do what they want and get what they want. The low person — the poor person — can never do anything.

But I'm not totally happy here either. Before I came to America, my dream was to come here to study.

I was 19 years old and I said, 'Better that I go to school.' But when I got here I didn't know anything about life in America. I didn't know how to go to school. Then I felt homesick and I'd get upset.

After that I met my husband. I needed a partner so I got married. Then everything changed. I had a daughter and then I had a son.

I stayed home as a housewife and could not go to school. At first we didn't make a lot of money, so I couldn't pay for a babysitter.

I got divorced from my husband because I couldn't stand him having another woman.

I had a dream that I could do some small business, but it's very difficult to make my dream come true.

No, I don't try to make it come true now...no more. Now I just want my children to grow up and study well. They're doing so-so in school.

After I moved to this apartment I was happier, more relaxed. There was more room.

Before I had one bedroom, but now I have three bedrooms.

When I was a kid my family was a very happy family, but in America my sister lived somewhere else and my brother lived somewhere else.

They had their own family, so we didn't get together all the time. The life here is too busy.

In Vietnam we were happy because my father had a job. We went to school. We didn't have to worry about anything.

Now my father is here but he cannot do anything. He just gets SSI (Supplemental Security Income). I feel upset for him because actually he can do something.

When he came here it was a big change for him because he doesn't know English. That was a big problem. If somebody doesn't know English when they come here, it's like they can't do anything.

My parents told us to study hard, enjoy life and be nice to people — to help people when they needed help.

I am happy when I make somebody happy — if I can help someone.

Sometimes I pray. I have my god — Guanyin. When I was a kid, Guanyin was in my mind because my family, my grandmother prayed a lot on every

Chinese holiday.

When I have no one to talk to I talk to Guanyin. I say something in my heart.

I don't like the person who burns the incense every day. I don't do that. I put it in my heart. Buddha and Guanyin are really the same. Guanyin means the good heart.

I like Castle Square because it's not that quiet. I don't like a quiet place. When I go outside I can see people. I feel comfortable when I walk through this area.

I like the trees and I like the people. If I see more people walking I'm happier. If a walk alone I feel tired.

In America the gun and the knife are easy to have. That's why I don't like it. I don't go out at night right now.

But in just these last two years it has changed. We have security now. Before I heard about a lot of bad things, a lot of robberies.

There are too many people here [in America] who can't control themselves. There's too much freedom.

Freedom is good but you can't control the people [if you give them too much freedom].

Vietnam is a small place. Everything is close together. People are closer. Here you go to work and you see the people at work, but after work you don't see them.

I know a lot of people, but it's not easy to get together. My next-door neighbors are best. We play mah jongg. Four people at least. We bet money sometimes.

Last night I won $2, but sometimes I win over $400. It depends. If you are lucky you can win more.

I go next door so I can still watch my kids. I don't like to go far away.

My future? I want my kids to study good and get a job. I don't think too much about myself. I don't worry too much about myself.

I just want for myself an easy life one day. Don't let me worry too much. When I have money it makes me happy. If I had a lot of money I would buy a house for my parents. I would like them to travel.

Don't let them worry. My parents worry. I don't think they're happy because I still have one sister in Vietnam. I see they worry about her. She's still on the waiting list.

If my sister were here, my mother would no longer worry. I don't like seeing my parents with a sad face.

When I have money I can make my children happy. I can make my parents happy. To do anything you need money.

I make little money, but I still try to make them happy. If they're not happy, I'm not happy.

In the beginning my family didn't like me going with Eddie. But for me, Eddie is just a good person.

I tried to stop because he's black — a different race. The Chinese don't like mixed couples. My family 70 percent accepts Eddie now.

In Vietnam, the Chinese don't like the Vietnamese people, and the Vietnamese people don't like the Chinese people.

Some young people like each other, but the old can't accept it. I don't know why.

But I don't care what the people say when we go out. When the Chinese people see us, it's like 'You're strange.'

In the beginning I felt guilty, but then I told myself — why? I didn't do anything wrong.

So if they look at me now I look back at them. Eddie does that too. I say, 'Hi.'

Now we don't care.

Chinese people don't accept living together, but now there's nothing they can do because I don't listen to them.

I need somebody to always be with me and Eddie is a nice person...he's nice to me.

But something is always different. Chinese people like to eat on time, at the same table. This feels comfortable. In Vietnam, every day we eat lunch and dinner together.

But Eddie doesn't understand this. In the beginning I felt upset, but now I say, 'How can I change people?'

If he's at home we eat together; if not, I save some food for him. In Vietnam we eat together, the whole family, it's very happy.

'Everything Here Was Yesterday'

IN A HARD-TO-FIND STOREFRONT on Hudson Street, a group of older men are playing cards and socializing — doing what their Syrian parents and grandparents did on this same street earlier in the century.

At one time the men lived on these Chinatown streets but they have long since moved to the suburbs.

As often as they can, though, they return to this neighborhood club to meet with their childhood friends.

"We're like lemmings, by instinct we still come back," says Bill Kameese of Brockton.

The club is the last flicker of a once thriving Syrian community. The men are in their 60s and 70s now — the last Syrians with a connection to Chinatown. All of them are retired.

The club still has 15 to 20 members, but there was "a time down here when we probably had 400," he says.

"This is the end of this," says Kameese, a grandfather with 16 grandchildren. "This is for dinosaurs."

"It's an unusual situation where you can get men in their 70s and 80s who still see their childhood friends," he adds. "Our fathers came in here to play backgammon and have Turkish coffee."

George Hadaya, the owner of the club and one of the few Syrians who still live in Chinatown, recently met with club members to decide on the club's fate.

The Syrian community was fading and he was unsure if there were still enough members to continue supporting the club.

Hadaya expected the worst, but the men wanted to renovate the club and reopen it.

The club had been open for over 100 years and closing it was "like losing someone in the family," says Hadaya.

But time was catching up with all of them, he says. "I'm the youngest one of the bunch and I'm 72."

Hadaya has lived his entire life on Hudson Street. "We had a coffee house," he says. "We had Syrian bakeries...the music would go all along the street here."

Men smoked water pipes and played chess. On Easter Sunday, the churches organized a parade. There were traditional fencing displays in the street.

A big part of Syrian life involved the Christian Orthodox and Roman Catholic churches they attended in the neighborhood, he says.

Many of the old residents still come back to search for traces of their past. "If I'm here I invite them in," he says. "If we see each other 10 or 20 or 30 years from now, it's like seeing a brother or a sister."

The grandparents and parents of this last generation of Syrians emigrated from the Middle East — most were Christians, but the community also included Muslims.

Many worked as peddlers. "My grandmother sold Calvin Coolidge's wife linen in the White House," says Kameese."

Hadaya says his father was born in Turkey, migrated to Syria, then made his way to Boston, where he worked as a door-to-door salesman.

Like Kameese's grandmother, he sold linen, lace curtains, and oriental rugs. Governor James Michael Curley was a customer.

"My father went to the governor's house and sold to him," he says. The Syrians were "go getters," he says, "business oriented" people.

The community also had its brush with fame. The woman aviator Amelia Earhart used to work with young people at the Dennison Settlement House on Tyler Street.

"I remember one time we were all around her car," says Joseph Sabino. It was a big convertible. "We thought she was someone special."

And then there was the writer Khalil Gibran, who lived on Tyler Street and attended the old Quincy School on the other side of the block.

"I knew his sister and I knew his nephews," says Sabino. "He was a wanderer."

After the war, the Chinese gradually migrated from Chinatown proper to the Syrian neighborhood on the south side of Kneeland Street.

"The Lebanese sold buildings to the Chinese," says Neil Chin, who grew up in Chinatown. "The two groups didn't really get together that closely until the Syrians started selling their property to the Chinese."

Chin says the two groups "looked after each other" in the 1950s, but also stayed in their separate worlds. "They kept to themselves and we kept to ourselves, though the younger generation often became friends."

Although the two groups lived separate lives, they still have fond memories of each other.

"They were great people to live with," says Kameese. "We used to carry flowers in their funerals."

For an earlier generation of Chinese, memories of Hudson Street come replete with the smell of Syrian bread baking, sidewalk chess games, and men smoking water pipes on the street.

In the 1990s, a reunion was held for former residents of Hudson Street both Chinese and Syrian.

It's a street and a time that lies close to the heart of both communities, especially since one side of the street was demolished in the 1950s to make way for construction of the Southeast Expressway.

"After the war they (the Syrians) all went away," says Hadaya. They went to West Roxbury, Brookline or Wellesley. "The kids were growing up. They wanted to better themselves."

Hadaya was one of the few Syrians who stayed behind, raising his family on Hudson Street and running his business out of an office there.

"I loved the area. I loved being in town. The nostalgia! I have memories I can never erase, I can never lose."

"I feel the Syrians should have stayed here and built a community here," he says. "We're right in the heart of town. There's everything available to us."

"It was a glorious area," says Mary Mahanna, who still lives in the Oak Street building in which she was born. "I can speak some [Arabic], but there's nobody to use it with anymore."

Mahanna, whose parents were born in Lebanon, remembers growing up in a secure close-knit neighborhood — the kind of neighborhood where clothes hung on lines and men gathered in coffee houses.

"Everybody knew each other," she says. "We never locked the door."

In the 1990s, Mahanna fought hard alongside Chinese residents to stop the New England Medical Center from building a garage across the street from her building on city-owned land known as Parcel C.

"Of course when they wanted to put the garage up here my voice was very loud," she says. "Parcel C was a big hassle, but thank God we won that."

Mahanna has also been outspoken in other ways, fighting hard to rid the area of the prostitutes who often kept her awake at night. "I've shouted at them from the window," she says.

But today, she adds, there's "no more sitting out in the front door like we did before...everything here was yesterday...it's never coming back."

'I Try to Be Fair, Just a Human Being'

EDDIE WATKINS SITS IN HIS APARTMENT on a section of Tyler Street in Chinatown that was once the center of a thriving Syrian neighborhood. It's a warm spring day in 1995.

Eddie has been working for the Syrian-American owner of the apartment building where he lives.

For a time he lived in nearby Castle Square. He practices kung-fu with a Chinatown martial arts instructor.

He is one of the few African Americans involved in the Chinatown community. In the 1990s, he often performed the lion dance at Chinatown events.

"My parents were very good. I learned a lot of discipline from them — a lot of respect for older people and for anybody period, for doing the right thing. My mother was a church-going person. That kept her and us focused on surviving.

There were eight kids in my family and I was the youngest. My father passed away when I was 13.

He had a fast car and wanted to race with it. They coached him into racing and that's how he passed away.

I was the one who ran out and said: 'Can I go,' and he said: 'No, you stay here with them.'

I stayed and pouted because I wanted to go. A few hours later we learned he had an accident up the road.

What keeps me going is God. My mother still goes to church every Sunday. When I visit [her] I also go to church.

I get my drive and self-esteem from her. She pretty much paved the way for me doing things on my own and not just waiting for somebody to give me something.

Being nice to people, treating people the way you wanted to be treated and should be treated.

Not forgetting that I should get the same in return. That's pretty much what keeps me going.

Five years ago I started taking martial arts — kung fu. That interest came when I was in Georgia. I first started karate there. I just liked the sport.

When I got older, I started looking at the inside of it, the benefits you can get from it, the understanding, the thinking, the wisdom of it.

In kung fu we do meditation. It allows us to relax mind and body — forget about certain problems. Not forgetting about it totally, but just relaxing your state of mind.

At that point you can try to find a way to solve a problem. Rather than just giving up and throwing in the towel you try something out of the ordinary. You're reaching, searching. It lets you step back and reevaluate the situation.

I'm kind of mixed now — a little Buddhist, a little Christian. I'm a Baptist, but I don't go to church here.

I still worship God as being the almighty God. I pray. I still do it the old-fashioned way, by kneeling near the bed or just dropping on my knees and praying. I talk, I read the Bible.

I also meditate. We bow to the Buddha — or something like the Buddha — but I don't worship two Gods — I only worship one.

When I pray to the Buddha, I'm bowing to the kung fu — to the kung fu ancestors there.

In Chinatown, you almost feel out of place sometimes, like you're on a different planet almost.

It feels a little different because you can't speak the language. But the people I know accept me. I do know that.

Most of the time when you walk into a room and a Chinese person is near you, you don't get too much out of him.

Number one, it could be what they've already heard about you...about whether you're black or white. There is a stereotype.

But if they know you it's acceptable; if they don't know you, then it's like, 'No, I'm not going to talk to this person, I'm not going to look at this person.'

At first you feel a little uneasy, upset even, but after it happens to you so many times then you just know what the reason is...you know why.

And pretty much, to tell you the truth, I really don't blame them, because so many things happen. You hear about the same people doing it. You can go out and see the same people doing something.

But the misunderstanding is that they're not all like that. Everyone is not like that.

But if they don't give you that chance to find out, they'll never know. That's what I see.

There are some things you can talk about and some things you can't talk about. If you're grown up, you're responsible for doing right or wrong. Trying to be a normal human being is up to you.

I just focus on me, and if a point needs to be made, or if something needs to be known, I just speak up and say who I am and what I do and what I am about.

Sometimes we do lion dances or kung fu. As long as they see you with the group and you have on a uniform and they know who you are, they respect you the next time they see you.

Having a Chinese girlfriend makes it kind of awkward when you go out and see people, especially Chinese.
Chinese people look at you like you have three heads. The blacks look at me, but they don't say anything...they just look, double look.

It's funny. I can really tell what the blacks and Chinese are thinking but the whites I can't tell, because when they look at you, they're trying to see through you.
They pretend they're looking at something else, but actually they're looking at you. But I've gotten used to that.

At first her mother was the one to convince, more than her father. It took a while for her mother to accept me.
But she's a nice lady and her family accepts me — father, brothers, and sisters, I'm part of the family now.
If they don't see me, they say: 'Oh, where's Eddie?' They're nice and I respect them...we get along.

Race? It doesn't really bother me anymore. Like I say, I went through that before and I know pretty much how people think about certain situations.
What color you are does affect you. But we all get up in the morning and see a human being there — never mind the color. I try to be fair, just a human being.
I'm the kind of a person who doesn't like to get involved too much in aggravation or pressure.
This is where the kung fu comes in. I isolate myself from these types of situations. If I see something like that coming towards me I go the other way.
If it's something that's going to involve me I will stay there and deal with it. If it's something I don't want to be involved in I isolate myself.

UNDOCUMENTED

Life in the Shadows

WHEN OUTSIDERS ARRIVE IN CHINATOWN to have dinner, most of them see only the colorful signs and restaurants.

They're unlikely to look beyond the storefront businesses to the upper stories of Chinatown's aging buildings where residents often live in narrow closely packed rooms.

On Beach Street there's a one six-story building where single men — many said to be illegal — rent rooms.

A little further south along Tyler Street are row houses where undocumented people are also said to live. These apartments are in three-story brick buildings that once were part of a vibrant Syrian neighborhood.

On some mornings, a slender white prostitute with a cigarette hanging from her lip ambles out of one building, often accompanied by one of the men who lives in the apartment.

She looks drawn and a little wired. A bemused look on her face, she seems to be talking to herself though on closer look her lips aren't moving.

Another resident who appears to be undocumented often walks up and down the street, his hair and clothes disheveled, talking to himself, pulling at his hair.

Late one afternoon he becomes enraged when a newspaper photographer take his picture while sitting on the stoop of a family association building on Harvard Street.

As the photographer snaps his picture, he waves at him to stop and immediately demands the film.

In the late 1990s, social service providers and others in Chinatown began to see an increasing number of people from China's Fujian Province living and working in the community.

People believe the Fujianese are entering the country illegally near New York and migrating to Boston.

"Lately you see more, you hear the dialect," says Chau Ming Lee, executive director of the Asian American Civic Association.

In the late 1990s, more Fujianese were starting to appear at the Civic Association to ask about political asylum and employment authorization.

Lee and others believe the Fujianese were moving to Boston because there wasn't enough work for them in New York.

Many Fujianese who have come to the U.S. illegally have been applying for political asylum and receiving temporary work permits.

Fred Chin, a court interpreter, says the Fujianese tend to be itinerant, moving along a corridor that runs from Washington D.C. to New Hampshire. "They go where the jobs are," he says.

Any slowdown in the Chinese restaurant industry tends to keep them moving, he says.

Rev. Denis Como, director of the Chinese Catholic Pastoral Center on Tyler St., says the number of Fujianese attending church services and activities at St. James the Greater Church in Chinatown began to rise in the mid-1990s. The worshippers included families and single men.

The Fujianese are "friendly" and "appreciative," he says. There have been Roman Catholics in Fujian since the 1600s, he says.

Chin believes many Taiwanese with roots in nearby Fujian Province have been investing heavily in Fujian since the opening of China. The growth of the Fujian economy has led to greater prosperity and the resources to hire "snakeheads" to smuggle Fujianese into the U.S., he says

Chin says the Fujianese tend to dominate Chinese enclaves in Malaysia, the Philippines, Singapore, and Indonesia, but have generally been viewed as outsiders in a traditional Toisanese and Cantonese district such as Boston's Chinatown. "Boston hasn't offered them anything to stabilize their situation," says Chin.

He says Fujianese and Cantonese haven't always gotten along well with each other. "I think there's a lot of tension," he says.

Some of that tension may be due to language: the Fujianese and the Cantonese speak different Chinese dialects, though some Fujianese learn Cantonese — the dominant language of Boston's Chinatown today — once they arrive here.

Once the illegals arrive in the Boston area, many tend to use the small storefront employment agencies scattered around Chinatown to find temporary under-the-table jobs in area restaurants and construction companies.

Chin believes the exploitation of Fujianese was underway by the 1990s because they were an attractive workforce for restaurants seeking cheap labor. Their illegal status put the migrants in a vulnerable — but valuable — position. The Fujianese are often paid less than other workers because of their illegal status, say several people familiar with their situation. "In that sense, they are meeting an economic need," says Chin.

The infusion of Fujian workers into the local economy has also forced some older workers out of restaurant jobs, says one woman who has worked for many years in Chinatown.

"They work very cheap labor, so a lot of residents can't get jobs," says the former teacher. "A lot of my older students who are getting into their 50s can't find jobs now."

"Almost every family (in some villages) has at least one or two people here," says one Fujian immigrant who agreed to talk about the local Fujianese provided her name wasn't used.

In China, most of the residents of some Fujian villages are elderly who are too old to work and must hire workers from other provinces to cultivate land for them.

The villages are empty because many young people have immigrated to the West. When young people migrate to the U.S., they often send money back to elders in the village, she says.

Life in Fujian today is neither very good nor very bad, she says. Although most people have enough food to eat, they often don't have much money.

If a villager finds a job and can earn a good living in a Chinese city, he will stay in China, she says. People only want to leave China if they think they can earn more money abroad.

Some who leave are adventurers, she says. They want to see the world and experience a different kind of life elsewhere.

While many Fujianese come to the U.S. illegally, others — including her — are here legally.

People who migrate illegally generally pay the "snakeheads" about $30,000 to be smuggled into the US, she says. Some pay the fee in China, others make their final payments in the U.S.

Many borrow money from relatives to pay for the trip, but the fee must be paid in full within a week of their arrival in the US. "Almost everybody pays right away," she says.

She tells of one smuggling event that started with a 20-day overland journey to Thailand. Members of the group climbed mountains and traveled in boats. They hiked at night and hid in caves during the day.

Some members of the group become ill along the way. They were bitten by poisonous insects or came down with other ailments. She knows of several people who died along the way because they couldn't get to a doctor in time.

Once the group arrived in Thailand, the journey became less demanding. They stayed in a hotel and waited for a commercial flight to take them to the U.S. The snakeheads provided them with passports for the journey.

As soon as they landed in the U.S. they contacted their relatives for help. The migrants first went to New York or Los Angeles, but eventually spread out to places like Boston.

"They feel those guys (the snakeheads) are not bad," she says. "They're just doing business."

Sometimes they will do small favors for the people being smuggled, she says. They'll make long-distance phone calls for them or buy clothes for them.

Once in the U.S., most of the migrants find work in restaurants. They live with a certain amount of fear, especially if they read newspaper stories about illegal immigrants being captured or see police snooping around their neighborhood.

But they also feel protected because they know there are many illegal immigrants living in the U.S.

She says they don't feel guilty about breaking American immigration laws. They think that if they don't break any other laws here "Americans won't catch [them] or treat [them] badly," she says.

"The people are very nice people," she says. "They just want to make money."

Many of these smuggled immigrants also arrive in the United States believing they will eventually find a way to become legal.

She says the smuggling organizations in China often tell the migrants they can apply for political asylum once they arrive here.

"A hundred percent of the people who come in here are economically oriented," says Chau-Ming Lee, who believes the undocumented tend to taint the image of legal immigrants because the public may sometimes conflate the two groups.

Widespread criticism of China's human rights record leads many illegal immigrants to believe they can be granted political asylum simply by claiming they've been victims of political harassment or forced abortions or sterilizations in China.

In the past, many illegal migrants applied for political asylum by citing China's one-child-per-family birth control policy.

To cut down on abuses among applicants for political asylum, the U.S. Immigration and Naturalization Service (INS) has made it more difficult for applicants to be granted asylum.

Under the new rules, asylum interviews are granted six to eight weeks from the time of application and temporary work permits are more difficult to obtain.

A work permit will be granted only if the INS determines the asylum application isn't frivolous.

Illegals can also become legal by marrying a legal resident or finding employment if they have a skill that's in demand here.

Occasionally images of life in the underground leap to the surface. In the 1990s, illegal Fujian immigrants were involved in several incidents in Boston's Chinatown.

In one, a Fujian immigrant was kidnapped by other Fujianese, apparently because he owned them money for his passage to the U.S.

Law enforcement officials say snakeheads seeking to collect smuggling debts often prey on illegal immigrants. In the 1990s, illegal migrants were paying snakeheads as much as $30,000 to be smuggled from China to the U.S.

In 1994, two men were abducted from a Chinatown apartment and later released, leading police to speculate that money had been paid to the abductors to settle a debt.

In another incident, a legal immigrant from Fujian Province was stabbed in the hand and ordered by his roommates in a Chinatown boarding house to withdraw $10,000 from his bank account at a Chinatown bank.

The bank alerted the police after the restaurant worker, Hok Thu Chan, told the bank teller that he was being forced to withdraw his money.

One man who helps Fujianese find work here says the snakeheads often cheat people and lead the migrants to believe they can become rich easily in America.

"They didn't know the truth," he says. "Many people come here and they cry, but they have no way to go back."

Many, he adds, must work four or five years to pay back loans they took out to come here.

A Boston-Bound Boat Intercepted

IN A FEDERAL COURTROOM a few minutes walk from Boston's Chinatown, three unlucky Fujian snakeheads are on trial for attempting to smuggle 109 illegal immigrants into the U.S.

If they hadn't been caught, the snakeheads would have offloaded the 109 immigrants from their ship onto a boat near Bermuda, which would then have carried the migrants to the Boston area.

Witnesses testifying against the three Chinese nationals painted a grim picture of a profit-hungry smuggling industry that charges exorbitant fees, provides inadequate food, and ensures beatings for passengers who step out of line.

The witnesses who testified were passengers on the boat who were attempting to enter the U.S. illegally.

The witnesses testified against Ben Lin, Mao Bing Mu, and Sang Li, who were charged with four counts of conspiring and attempting to bring illegal immigrants to the U.S. for profit.

The men pled not guilty to the charges. Three other men, Hui Lin, Yiu Ming Kwan, and Nai Fook Li, had earlier pled guilty to the same charges in federal court.

The indictment alleged that Hui Lin, Yiu Ming Kwan, and Nai Fook Li made arrangements in Boston to have a fishing boat leave Massachusetts and rendezvous with a ship from China that was carrying illegal immigrants.

The Massachusetts boat planned to offload the immigrants and carry them to the Boston area. From Massachusetts the smuggled immigrants were to be transported to New York City.

In August 1996, the Xing Da, a cargo freighter loaded with about 105 illegal immigrants, departed from China.

On October 2, the U.S. Coast Guard boarded the Xing Da near Bermuda and transported the passengers and crew to Quantanamo Bay, Cuba, where they were interrogated.

Most of the Xing Da passengers were deported to China, but four remained in the U.S. to testify as government witnesses against Lin, Mu, and Li.

In return for testifying against the crew members, the witnesses have been granted immunity and will be given the chance to obtain visas to stay in the U.S.

One of those witnesses is Fu Chang Ni, who is questioned by Assistant U.S. Attorney Susan Hanson-Philbrick and attorneys for the three defendants.

Fu Chang Ni testifies that he left his hometown in China's Fujian Province on Aug. 11, 1996. He says he had met the defendant Sang Li (whom he called Ah Bin Mo) in a hometown social club.

He says Li asked him if he wanted to go to the U.S., and Ni said he did. Li told him he would need to pay $24,000 to make the journey.

Lee hadn't enough money at the time, but says he planned to borrow it and pay it back by working in the U.S.

"I had planned to borrow that money from loan sharks," he says.

Ni says he would need to pay back the principal and interest at a monthly interest rate of $3 per $100.

In China, Ni says he was employed as a farmer near Guangtao and as a construction worker when work was available.

He says he could earn between 1,200 and 1,300 yuan a month when he worked as a construction laborer — which is a good wage in China.

About 10 days after meeting with Li in the local association, Li told Ni he would be leaving for the U.S. the following night.

On the night of his departure, Ni waited with a group of people along a roadside. Li arrived in a van and took the group to the seaside where a boat was waiting for them.

They boarded a wooden boat and traveled on it for four to five hours before being transferred to the Xing Da.

The freighter then began its long journey east around the southern tip of Africa and across the Atlantic toward Bermuda.

Ni says most of the passengers on the Xing Da were confined to the "hold," a windowless cargo area below deck where the passengers slept on mats.

In the first stage of the journey, Ni was allowed to remain on deck, but later he and other passengers were forced to remain below. Only those willing to deliver rice and water to other passengers were allowed on deck.

The passengers were divided into small groups and fed rice and preserved vegetables during their journey.

Ni says he often shared a bowl of soup with his group but had very little drinking water. "I rarely drank water above deck," he says.

Ni says he knew two of the snakeheads on trial before the journey began. He often saw Li around his hometown and had attended school 20 years earlier with Mao Bing Mu.

When Ni became seasick and could no longer work on deck, Mu told him he would have to return to the hold.

At about the same time, Mao Bing Mu saw Ni steal about 10 packages of preserved vegetables. Ni says the Xing Da passengers were not given enough food to eat during their journey.

After he was confined to the hold, Ni says he occasionally went on deck to brush his teeth. One time Mao Bing Mu saw him and called him over.

"He started hitting me," he says. "He dragged me by the collar and started punching me all over here (pointing to his chest and back).

Ni fell to the deck and Mao Bing Mu and another snakehead beat him with a stick. "They started kicking me," he says.

He says one of his attackers said: "I'm going to beat you to death" for stealing food and refusing to work.

Ni says he saw two other people being beaten during the journey, including a friend who also testified as a government witness.

Hanson-Philbrick asks Ni if he knew he would be entering the U.S. illegally. Ni says, yes, he knew what he was doing.

"I would be traveling by boat and I didn't have any documents at all with me," he says.

The defendant's attorneys repeatedly suggest during their questioning that Ni is lying to protect himself and to make it easier for him to remain in the U.S.

Ni says he doesn't want to return to China because he fears the defendants' families will take revenge on him or members of his family for testifying against them.

Another witness, Yen Chin Chen, alleges that Sang Li threatened to kill the witness's wife and children in China for testifying against the snakeheads.

"Under the circumstances I don't wish to go back to China," Ni says.

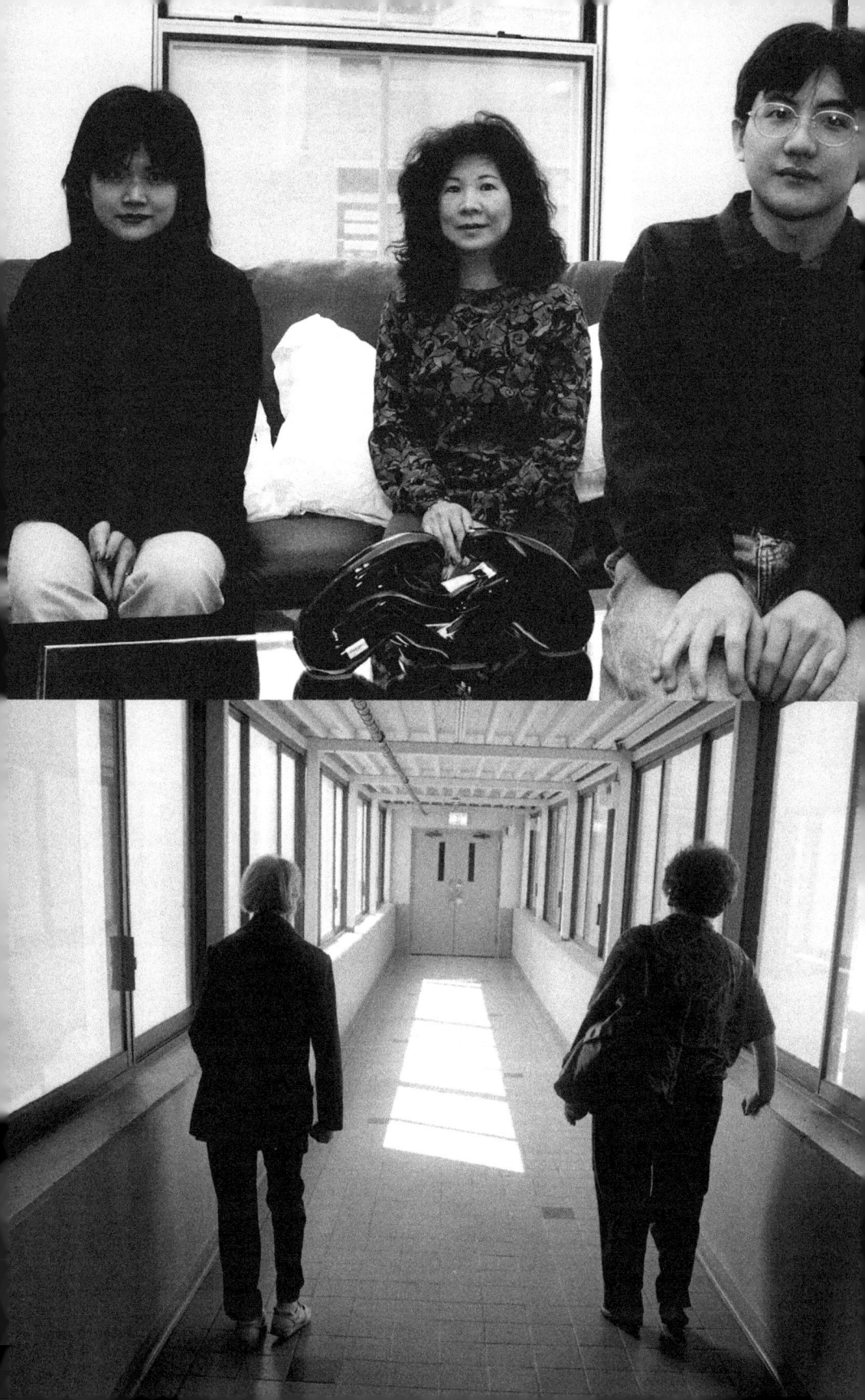

FAMILY MATTERS

Two Worlds Meet in the Family

THE PHONE RINGS IN THE HOME of Daquang Chu in an elderly housing complex in Chinatown.

His daughter-in-law is calling from her home in nearby Quincy and wants to know how her brother-in-law did in a job interview she arranged for him today at the factory where she works.

Not long ago he and Daquang Chu's daughter immigrated from Guangzhou, China, but in recent days, he has been growing disheartened by his new life here.

He can't find a suitable job and is worried about violence and a lack of rigor at his son's public school. He has even written a 12-page letter to his parents-in-law explaining why he wants to return to China.

To strengthen their son-in-law's resolve, Daquang Chu and his wife, Chen He, remind him of the success of their five other children who have immigrated to the U.S. over the last decade and a half.

Their goal now is to ensure that this last daughter and her family remain in the U.S. with the rest of the family.

In the Chus' extended family, everyone chips in to help the new family adjust to life in America. In many Chinese immigrant households, family dramas like the Chus' are the rule rather than the exception.

Many Chinese say the guiding principles of China's traditional culture are rooted in Confucian philosophy. Confucius taught that fulfilling one's allotted role in the family and society was the key to group harmony.

At the heart of the philosophy is an emphasis on self-cultivation, self-discipline, education, and respect for elders.

Chinese culture tends to encourage children to obey elders and put the well-being of the family before their own needs and concerns.

In America, immigrant parents are often determined to give their children the kind of education and job opportunities that were unavailable to them.

The value of education is so deeply rooted in Chinese culture that even parents who have not been educated themselves in China are eager to have their children educated in America.

In China, a working woman will pay for a younger brother's education, while a son who immigrated to America will generally invite his parents and siblings to follow him abroad, often housing and supporting them once they have arrived here.

"People will sacrifice for their family members," says Bak Fun Wong, the principal of the Quincy Upper School in Chinatown.

In China, people unable to support themselves traditionally could not depend on government for help, as in many contemporary industrial societies. "Their fall back would be the family," he says

"Chinese families, I think, are very good training for team work," said Ting-Fun Yeh, who worked for a city agency in Chinatown. "The bad thing is the individual can be stifled, but the plus side is you do learn to tolerate" the shortcomings of others and gain an awareness of your own.

In a Chinese family, explains Daquang Chu, "if you do something wrong, you have to criticize yourself."

A misbehaving son or a daughter reflects badly on the parents, who lose "face," he says.

People conclude that the child has misbehaved because the parents have failed to teach the child well.

For rural Chinese, emphasis on cooperation and clearly-defined family roles was as essential to cultivating the earth as the rain and sun.

"When you start as an agricultural society," says Yeh, "you just have to work together."

Yeh vividly recalls observing an American mother ask her four-year old child his opinion as she was about to make a decision. It was something many Asian-born Chinese parents wouldn't do because it blurs the line between parent and child.

Even I can't make that decision," laughs Yeh, who grew up in Taiwan and originally came to the U.S. as a student.

The centrality of family in Chinese life is embodied in China's folk religions. Shrines containing representative images of village ancestors are commonplace across rural China.

Similar shrines are also on display in Chinatown homes and family associations, which in their heyday served as substitute families for Chinese sojourners living abroad without their families — often because of restrictive immigration laws that discriminated against Chinese.

"The ancestor played the role of Christ, of God in religion," explains Yeh. "In China when you talk about afterlife, (it means) you go back to your family. It's to your ancestors that you go for a blessing."

Even now, she says, a visit to the home of her uncle in Hong Kong begins

with paying respects to her grandparents by kowtowing before the family ancestral shrine.

Such respect for ancestors in Chinese society is in part the result of the care many elders show in life towards the next generation and to the preservation of family unity.

In many immigrant households grandparents play a critical role in supporting family stability by caring for grandchildren while their parents are at work.

Since she immigrated from Toisan in Guangdong Province in 1983, Chen He has cared for at least six of her 10 grandchildren.

Before her son Ming Chu's parents-in-law arrived from China earlier in the year, she had been caring for his 2-year-old son Alex in her South Cove Plaza apartment every day while he and his wife Ling were at work.

Every morning Ming and Ling would drive to Chinatown from Quincy to drop off their son.

At the end of the day they would return to the apartment to pick up their son and she would serve them dinner.

Her husband, Daquang Chu, has also been actively involved in the care of grandchildren.

Every afternoon he would walk to a school bus stop in Chinatown to meet his granddaughter, take her to his daughter's home nearby, and stay with her until her mother returned home from work.

"We try to respect each other and work as a family," says Daquang Chu. "Because the family members try to help each other, it makes the transition smoother and quicker."

In a Chinese family, he adds, harmony is the key to well being and survival.

Like an increasing number of Chinese elderly in the U.S., Chen He and her husband prefer to live on their own in a senior housing complex in Chinatown, but that doesn't diminish their role in the life of the family.

Every day they see at least one of their children and are often in touch with them by phone.

Even small events in the family are not beyond their view. When her immigrant grandson tried to pierce his ear, his grandmother found out about it and immediately expressed concern:

"He's wrong. He shouldn't do it. He's only 12 years old," she told her son.

At the age of 7, Constance Lum, a counselor in Chinatown, immigrated with her family to Honolulu from China's Guangdong Province.

Lum recalls her parents working "from morning to late at night" in restaurants and hotels when they first arrived in Hawaii.

The family was unable to spend much time together because of the long hours of work, but she says she always felt a "sense of stability in the family."

Although she found it hard to talk about "personal" things with her parents and became frustrated when they couldn't understand what she was going through at school, she admired their self-reliance, respect for education, and sense of responsibility.

In her family everyone was told they had to cooperate to ensure a stable family life.

After watching her family struggle to make a new life without the benefit of wealth or the ability to speak English, she feels that much can be accomplished through cooperation and discipline.

Her Chinese upbringing and her family's experience has taught her that people shouldn't spend a lot of time blaming others for their circumstances but should instead concentrate on working hard to change them.

America, she says, is still a young culture and hasn't really developed a stable set of time-tested values to avoid some of the social problems that have beset the country in recent years.

But Lum says she also experienced her share of family tensions while growing up. Language and cultural obstacles sometimes exacerbated the generation gap. "I wanted them (her parents) to really understand what we were going through," she says.

Often she had difficulty explaining to her parents the challenges she faced navigating her life at school and outside the family.

She was also wary of certain traditional "Confucian" values promoted by her parents.

For example, she didn't believe that wives should obey their husbands and girls should aspire to be "the ideal Chinese good daughter." Such a daughter doesn't go out on dates and uncritically agrees with her elders.

She says her father tended to have expectations of her as a girl. He would tell her to wear more dresses and not to practice kung fu. He told her not to go out hiking with friends "because that was a boy thing to do."

Lum says she sometimes had to assert her independence and individuality, particularly when she moved to Boston in the 1990s.

"My mom did not really approve," she says, "but her father was more willing to accept her decision because it included a plan to go to graduate school."

Chinese emphasis on cooperation has been a key ingredient of the ability of Chinese immigrants to thrive in the US, but it has also been a thorny issue for some of their children.

Growing up in America, these young people inevitably come under the sway of American individualism.

Children who sidestep the wishes of their parents and pursue more personal modes of expression often end up feeling intense guilt for their transgressions.

If a Chinese child's personal concerns clash with those of her parents', the child's opinion may be discounted and the parents' word considered final. Children will tend to avoid being direct and saying what they really believe in order to preserve family harmony.

"I think what you do is you don't tell the truth," says one Chinese woman who felt compelled to conceal from her parents the identity of a non-Chinese boyfriend because she knew her parents preferred her to date only Chinese men.

"Why could I not tell them? Why did I live a life of lies? That brings us back to the whole issue of control — of the power the parents have over the kids," she says.

Telling her parents the truth would have hurt them and made her feel guilty. They had immigrated from China and had worked hard in their business.

Like many Chinese parents, they had sacrificed much to ensure a better life for their children. She felt she owed them something.

But sometimes it seemed that "you owed them your life" and that was perhaps too much, she says.

The cultural legacy of Chinese Americans may also have an impact on their life in the workplace, says Bet Key Wong, who grew up in Chinatown.

"Our parents taught us not to make any waves and to work hard," she says. But in America, "you do have to make waves."

Wong suspects that some Chinese Americans may be passing up out-of-state promotions because they're afraid to leave behind their aging parents, while those who do relocate often feel guilty for abandoning them.

Chinese families, meanwhile, are not immune to the pressures facing the larger society.

The number of divorces, teenage pregnancies, and single-parent families is growing among Chinese, says Rev. Thomas Lee of the Boston Chinese Evangelical Church in Chinatown.

"The fact that there's an Asian women's shelter shows that all Chinese families aren't the same," notes Anita Hum, an English teacher in Chinatown during the 1990s.

In a study of Chinese students in the Quincy public schools, May Quan Lorenzo, a Chinatown therapist, found that Chinese students were doing well in school and were generally well-behaved but identified fewer role models and have "very low self esteem, compared with the white students."

Lorenzo worries that some of the children do not look up to their parents, who may be working six days a week in restaurants and haven't the time — or in some cases the language and cultural resources — to guide them through their bicultural worlds.

The children of immigrant parents are also quick to point out the shadow side of the Chinese family.

Lum says she has known families whose homes were "like hotels" and whose primary focus was earning money.

And that much toted Chinese respect for elders doesn't always live up to the ideal. Elderly immigrant parents sometimes feel isolated and alone in their new environment because their children are too busy to spend time with them.

One Chinese woman believes the Chinese tendency to focus excessive attention on their own family leads to an inward turning, a family-centeredness that ignores the concerns of the larger society.

While children are taught to work together, the context tends to be the family. The result is that many immigrant Chinese are willing to contribute time and energy to the family, but not to activities of interest to the broader community.

In Chinatown, some social service workers complain that Chinese students tend to spend most of their time focused on earning money and contributing to the well-being of their families.

What happens outside the family unit tends to be of little interest to them.

Chinese Americans continue to refine their strategies to address these cultural conflicts.

"Even though I believe strongly in family ties I think I've adopted the idea of giving children more independence," says Hum, who adds that in her family her parents usually had the final word.

May Wong, a clinical social worker, wants to instill in her children a respect for traditional Chinese values such as family cohesiveness and self-sacrifice while also emphasizing traditional American values.

"They have to kind of think of themselves (and) be a little more aggressive, a little more opinionated, to do what they can to survive," she says.

Wong believes that a new "Chinese American culture" is emerging in which the strengths of both traditions are honored.

"I try to integrate the best values from the Chinese and American cultures. It's difficult at times."

"The more you learn to work with restraint — to work with discipline," says Yeh, "the more you gain from it.

"A creative society not only depends on originality and experimentation, but also requires personal discipline to realize one's design."

That "doesn't mean we negate the good points of American society," Yeh says. An openness to freedom of thought and the opportunity to be creative are highly valued by Chinese Americans, she says.

These also happen to be qualities that may not be given the respect they deserve in Asian cultures, says one recent immigrant from Mainland China.

Lack of respect for the young and excessive control by the elders tends to stamp out new ideas and stifle China's progress, she says.

What many Chinese Americans are seeking is a balance — itself a recurring idea in the history of Chinese thought — between the ideas of restraint and cooperation on the one hand, and freedom and individuality on the other.

In return for the opportunities offered by American life, says Yeh, Chinese Americans — like all immigrants whose ideas have enriched the American landscape — may have "something we can give back."

That something, says Bak Fun Wong, could be the joining of these two traditions, each with a set of unique strengths.

"I think the balance of the Eastern and Western cultures will be seen as the contribution and the impact we can have on this society," he says.

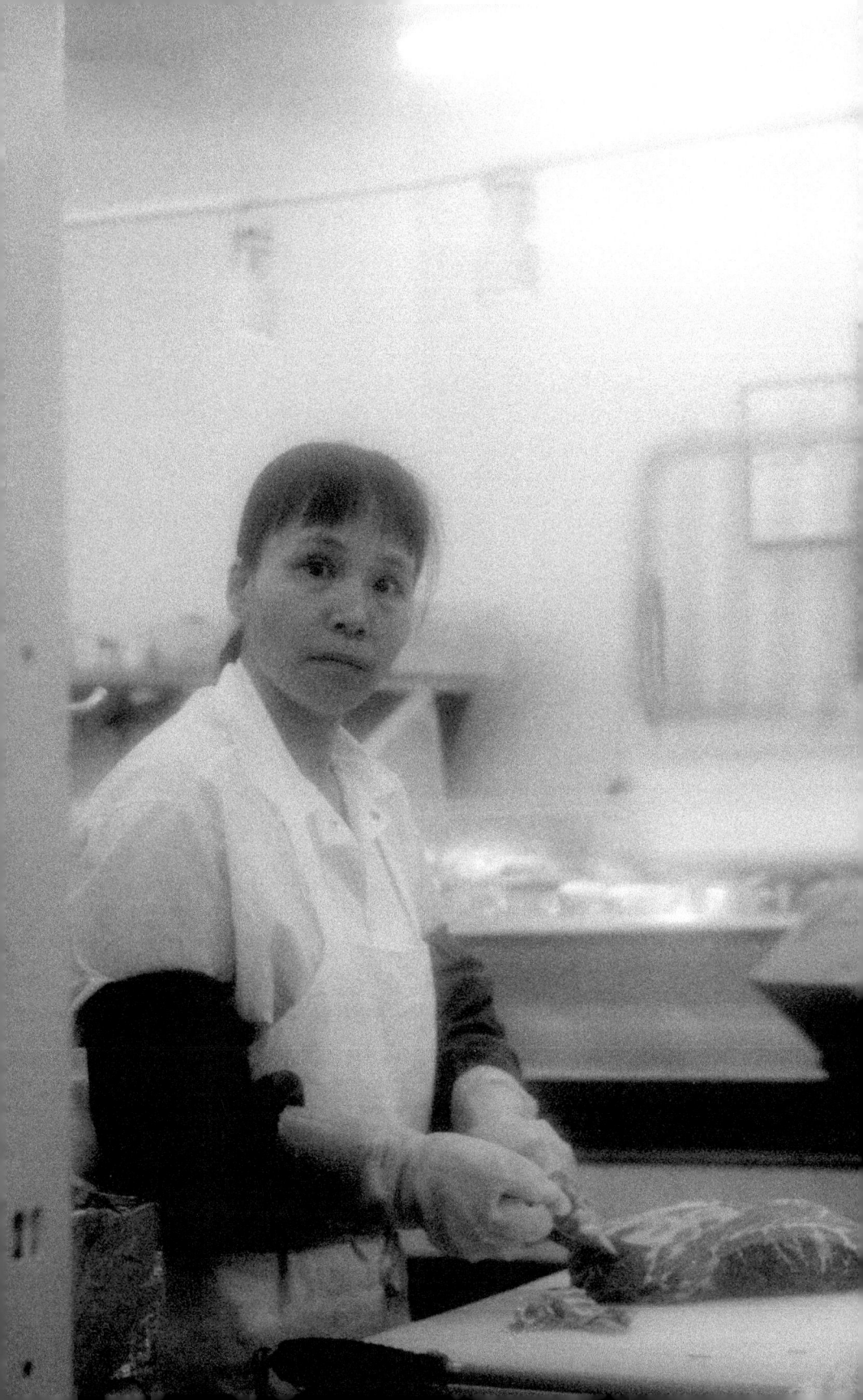

'This Bridge I've Been Trying to Build'

CHINESE YOUNG PEOPLE CONTINUE to maintain a deep-rooted belief that it's important to care for their parents in old age.

Although Elena Choy had recently been married, she was still spending most of her time taking care of her mother — who had Alzheimer's disease — in the family's home on a narrow side street in Chinatown.

Seated in the redbrick building where she had grown up, Choy tells her family's story on a snowy winter day in 1999.

"I was born in Peru and adopted by Chinese parents. The three of us immigrated from Peru at the end of 1969 and lived on Tremont Street in the South End.

My parents had earlier immigrated to Peru from China. My father went there when he was a young man and later returned home to marry my mother. Twenty years passed before she joined him in Peru.

From Tremont Street we moved to an apartment above the Eldo Cake House in Chinatown, and later my parents bought this place on Harvard Street.

Like a lot of Chinese men, my father worked as a cook. He eventually became a partner in a restaurant in South Attleboro which is still operating.

My mother worked mostly as a lacer of wine skins. The skins were in the shape of a bladder. At the time it was kind of a hippie thing. They had a leather covering and lace up the sides. She used to tie the laces on the side for the strap. They made those at the House of Taurus in the Leather District.

I went to the Quincy School at 90 Tyler St. until busing began. I had a few very good friends, and we all went to school on the same bus and came home on the same bus.

During that time I knew mostly Chinese kids from the neighborhood. It wasn't until college that I made other friends.

Chinatown at that time was very much a neighborhood unto itself. People lived here and socialized here and bought their groceries and did their things here.

But nowadays, you have this huge community. Chinese and Asians now use Chinatown as an open-air mall. They shop and eat in the restaurants and walk around and enjoy seeing other Asians.

But they don't live here. So I think that's really strained the neighborhood in many ways because of the parking and the congestion.

In the mid-'80s I went to Tufts University. I lived at the school, which was a big change, a rude awakening. For the first time it was clear I wasn't as comfortable being from an immigrant working-class background. As a child it was less obvious to me where I was in relation to the rest of society.

It's never easy to encounter the class wall but I think that after you get through the initial shock, you feel comfortable in your roots.

You can judge — irrespective of the class to which you belong — who are the good people and who are the bad people, what is moral and what isn't. Chinatown became a familiar and comforting place for me.

After the Tufts experience I felt a greater need to make a bridge between those two worlds.

But that was very difficult. I felt they couldn't (couldn't more than wouldn't) extend themselves to meet me in my new world. So I had to go back and build that bridge myself.

I think they felt uncomfortable leaving their world. Once, for instance, I bought them tickets to go to a Boston Celtics game because they loved to watch the Celtics on TV. I thought it was a great gift, but they didn't want to go.

They said it was nighttime and they weren't interested in going out at night. They thought it was a big hassle and said the seats weren't great. They could have a better picture on TV. So they couldn't or wouldn't.

I tried to bring them to American restaurants to eat. One time I brought them to Newbury Street. My mother just took one look and said:

"I'm not eating here."(I think it was really the Alzheimer's.) So we had to come back to Chinatown to eat.

These are just a few examples of the ways I tried to let them have experiences outside of Chinatown.

I did bring some white friends home. They were female, so that was okay.

After college I worked for a year and lived outside of Chinatown on Beacon Hill. I knew that was very difficult for them. They didn't understand why.

I brought my mother over there one time. I was surprised she even came with me. She was so hurt and so angry. I think that was the first time I'd seen her not being able to express herself. She was a no-holds-barred kind of person.

But this time I could see she was so upset by this whole thing that she couldn't even articulate, couldn't even yell at me. She'd lost control at that point because I could pay for myself.

According to them, there was space at home, so why would a single, unmarried daughter choose to live not far away when there was space at home.

I don't think they understood there may have been conflicts between us all that time.

I lived there for about a year before I entered a two-year master's program in urban studies and planning. I moved to Cambridge and also started dating Eric whom I eventually married.

It was while I was in graduate school that it suddenly hit me. I decided I was going to move home to take care of them. They were getting old – my father was in his late 70s and she was about 70. I would merge my world with theirs.

I had a vision of this atomic fusion in my head. Whatever happened, I was going to be fine with the move and we were going to live through this however it was going to be done.

Eric said, 'Why are you moving home? You're crazy.' But when he met them I think he finally understood that they were quite old. With that kind of goal in mind I moved home after finishing graduate school in 1990.

But I wasn't prepared at the time. We didn't know she had Alzheimer's.

My father became sick in 1993; he had a heart attack in the middle of the night. I was living at home at the time and was in the apartment when it happened.

My father had been a smoker for a long time, but he had stopped smoking about two years before he had the heart attack.

He said, "Why did I stop smoking? It gave me the heart attack." This is the kind of humor you need.

We managed to get through that crisis and my father came home. But my mother had Alzheimer's at that point and had stopped sleeping at night. That was hell because I still had to go to work in the morning.

One night I was up washing clothes and she fell into the bathtub behind me. She hit herself on the faucet and got a big gash and it was horrible. Blood was all over the place.

My Dad got some kind of Chinese powder – Chinese medicine – and he put it on her and it stopped the bleeding.

She had this big gash but by the time the EMT's came she had stopped bleeding. They brought her to the hospital for a concussion.

I said, "Oh, he put this stuff on her, I'm sorry, he just did it, I don't know what he put on, I'm sorry you have to clean it up right now."

And they said, "Oh no, it stopped the bleeding. That's great!"

When we brought her to the hospital with a gash in her head, she was screaming bloody murder because she didn't know what was going on and they were stitching her up and I just couldn't bear it.

I mean I tried to be there but I couldn't bear it. I had to go outside but I still could hear her as they tried to stitch her up. It was horrible, horrible.

We eventually started patching together 24-hour care for her, and we've maintained that up to this point. I'm part of that care. I've been able to do this because of my persistence and advocacy to keep her at home.

The people who come in to help her are the best people. We are fortunate in this community to have people, mostly older Chinese women, who are willing to do this job.

It's not the worse job because the wages aren't too bad and it does come with some benefits versus other jobs in the community.

You can count on them. Many give a lot beyond the job.

But it's a fight for people who try to keep their family in the home because it's difficult to get either Medicare or Medicaid to pay for some of these services. They don't want to pay for chronic need; they'll pay for acute care only. You have to patch together whatever you can.

There's also the medical profession. Many medical people think that if you have a bad apple in the bushel you have to take that away because it's going to affect the other people, the other apples — in our case maybe my father and me. So I think it's sort of American or Western thinking.

But the way I look at it is, we as a family unit should enjoy life together and suffer together. Whatever happens we should endure it together. And that's the way I've seen it play out.

It's been an amazing journey these last nine years! It's very difficult to do what I'm doing and I guess it's not right for everybody. But I think people should have the option of keeping family members in the home if that's what the person wants.

My understanding is that most elders want to stay in the home, so I think the option should be there.

Maybe in some ways I'm more Chinese than I think I am. I always think of myself as being so Americanized. I think I'm scared to think of myself as Chinese because I'm afraid that I don't know exactly what that means.

But I do know what it means to be American, and I think that's more comfortable for me. I think that's an interesting part of me that I have to explore sometime soon.

I think I try this hard because of this bridge I've been trying to build. I think I've succeeded at least in my own eyes.

Eric met my father before he died and actually spent quite a bit of time at my house. So that piece of it was resolved more or less, and things were good.

My father accepted Eric and we'd go out. He would have him over and cook him whatever he wanted.

I also brought my dad to my workplace and had him meet people there and that was also very good. This was about a year before he died, so I think that was a success.

In my mom's case I really think that without this disease I wouldn't have had the opportunity to be able to express the love I have for her. And I think that's also a success.

Many people in the community don't know about Alzheimer's disease. They think it's craziness or they think it happens because somebody has done something horrible in their past life. They think it's caused by evil spirits.

They think: "Well, you must have caused your mother a lot of conflict and upset. She was worried about you for not getting married and that's why she has this illness."

But that's a horrible burden to put on me. People need to be educated that this is an organic disease. When you examine the brain of people with Alzheimer's you can see very clearly the tangles. It's like seeing somebody with bad lungs, with emphysema.

Taking care of my mother has been a challenge, a mental challenge. It's like being an athlete running a marathon.

I'm not a religious person but it certainly has a spiritual component. It becomes a way of living and showing what your values are.

I'm hoping to be able to keep her at home till the end. You need those values to get through it, because it's just overwhelming.

The bar keeps getting higher. You have to energize yourself to do it. Otherwise you couldn't...you really couldn't. You have to trick yourself mentally to do it.

'I Was Never Submissive, Even in Vietnam'

IN THE SUMMER OF 1998, Jennifer (a pseudonym) was working in a social service agency in Chinatown.

An ethnic Chinese, she was born in Vietnam and left there on a boat when she was 9 years old.

She came to the U.S. as a refugee when she was 13.

My father was put in jail because he was trying to smuggle the whole family out of Vietnam. My mom left soon after my father was put in jail.

I was 1 1/2 when my mother left with my sister so that I ended up spending my childhood with my grand-mom.

I was an orphan when my grandmother took care of me. She let my aunt take care of me.

My aunt was really young back then and she took care of me whenever she could. But it was a difficult life for me when she couldn't.

We didn't find out until much later that my mother was actually staying not that far from my place.

When I was 5 years old my father was very sick and was released from jail. At that time we didn't quite know what his condition was. We later found out that he had cancer.

So we spent a lot of money and treated him but he didn't make it. I saw him for one year and then he passed away.

He was fine in the beginning, for a few months, but then he began to get really sick.

He had throat cancer. You could see blood running through his nose and he couldn't even talk. I was 6 when my father died.

Before he passed away he asked my grandma to locate my sister. He wanted my sister back.

So they found my sister somehow and forced her to stay with us. I don't know how they found her. They never tell kids a lot of things.

After my father passed away I went to school and we began to think about why my father tried so hard to smuggle us out of Vietnam even though he knew it was illegal. He knew that if he got caught he would be put in jail for life.

When I went to school I kind of understood why — Chinese in Vietnam back then — I don't know about now — were not allowed to attend university. It didn't matter how good your grades were.

I didn't attend a Vietnamese school because they don't see us as equals. I

went to a private Chinese school.

So we began to ask questions about my future. Even if I got a good education there would be no way I could get a good position in Vietnam. You have to have money to bribe people to get a job in an office.

So my aunt and grandma decided to follow my father's wish. My aunt and I tried to escape from Vietnam by boat.
It was very confused on the way to the boat. It was night and we had to walk a distance in water before we could get on the small boat.
As we were walking we heard the police car coming and everyone rushing and I was just walking and walking and I grabbed onto someone's leg and they pulled me on the boat and we just stayed there and it was confusion.

I didn't find out until much later that my aunt hadn't followed me. She didn't make it to the boat because the boat left early. I was with her when I was going to the boat and she got left behind.
Not until morning when everyone had calmed down did I start to get my senses back.
We were kind of safe then and I looked around and kept looking for my aunt but I couldn't find her.
I was crying, crying, crying, but there was nothing I could do. They weren't going to turn back and put everyone on the boat in jeopardy. So you just had to go on.

The boat broke down on the second day. We had been chased by pirates and outran them but the chase took its toll on the engine, which couldn't be fixed.
We thought we were going to die, but luckily an American boat passed by and saw us.

We burned all of our extra clothes and they stopped and rescued us and took us to Malaysia. This was 1987.
I stayed in the refugee camp in Malaysia for two years and then was transferred to a camp in the Philippines. I spent seven months there, then came to the U.S. in 1989.

An American lady adopted me. She belonged to a church that had been adopting orphans from refugee camps. She never saw me before she sponsored me.
At the airport, I didn't know how to speak a word of English and she couldn't speak my language.

I don't even know how we recognized each other. She had a sign with my name written on it. This was July 1989.

So she took me home. I had every kind of feeling at the time. I felt angry and I felt scared, but I also felt happy.
My uncle was in the U.S. I didn't know why he couldn't have sponsored me. Why couldn't I stay with him?

How come I had to go through all these difficulties and still have to stay with a stranger?

But I felt happy because now I finally could start my life. In the refugee camps, I didn't have to go to school if I didn't want to.
I didn't do anything during that time and had really fallen behind in my education. That time was totally wasted.
So I was happy because now I knew I was secure. I was 9 years old when I left Vietnam but by the time I came here I was 13.

I learned English fast. I had to speak English at school. I took English as a second language and got laughed at a lot because I couldn't say anything. When I spoke I said it all wrong.
But somehow I don't know how I got straight A's throughout junior high school.
The textbook was so difficult. I had to translate every single word in the textbook to read it.

At the end of junior high school my family came to the U.S. and I had to go back and live with them.
My grandma said I owed her and my aunt something because they were the ones who raised me when I was a child.
I lived with my foster mother for two and a half years before going to live with my grandma again when I was 15.

The American lady really understands me. She sees me as an equal even though I'm younger than her.
She encourages me to speak my mind. When I speak I look her in the eyes. When I disagree with her I tell her.
She encourages me to be my own person, to let me develop, to build up my self-esteem and make me feel confident. I have very low self-esteem.

My aunt and grandma, on the other hand, are very controlling people. They want me to be submissive. So it's totally like north and south. One person encouraged me to be my own person, the other group wanted me to be totally submissive.

I was supposed to follow everything my grandmother and aunt told me. I should always say yes and shouldn't look in their eyes when I talk.

I felt crushed because I wasn't allowed to have my own ideas. In their eyes I was a very rebellious person. They said I was too Americanized. They said I had forgotten my roots. My roots are Chinese, yet I don't act like one.

And I would think: You are ignorant...you cannot force me to be whoever and whatever you want me to be.

I got exposed to both the Chinese and American cultures. I should be free to choose elements I like from both cultures and be myself and make my own choices.

It was a rough time. They constantly hit me and tried to make me be submissive, but they stopped after I tried to commit suicide twice.

I was so tired. If I couldn't be my own person I would just die. My grandma had a whole drawer filled with medications.

One night I volunteered in school and my grandmother and aunt waited for me to come home. They yelled at me and said, "You're so stupid."

They didn't like American people back then. Now they're okay, but back then they would say:

"You're so dumb, you help those American ghosts. What do they do for you? They don't do anything for you. They don't feed you, they don't put clothes on your body. When you don't have money they don't help you. So why are you doing free things for them?"

I survived that suicide, the first one. The second one was when my foster mom tried to contact me. She tried to ask me to go back with her because she said she missed me and I missed her too. I missed the carefree lifestyle, and I missed the affection too.

I know now that every single member of my family loves me, but I didn't understand their way of expressing their love back then.

I was very young. I didn't know how they expressed love. I always thought they didn't love me.

My foster mom is different. She used to give me hugs and would tell me every night that she loved me.

So back then I thought my foster mom and my sister and my boyfriend and my father were the only people on earth who cared about me.

I really wanted to go back to my foster mom, but my grandma and aunt wouldn't let me.

They said, "We raised you up; you owe us something. If you raise a dog, the dog will wag its tail when it sees you. But you don't even know how to be grateful for what we give you."

After the second time I said, Okay, somehow, someone out there doesn't want me to die. I tried twice and I'm not dead yet.

I said, Okay, I won't try it anymore, and committed myself to school and worked really hard at school. I got straight A's through high school and met my present boyfriend.

When it was time to go to college I had developed into my own person. I was strong.

There was nothing my grandma and my aunt could do to me because they knew I didn't even fear death.

So if I didn't fear death, then what did I fear? So they totally gave up on me.

I came to Boston to find myself again — to develop who I am even though my family kind of opposed it.

But they knew it was no use to try to stop me because I was beyond being rescued. I was beyond help.

Now we have a very good relationship. We don't see each other that often but I still call and talk to them and kind of counsel them when they have problems. I help them solve their problems.

When they need money I send money back. They're not trying to control my life now.

My two aunts work in a factory. They don't speak much English. My whole family works in the factory.

My grandma is taking care of the babies. I stay in touch with her too.

The U.S. fits me well because I am a carefree type of person. I speak my mind. I believe that as a woman I am equal to a man. I believe I am capable and that if I put my mind to something I can succeed.

I want to get into the human resources field. I will go back to school to get my master's, maybe an MBA, even a Ph.D. I can make a life for myself and have a career. I love the freedom.

I could not have all that in Vietnam. In Vietnam women stay home and cook. And men — no matter what they say — expect you to be submissive.

When you're at home you 're submissive to your family; when you're married you're submissive to your husband; when you get old you're submissive to your children.

So women are always very, very submissive, but that's not me. I was never submissive, even in Vietnam.

Late-Life Americans

THEY LIVE IN HIGHRISE APARTMENT buildings scattered around Chinatown. Many dress in the dark clothing of post-revolutionary China.

You see them on the streets and in the markets, often with very young children or other elderly.

Early in the morning some perform tai chi chuan and other exercises on nearby Boston Common.

The elderly make up a significant portion of Boston Chinatown's population. Most are poor and living on Supplemental Security Income (SSI), Food Stamps, and Medicaid.

Many came to the U.S. late in life to join children who migrated earlier. They often spend much of their time caring for grandchildren — at least while the children are small.

Childcare in America is expensive and Chinese grandparents offer the perfect solution for struggling young immigrants.

But once their grandchildren grow up and the grandparents are no longer needed to care for them, many elders suddenly feel unwanted.

In China, many elders live with their children, but here in America life is more complex.

American lifestyles and values sometimes clash with traditional Asian values.

There are pressures in daily life here that are unknown to people who have spent most of their lives in a slower-paced Asian society. People in the U.S. don't have as much time to spend with their aging parents.

When President Clinton signed a welfare reform bill in 1996, it brought into relief the precarious living conditions of many immigrant elders.

The welfare measure included a provision barring non-citizens from receiving Food Stamps and SSI, which are the primary sources of support for many Asian elderly.

On a fall night in 1996, many older Chinatown residents attend a meeting at the Quincy School to find out how the new government welfare measure will affect them.

Most of those attending are over 60 and living in subsidized housing in Chinatown. Most receive SSI and Medicaid.

If they don't have access to SSI they will have to turn to their children for support.

Although some immigrant families in the Chinese community struggle financially and can't afford to support more people, others have the resources to support their aging parents.

Ruth Moy, executive director of the Greater Boston Chinese Golden Age Center, believes that if benefits for the elderly are unavailable, families would be less willing to sponsor their elderly relatives and the result would be a reduction in immigration.

Bao Xian Cai was 67 when she immigrated from Guangzhou, China, to join her son here in 1986.

When she first arrived in Boston she worked as a dishwasher in a Chinese restaurant — a typical job for immigrants with few work skills. She worked there for seven years, she says.

But once she became eligible for SSI she no longer had to worry about working in a restaurant.

She and her son share an apartment in Chinatown's Mass Pike Towers, one of Chinatown's subsidized housing developments. They live on her $506 monthly SSI payment and his income, which she says is unstable.

She says her son has an illness that limits his ability to hold a full-time job.

Bao says she is studying to become a U.S. citizen but is worried about the future. If she lost her SSI, she would have to go out and find a job again.

Social Security isn't an option because she hasn't worked here long enough to qualify for it.

Mrs. Lam, another Chinatown resident who has come to the information meeting, is also concerned about losing her benefits.

The 72-year-old woman says both she and her husband rely on SSI for their income.

Lam came to the U.S. from a village in China's Guangdong Province in 1984. Her sister agreed to sponsor her and her husband, though unlike other older immigrants who follow their children to the U.S. the Lams preceded their children here with plans to eventually help them immigrate too.

When she and her husband arrived in the U.S. they worked in restaurants and factories (pharmaceutical and leather goods factories) — typical jobs available to older immigrants who come to the U.S. with little knowledge of English and limited education.

She says she retired six years later when she became eligible for SSI. If she loses her SSI now she worries she will have to return to her village in China.

"My children also have a very difficult life here," she says. "It would be difficult for them to support us."

Lam says she is studying to become a citizen but is worried she won't be able to pass the English-language component of the citizenship test. She had very little schooling in China and can barely read and write Chinese.

She says she recently passed the English multiple-choice section of the test by guessing and carefully studying how the questions were arranged.

She says she answered the questions correctly without really knowing the meaning of the words.

While most of the people who have come to the meeting tonight are elderly and worried about losing their SSI benefits, Mrs. Lee is here because she's worried about losing her welfare benefits.

Not long after her arrival here from Hong Kong in 1979, her husband died and she suddenly found herself in a new country with two small children to raise.

Lee applied for welfare to support them and has been receiving it on and off ever since.

Now state and welfare reform measures mean that Lee, who has only one child living at home now, must discontinue collecting welfare next year.

She says she is close to completing a two-year associate's degree at Bunker Hill Community College in Boston and has a small income from delivering newspapers in nearby Quincy.

Over the years Lee has done volunteer work in Chinatown and held a number of part-time jobs, but none of the jobs seemed to suit her or provide her with enough income and health insurance to support her family.

She says her husband's sudden death and her lack of English skills and education have held her back over the years.

"Even though I doubt my future, I just keep going," she says.

Lee says few Chinese receive welfare or look favorably on those who receive it. Even her brother, she says, is critical of people who refuse to work and make a habit of receiving welfare.

"I don't see the Chinese [receiving welfare] very much," she says. "They feel shame," or else are "afraid the government will throw them out [if they do]."

The women who have come to the Asian American Civic Association today to start the lengthy process of becoming a U.S. citizen are all in their 70s or 80s.

They're willing to go through the citizenship process to avoid losing their

SSI and Medicaid benefits.

One 75-year-old woman has come to the agency with her daughter to fill out an application form.

She takes a seat in front of a white background screen to have her photo taken.

Taking the citizenship test will be less stressful for her because she can take it in her native Chinese. She has this option because she is 75 years old and has lived in the U.S. for 19 years.

But she is still worried about the test, worried that she won't remember the answers to the questions.

Although she has been in the U.S. for two decades, she only recently decided to become a U.S. citizen.

Like many elderly Asians, she's going through the process now to protect benefits threatened by changes to U.S. welfare regulations.

She immigrated to the U.S. from Myanmar in the 1970s and worked for nine years in garment factories in Boston.

Because she didn't work long enough to accumulate the required 40 work quarters to be eligible for Social Security, she instead was able to collect SSI, a government welfare program for the poor, elderly, and disabled.

Many Chinese elderly have a deep fear of the English-language section of the naturalization test, says Peter Jae, who runs citizenship classes in Quincy.

While Jae believes it's useful for new citizens to know English, he questions the value of requiring citizenship applicants to learn the language so late in life.

He says many pass the test by memorizing key English words and sentences — but they can't really speak English.

Although some immigrants don't want to invest the time and effort required to learn English, others are illiterate in Chinese and struggle to learn a second language.

Jae recalls the case of one 92-year-old woman who recently came to him seeking help to become a citizen.

Members of her family wanted her to apply because they feared she would lose her SSI.

He counseled her family to avoid subjecting her to the rigors of learning English at such a late age. "Why give her this hard time?" he says. "Just give her a little money."

"I think the elderly come because of the family," says Jae. "If you bring them here, you should support them."

Alone in the New Land

WHEN THEIR DAYS CARING FOR grandchildren are over, many older Chinese — including some from surrounding cities and towns — end up living alone.

"I think most of them have children over here," says social worker Wendy Lam of the Greater Boston Chinese Golden Age Center, which runs daytime social programs for seniors in several housing complexes in Chinatown.
"Sometimes the elderly prefer to live alone," she says. "They want their own space."
Others, however, believe they will live with their children once they arrive in the U.S. and are disappointed when things don't work out as planned.
In some cases, their children don't have enough space for them in their homes; sometimes elders find it difficult to get along with grandchildren who are growing up under the influence of an American culture that feels alien to them.
"It really upsets them," says Lam. "They expected maybe they could stay close to their family."

Peggy Yang, 74, often comes to Hong Lok House in Chinatown to serve as a peer counselor for the elderly.
She says family conflicts aren't generally a problem when the grandchildren are young because the elders are still valued as caregivers.
"When they (their children) have babies, they want the parents to take care of them," says Garrett Tu, a Chinatown social worker.

But when the children start to grow up, the elderly become more of a burden and space in the house becomes an issue. Conflicts arise and the elders may no longer feel valued and wanted.
Their Americanized grandchildren may not like their Asian-born grandparents telling them what to do.
The elderly, on the other hand, find it hard to tolerate some of the behaviors of American teenagers.
Conflicts over food and other differences start to upset family harmony. Conflicts with in-laws also become a major problem.

Social workers say some older immigrants come to America with illusions about life here. Some expect too much from their children, who are also struggling to make new lives in the U.S.
Many elderly believe it's their right to be taken care of by their children and the U.S. government.
In China, three generations often lived together in the same house. The

young respected the authority of elders and obeyed them even as adults.

But here in the U.S. — and increasingly in China as well — that tradition is coming under pressure.

In the U.S. the elderly have the option to move into elderly housing and support themselves with the help of other social benefits, making it possible for young and old to live apart if that is what they prefer.

Chinatown's social workers say it's sometimes hard to get children involved in the lives of their elderly parents.

"They think it's our responsibility to take care of them," says social worker Garrett Tu.

"We ask them to come to their birthday party, but they say, 'I don't feel comfortable there,'" says nurse Mary Leung.

Chinatown social workers say the elderly start to feel isolated and abandoned if their children don't express concern for them. Many find it difficult to ask their children for help.

"They seldom have family support," says Kun Chang of the Golden Age Center. "Their families should come to visit them."

"They say Chinese have good family values, and that's true," he says. "Unfortunately here (in the U.S.) it really changes."

Chang and others believe the changes can be attributed in part to the way people live in America and the pressures placed on families here.

American life is fast-paced. People are always busy. Everyone thinks there's not enough time in the day here.

In America the elderly are expected to be as independent as their children.

"Their children are also under great pressure," says Chang. "It's very difficult here to earn a living, to raise children."

"There's a growing elderly population among Chinese," he says, adding that their age is growing.

In an earlier era Chinatown seniors tended to be in their 60s and 70s but now they're in their 80s and 90s, says Chang.

Many are frail and have more serious health problems, including Alzheimer's disease and dementia.

"I really see more cases in the community and they really need a lot of services," says Chang.

The elderly prefer to live at home for as long as possible and generally dread the thought of going to a nursing home, where they believe their quality of life will decline rapidly.

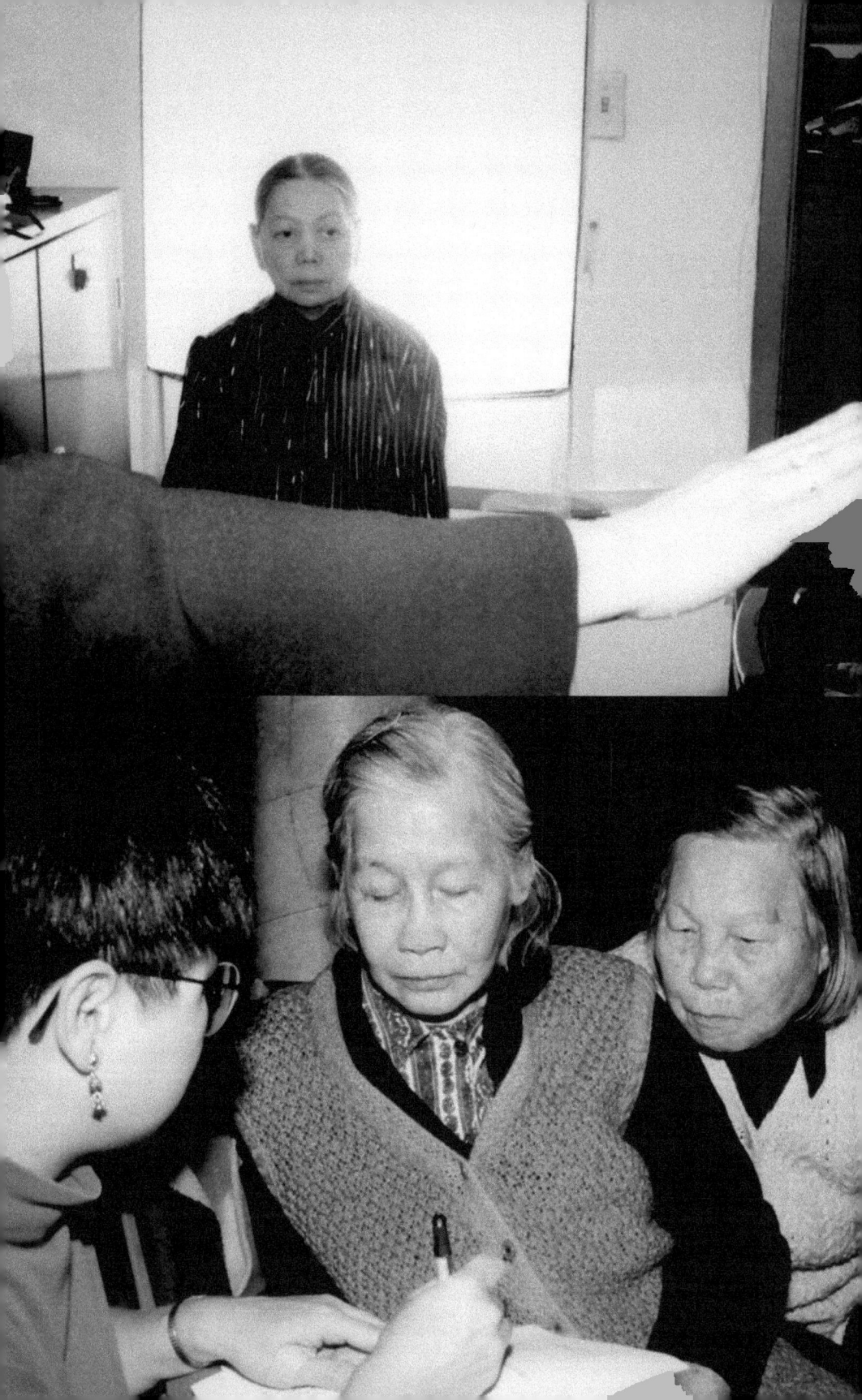

Everyone Here Is My Friend

LEE SHUN TAI'S FACE LIGHTS UP when she picks up a playing card. She has a smile fixed permanently on her face, illuminating her 97 years.

With a fan-shaped set of cards held firmly in her hand, she talks quietly to her card-playing partner who sits beside her.

Every weekday morning Lee comes to Quincy Tower in Chinatown for a full day of activities and socializing with other elderly friends.

"They love each other," says nurse Mary Leung of Lee Shun Tai and her friend. "They keep each other company."

Lee Shun Tai was already in her 80s when she made the long trip to America from a village in Toisan, China.

She remembers how surprised the customs official was to see her standing there waiting to enter the United States on that day in 1981.

He asked her how someone her age could make such a long and difficult trip. At the time, she said, she didn't think anything of the trip or of coming to America at such a late age.

But getting to America was easy compared to the work that awaited her in America.

Lee thought she was just coming to the U.S. for a vacation with her daughter but ended up staying here to help care for her granddaughter.

From that point on her days were filled with housework and carrying a child around on her back.

Lee says she hasn't any regrets about her decision to stay in America. She likes it here and saw no reason to return to China.

In China, she had to chop wood and work hard in the fields as a village farmer. In America her life was much easier despite the hard work of caring for a child in her 70s and 80s.

Now Lee lives in elderly housing in Chinatown. Her granddaughter and daughter regularly come by to visit her, and she sometimes stays at her daughter's home.

Lee says she prefers to live alone now, joking that if she lived with her daughter they would probably end up bickering about one thing or another.

Her nights are a little lonely, she says, but during the day she has a lot to do — a lot of friends to pass the time with.

Everyone here in the room is her friend, says Lee with a smile and a wave of her hand.

Sheng Xiong Xiao, 76, makes the trip to Hong Lok House just about every day now.

He says he didn't find it difficult to adjust to life in the U.S. but knows that some immigrants haven't been as fortunate.

He knew one person who used to tell him that living in the U.S. was like living in a prison.

He didn't know the language or the culture, he had nowhere to go, no way to feel comfortable and connected with the life around him. Unable to adapt, he eventually returned to China.

But Sheng says he's happy to be living here. He has freedom and doesn't need to worry about health care and financial matters because he receives SSI and Medicaid.

He suffered during China's Cultural Revolution and appreciates this country's democratic traditions.

When Sheng and his wife first came to the U.S. they lived with their son's family in Quincy, but now he prefers to live on his own.

Living on his own makes him feel more independent, more capable of taking care of himself. "I feel more comfortable living separate," he says.

The dancers move cautiously across the floor. They don't know the steps exactly, but they're eager to learn.

Kim Sit often spends time helping them remember, guiding them through dance steps familiar to them from their youth.

Slowly now the ballroom at the Chinese Cultural Center in Chinatown is filled with dancers.

The music is turned up, the dancers seem more sure-footed, the conversation is suddenly livelier.

Kun Chang stands nearby, watching the dancers spin and balance, impressed by their energy and skill.

"This kind of development is recent and represents a "more active type" of socializing for the Chinese elderly, he says.

"I think they like to have more activities, but they're looking for someone to organize for them," says Chang.

In China, the government tended to make decisions for them and provided most of the benefits, but in the U.S. there's a more democratic tradition and people are expected to act more independently.

"They're mostly looking for free services," says Chang. "They believe that when they come to this country everything is supposed to be free."

Chang says the Golden Age Center now asks the elderly to pay a small fee for certain events so they won't take them for granted.

Social workers tell them now that "everything is not free" and that government funding isn't endless.

One participant in the dance party today complains that activities in the U.S. often require money.

In China the activities are free and more extensive than those here, she says.

Ci Ci Huang, 71, lives with her husband in an elderly apartment in Kenmore Square.

Huang, who arrived in the U.S. 13 years ago, spends her days taking long walks and participating in activities like this Thursday afternoon dance party.

Huang was raised in Taiwan and is the mother of three children. She says she and her husband prefer not to live with their children here.

It's not always easy for parents to live with their children, she says, especially when in-laws are involved.

Although many Chinese elders now have more free time to pursue leisure-time activities like dance parties in Chinatown, many continue to spend time caring for grandchildren or spouses who are ill, says Chang.

"A certain number of people provide a very vital service," he says. "These elders have little free time because of their family responsibilities."

Sojourner Families

IN THE EARLY DAYS OF BOSTON Chinatown, residents were mostly single men living abroad without the security and comfort of family life.

Most of these sojourners came from Toisan in China's Guangdong Province and many shared the same family name.

There were Wongs and Chins, Leongs and Lees, Woos and Yees.

In the Chinese villages where many of these residents were born, most of the villagers shared the same family name and generally saw themselves as members of the same extended family.

When these travelers arrived in America, they tried to recreate a sense of family by establishing the family associations found today on the upper floors of buildings on Beach Street and Tyler Street, Hudson Street and Harrison Avenue.

In the early days, the associations wielded substantial political power in Chinatown, but over the years their power has diminished as conditions in Chinatown have changed.

Although the associations continue to send representatives to the Chinese Consolidated Benevolent Association, their power today is a shadow of what it once was.

Reforms in the immigration law in the 1960s and support for family reunification gradually led to the weakening of the associations.

The era of the single male sojourner has mostly passed in Chinatown. Villagers migrating to the U.S. from rural China bring with them extended families now, abolishing the need for surrogate families here.

But today's family associations in many ways continue to be vibrant organizations, serving as daytime gathering places where retirees socialize, read newspapers, play mah jongg, and chat.

Although mah jongg is often criticized for its association with gambling, it's still the dominant activity in some associations.

In recent years some of the larger associations have been rethinking their goals and seeking ways to attract younger members.

In the 1990s some chose younger presidents such as Wilson Lee, who eventually took advantage of the connections he developed as president of the Lee Family Association to become president of the Chinese Consolidated Benevolent Association.

"The mission has changed to accommodate the needs of today's society,"

says Lee of the associations.

In the past the associations were available to mediate disputes, help members out in times of trouble, and arrange to have the bodies of the deceased returned to China for burial.

But many of these original services are no longer needed or are provided by Chinatown social service agencies.

Instead, today's associations are being reborn as carriers of Chinese culture to a new American-born generation who have largely lost touch with their roots, says Lee.

Still, some family association traditions may not sit well with members raised in the U.S.

In the 1990s, some clubs were still providing separate clubs for women, allowing only men to become members of the main associations.

Financial concerns have also been an issue. Many associations own property that generates substantial rental income, but in some cases there has been little oversight over association finances.

Critics of the associations believe that some of this income should be used to support social services.

Beverly Wing, whose father and grandfather were officers in the Moy Family Association, says she and her brother have had limited contact with the association, in part because they felt that input from the American-born generation was generally not welcomed.

She is also uncomfortable with the male-centric attitudes of many older Chinatown organizations.

Women, she says, have typically been given less status in family associations, where membership is often restricted to men.

She believes today's associations should be focusing more resources on providing services to help Chinese families adapt to American society.

Trouble at Gee How Oak Tin

IT'S A TYPICAL MORNING AT THE Gee How Oak Tin Association in Chinatown — the family association for the Chin, Woo, and Yuen families.

The association's club is in a building it owns above a Chinese herbal medicine shop on Harrison Avenue.

A group of men sit at a long table in the middle of the room, some talking, some reading newspapers.

A woman and her small son drop by to talk with some of the members.

The woman's husband recently died and the association has been helping

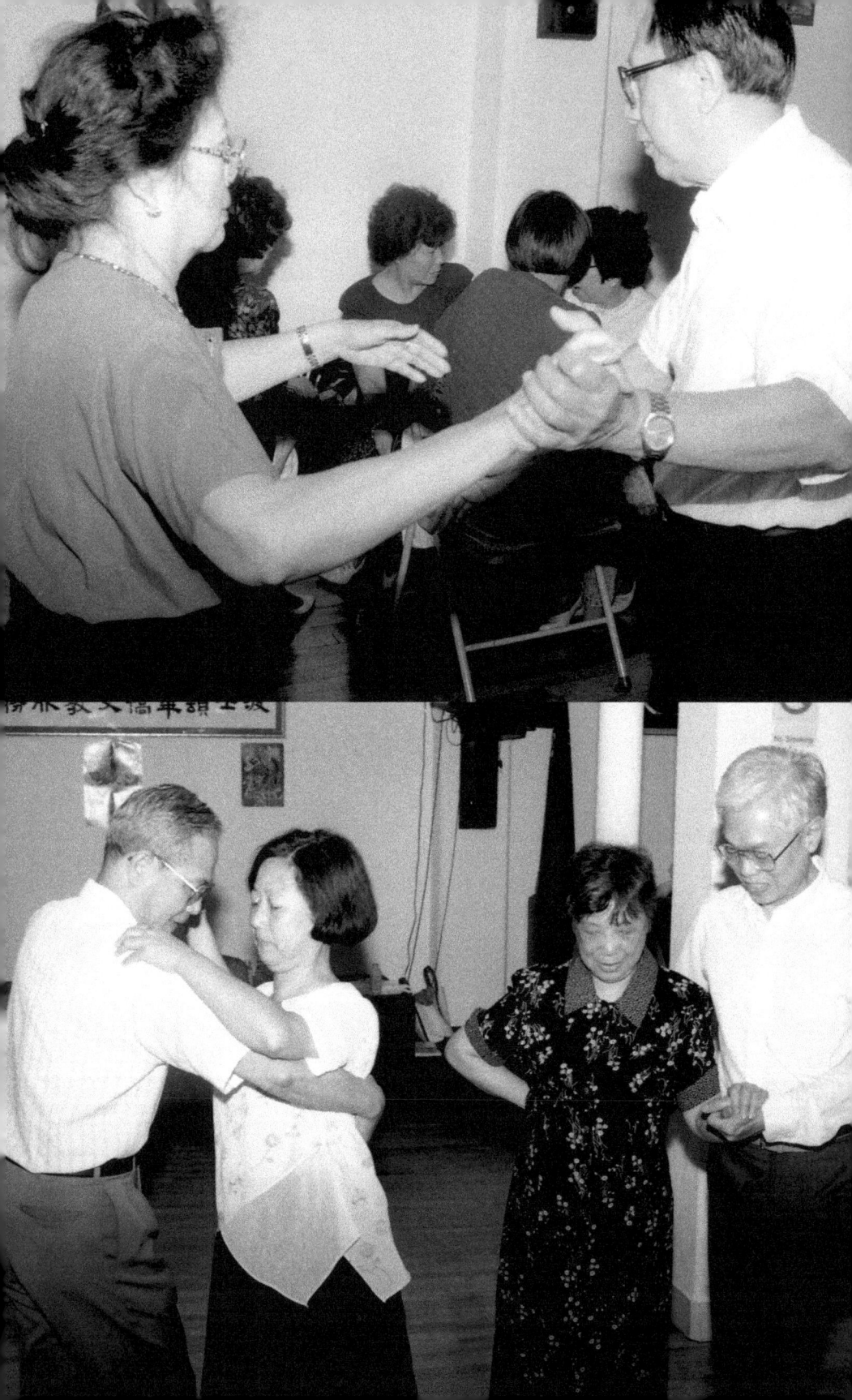

her find a new apartment and obtain government aid.

It's the kind of work that family associations have typically been known to provide in the past.

Photographs of past leaders and slips of paper with the names of contributors are attached to the wall.

At one end of the room is the association altar, which contains an ancestral image and a receptacle for incense.

Every Chinatown association has a similar kind of ancestral altar to pay homage to family ancestors.

The centerpiece of family association ritual involves the veneration of ancestors. On important Chinese holidays members pay their respects to ancestors by lighting incense and kowtowing before the altar.

Members also pay their respects to earlier generations by visiting the cemetery on Ching Ming, the Chinese day of the dead.

Raymond Chin, who served as the association's vice president, says the association is trying to provide new services for its members.

Elderly members now have access to a special health insurance plan and the association is also considering providing English classes.

Chin believes women should be allowed to become members but says the national association and some older local members want to continue limiting membership to men.

"We're trying to change and get some young people in here," he says. "If we have a good crowd to handle the association, we can do lots of things."

The Gee How Oak Tin Association is perhaps the wealthiest Chinatown family association, owning four buildings in Chinatown — at 23-27 Tyler Street and 77 Harrison Ave.

Richard Chin, Gee How Oak Tin's English secretary, favors using association resources to help the Chinese community deal more effectively with the mainstream world.

In the past Chinatown was isolated, he says. "They just didn't understand what was available to them."

Chin says he and other American-born Chinese tended to view the family associations as organizations for "the old fellows and the foreign born.

Hopefully, with the help of the American-born we can bring this into the 21st century," he says.

But in recent days, trouble has been brewing at Gee How Oak Tin. Signs

mysteriously appeared one morning urging members to avoid discussing subjects unrelated to the organization and to think about their own mistakes.

"In other words you're not supposed to talk, period," says one man, who, like the others present in the club on this June morning in 1997, doesn't want to be identified.

"It's a violation of free speech," says another.

The club members believe Kwong Hon Chan, the organization's new vice-president — or acting president — depending on your point of view, is responsible for placing the signs on the wall.

Although they don't want to give their names, the men are eager to talk about the factional fighting that has erupted within the organization.

Many people in Chinatown already know about the conflict because word spreads fast in Chinatown and stories have appeared in the Chinese newspapers.

On one side of the dispute is a faction led by Billy Chin, who has served as the organization's president as well as president of the national Gee How Oak Tin Association.

Allied with Billy is his younger brother, Frank, an officer in the national Gee How Oak Tin Association.

Kwong Hon Chan, the elected vice-president and owner of Wings Communications, is also a member of the Chin brothers group. Chan's father owns the Wing Fook Funeral Home — the first Chinese funeral home in the Boston area.

Opposed to the Chin brothers is a faction led by Raymond Chin, who appears to have the support of many of the men who regularly use the Harrison Avenue club.

In a letter distributed in Chinatown and sent to the national Gee How Oak Tin Association, Raymond Chin criticized Billy Chin's efforts to maintain control of the association and accused him of using the organization's resources to further his own interests.

In contrast, Raymond Chin pitches himself as a progressive who wants the club to provide more social services and allow women to vote.

Only in recent years has the association begun to adapt to changing times, he says.

For years the Harrison Avenue club was closed during the day and records of the association's finances were scarce.

The recent flare up at Gee How Oak Tin began during last year's association election but is part of a broader feud that swept through Chinatown during the 1990s.

The same two factions in conflict at Gee How Oak Tim were also battling for control of the Chinese Consolidated Benevolent Association and throughout the Chinatown business community.

In the 1996 association election, Hin Lee Chan was elected president with 270 votes. Over 150 people voted in the election, far more than in earlier elections.

The runner-up in the election was Kwong Hon Chan, who received 164 votes and was made vice-president.

Raymond Chin was also seeking to become president but only received 149 votes, not enough to become vice-president. Raymond Chin and Hin Lee Chan are allies and competed as a team.

The men who use the club are angry that Kwong Hon Chan, a virtual outsider, was able to enter the election out of nowhere and win enough votes to beat Raymond Chin to become vice president.

One of the men claims that Kwong Hon Chan's association with a funeral home isn't a plus in his favor either.

Having an officer associated with death performing rituals on Chinese holidays isn't a good omen, he says.

Raymond Chin and his supporters say the election was unfair because Billy Chin brought in people to join the association and vote for his chosen candidate, Kwong Hon Chan, on the day of the election.

They argue that new members should be required to wait three months before being allowed to vote in an election. They say that some of the people who voted in the election weren't even Chins and allege that the Chin faction paid the membership fees of some of these new members and voters.

Hin Lee Chan, meanwhile, was caught in the crossfire of the factional fighting. "He was an unsuspecting person in this situation...The other side wanted to control the association," says one member.

"Every time we had a meeting they argued. People always bring up the negative aspects. They say he (Hin Lee Chan) doesn't know what he's doing."

At one point there was a dispute over the renovation of space for a new Chin Wing Cheun Association club at 25 Tyler St.

The Chin Wing Cheun Association was originally an independent Chin family association that was incorporated into the Gee How Oak Tin Association. Chin Wing Cheun has space on the top floor of 27 Tyler St. that hasn't been used for many years.

Raymond Chin and others were apparently trying to revive the Chin Wing Cheun Association and move it into its former space at 27 Tyler St.

Billy Chin opposed the plan, arguing that the money should be used to renovate the Harrison Avenue building for the national Gee How Oak Tin convention to be held in Boston that summer.

Billy Chin says his opponents want to renovate the Tyler Street space "so they can set up another club over there."

He argues that the Chin Wing Cheun Association hasn't been active for over 30 years.

Angered by the Billy Chin faction's election tactics and the conflict over the renovation of the Chin Wing Cheun space, Raymond Chin had articles of incorporation filed to revive the Chin Wing Cheun Association at 25 Tyler St., with him as president.

Once the incorporation was complete, Hin Lee Chan scheduled a special meeting of Gee How Oak Tin members for May 23, 1997, at the Dynasty Restaurant, which is owned by the family of Wilson Lee, president of the Chinese Consolidated Benevolent Association.

Only about a hundred of the organization's 600 members attended the meeting. Those who were present, however, did the unthinkable by voting to transfer three of Gee How Oak Tin's properties, at 23, 25, and 27 Tyler St., to the newly incorporated Chin Wing Cheun Association for $1 each.

Raymond Chin said two of the buildings originally had belonged to Chin Wing Cheun, but a judge later said only one belonged to it.

Raymond Chin justified the transfer of the third property on the grounds that rental income from the other buildings had been misspent over the years.

One Billy Chin critic notes that former president Roman Chan's Kirin Produce Co. rents space in one of the Tyler Street buildings while a Billy Chin relative operates a restaurant in another space.

The factional infighting reached a climax at a Gee How Oak Tin meeting held on June 7.

A bitter argument over the recent property transfer erupted between the two factions.

People were shouting at each other. Things were getting out of control. Someone called the police.

Hin Lee Chan's supporters say he was unable to follow his agenda because his opponents kept disrupting the meeting.

Hin Lee Chan adjourned the meeting, but Billy Chin's faction refused to leave.

"They saw the situation was not their situation," says Billy Chin of his opponents' decision to end the meeting.

Billy Chin then urged Kwong Hon Chan to take charge of the meeting. Once he did, the group voted to suspend Hin Lee Chan as president for allowing the transfer of property to take place and made Kwong Hon Chan acting president. They also voted to change the locks at the club at 77 Harrison Ave.

After the transfer of the property, six members of the Billy Chin faction, including Kwong Hon Chan and Frank Chin, filed a lawsuit against Hin Lee Chan and Chin Wing Cheun in Superior Court. The civil suit sought the return of the transferred property.

The Chin brothers said president Hin Lee Chan and members of the opposing faction hadn't the authority to transfer the buildings to Chin Wing Cheun.

Many Oak Tin officers and board members didn't know the buildings had been transferred to Chin Wing Cheun until Gee How Oak Tin tried to collect rent and the tenants informed them they had paid it to a new landlord, says Billy Chin.

After the June 7 meeting, the locks at 77 Harrison Avenue were changed by Billy Chin and his supporters. The Association's hours were also changed to require members to leave by 2 p.m.

The Billy Chin faction also took an ad out in the Sampan — a bilingual Chinatown newspaper — to draw attention to the dispute, charging that the association's property had been given away illegally.

The Raymond Chin faction sought an apology for the ad, but the Billy Chin faction answered with a lawsuit.

The group sought an injunction to have the buildings returned to Gee How Oak Tin, but the judge refused and reinstated Hin Lee Chan as president.

Initially the judge appeared to rule in favor of the Raymond Chin faction, but the outcome would be quite different.

Billy Chin attributes Oak Tin's current turmoil in part to personality conflicts that developed earlier between former vice-president Raymond Chin and former president Roman Chan. He denies that anything inappropriate occurred during the election.

He says no one was paid to join and vote. Some new members are Chins but they don't have the Chin family name because they were "paper sons" who immigrated to the U.S. under assumed names.

One ploy to enter the U.S. in the last century was to claim you were the son of a U.S. resident.

Billy says new members can join the association on the day of the election because the organization's bylaws don't prohibit it.

"We don't have to be crooked to win the election," says Billy Chin. "We do know more people."

He admits that he and Frank campaigned hard to bring in more people to vote for Kwong Hon Chan, but he says this was a legitimate campaigning tactic. What they did wasn't unethical, he says.

The Chin brothers have been criticized in the past for rounding up large numbers of voters on the day of the Chinatown Neighborhood Council election in order to get their slate of candidates elected, but both Billy and Frank argue that such tactics are a legitimate part of the democratic process.

Billy says he urged his people to vote for either Hin Lee Chan or Kwong Hon Chan, but not Raymond Chin.

He says he didn't know Hin Lee Chan before the election but wasn't opposed to him either.

He says he is opposed to dividing the Chin association into two groups and questions how the Woo and Yuen members would feel about the transfer of the Oak Tin property to a strictly Chin association.

He says the intention of the transfer is to create a new association so that members who oppose his faction can "become their own kingdom."

Billy says he disagrees with the way Raymond Chin and Hin Lee Chan have handled association business. He supported Hin Lee Chan's removal because of the consequences of his actions. "Do you want him to continue — continue to make mistakes?" he says.

Although Billy says his group had the authority to remove the elected president, his critics describe the action as a "coup d'etat," an organized effort by one faction to maintain its long-standing control of the organization and its property.

In 1998, however, Superior Court Judge Margot Botsford releases a ruling on the case. Both sides seemed to claim victory, but Billy Chin's prediction that the court would rule in his favor turned out to be closer to the truth.

Botsford rules that the sale of the three buildings to the Chin Wing Cheun Association was void and that the buildings at 23, 25, and 27 Tyler Street must be returned to the Gee How Oak Tin Association.

She says Oak Tin members could vote to validate such a transfer of property, but it would have to be done differently.

"Under applicable common law principles," this vote was invalid because the meeting notice didn't make clear to the association members that the meeting was being called to consider the transfer of the property, she says.

The judge also rules that president Hin Lee Chan failed to fulfill his fiduciary duty to protect the assets of Gee How Oak Tin and act in the best interest of the corporation he was serving. Another victory for Billy Chin.

But Botsford agrees with the defendants (the Raymond Chin faction) "that the suspension of Hin Lee Chan as president on June 7, 1997 was unauthorized and invalid."

She says suspending the president could only be accomplished in a formal meeting for which proper notification had been given.

The judge also says that allowing people to join the organization and vote for new officers on the same day "invites some chaos and abuse, and in my view should be avoided."

She said lack of organizational bylaws was the cause of much of the Gee How Oak Tin turmoil.

FINDING YOUR WAY

The Long Way Home

HE FEELS UNEASY TALKING ABOUT the past. He is still struggling to find his way in America and reach his goals here.

In his job as a youth counselor at (Boston Asian Youth Essential Services) in Chinatown, he tries to help young people avoid some of the pitfalls he experienced when he first came to the U.S. as a refugee from the hill country of Laos.

He understands the world young immigrants have to navigate, the two cultures they need to balance in everyday life.

"One night I was sleeping, I heard guns going off in the village. The communists came in.

Two or three months later they moved us to the lowland — they didn't want us to live in the highland because they thought we were supporting the rebel army.

My village was against the communists. My father was serving in the rebel army against them. My brother and so many other people were doing the same thing.

They couldn't come home because the communists had targeted to kill them in our small village.

There was one man who was forced to dig a hole for himself in the cemetery. They put him inside the hole.

I remember it like a dream. They forced us to stand around the hole.

They said, 'If you don't tell the truth this thing will happen to you one by one.'

And they shot him right there, right in his head. I was around 5 years old.

After that, my father and brother were forced into a re-education camp, and we were moved to a new village.

A lot of people died there because it was not our ancestors' land. We believe in ancestors. We believe ancestors are not really ghosts even though we call them that.

Most of the people who went to the new land died and wanted to leave. That's why my two friends and I left when I was 9.

I didn't even know which way was Thailand. We just took off. We walked one month in the jungle before we reached the Mekong River.

My two friends and I swam across the river. My two friends drowned.

In Thailand I was forced to serve in the army for almost three years. I was going back and forth across the border trying to fight the communists. A lot of my friends passed away during the civil war.

Eventually I escaped from the army and went to the refugee camp. Then I got accepted by the United Nations program and came to America.

I came into San Francisco airport in 1990. I went to live with my friend who had come here earlier.

When I first arrived I believed that America was a place where people could have a better life and a better future, a place where I could reach my goal and realize my dreams. I had that in my head.

The kids I knew got involved in gangs and ended up on the street a lot. I felt it was really cool to hang with those powerful guys. It made me feel I was a big man.

My friends formed a group called the KB or Khmu Boys. Our group was made up of Laotians and Khmu kids.

We weren't at war with particular groups. Sometimes you'd meet with blacks; sometimes you'd meet Hispanics; sometimes you'd meet with whoever was trying to mess with you. You would just start to fight.

I wasn't involved in any of this. I just liked being there. I liked the thrill of being on the edge of life and death, but I didn't want to get shot.

One night there was a fight. My friend smacked one of those Cambodian kids with a baseball bat and they arrested him. They put him in court for smacking him.

When I went back home my friend kicked me out. He said: 'I wanted you to come to this country to go to school or go to work, to earn some money and go back home to see your family; I didn't want you to come here and do all these things.'

After he kicked me out I was sitting outside the house wondering where to go. I was still thinking about the day I had come to this country.

It seemed like paradise and I really liked it so much, but all these things got mixed up and I met with these bad people here and they forced me to become more like them.

If I could just have had two or three good friends who said, 'Okay, you go to school, you do this and this and this.'

Instead of going the way I went I could have gone another way.

My friend who threw me out told me about this friend in Boston and bought me a ticket to go there.

He said, 'You go to Boston and live with this person. If you're going to do it again, I don't know what he's going to do to you.'

So I came here in the autumn of 1990 and he put me in school, in Brighton High. I started in the 10th grade — started back to my ABC's and counting one, two, three.

I wanted to change but I couldn't really do it alone. I needed someone to guide me.

My friend said: 'You go to school...if you're lucky you can graduate and go to college...if not, you'll just go to work when you graduate.'

I had my commitment. I told myself I was going to graduate from high school. I went to school in the daytime and went to work in a Thai restaurant at night. I went to high school for three years and graduated.

While I was in high school I joined a program called Upward Bound. There was a lady there who helped me a lot — helped me to go to Bradford College.

I wanted to go to college. I wanted to show my friend that I could do this.

It wasn't that I couldn't have done it before, but I just needed help. I needed a guide. I needed a role model, somebody who could say to me, 'This is how you do it.'

I had my commitment and my faith. My friend would say, 'You're never going to graduate from high school. I was born here and I never graduated from high school.'

And I would say, 'That is you, but this is me, this is my commitment.' I said, 'I can do it,' and I did.

Faith helped me cross the Mekong River safely that day. I prayed to my father for help: 'Please let me cross safely from here to there.'

That was my belief, my faith. We believe in our ancestors. I made it across the Mekong River even though my two friends drowned that day.

I graduated from Bradford College in '97 with a degree in psychology and political science.

Now I'm working at Boston Asian Y.E.S., a non-profit organization in Chinatown that provides prevention and deterrence services for kids and their families. We work with kids who are facing difficult problems.

My job is to reach out to the kids. I try to talk to them and build up a relationship with them. I try to find out what their problem is and help them.

Sometimes a kid doesn't want to tell you anything. Even though they have problems at home they will say they don't have any.

These kids have a hard time staying in school. Some have a problem with their parents. The parents are maybe forcing them to stay home to do their homework when the kids don't really want to do it.

There's a cultural difference. The kid is facing these two worlds. He lives in America but the parents want him to be like they were back home in Asia.

The kid will say: 'No, this way isn't right, you control me so much, I have to get out.'

A kid will think, 'Oh my parents don't know anything. I feel just useless being home and now they try to control me. For what? If I have a problem with my homework they can't help me.'

But I try to explain to them that their parents came from a different place. That's why they can't help you with your homework. They can't help you deal with this schoolwork because they've never been in school themselves.

It's really frustrating. Some kids will say 'yes, yes, yes,' but two or three days later the parent calls again and says 'my kid hasn't come home and hasn't gone to school.'

I'm having a hard time trying to figure out what method is effective to help the kids at least stay in school or listen a little bit more to others.

I always give them my own life as an example, but sometimes that doesn't work because I'm the exception. I want them to think like me, but they can't do that.

I tell them I've been in a bad situation too. I ask them why can't they just change their mind?

'You're just stuck like that forever,' I say. I always put myself as a role model. I tell them that if I could do it, then they can do it too.

I have not finished my dream yet. There are a lot of things I still have to do. My dream was to get out of school and go to work and save some money and go home, but it hasn't worked out that way.

I'm in debt for $26,000 in student loans and my living costs are a lot, which is why I can't accumulate enough money to go home.

I have no idea where my family is. I haven't seen them in 15 years. I still remember...this guy came home...I was playing outside my hut. I told my mother and sister and they all screamed and cried.

I asked them what happened because I knew that near my home a lot of people died every day and I was just hoping it was not someone in my family.

When I got home my sister was crying. I said, 'Why are you crying?' and she said, 'Our father has died.'

It doesn't affect me because I don't see it. To me it's like a dream. I'm trying to absorb how it works but it doesn't make me cry even though the pain is still in my heart.

When I first came here it was paradise, but now it's not. When I first came I saw people driving nice cars and thought I would be able to get a car as long as I went to work to make money. It's not like back home where no matter what you do you will never get it.

That's the one thing that's paradise. You see a lot of people who have nice clothes to wear and are nice and very intelligent.

It doesn't mean our people are stupid, but the people here know a lot of different things. They have education.

But the bad thing right now...the thing that I think is hell is that I'm just trapped here alone. Everything is me, me, me. Student loans, house, food, clothes — everything is kind of me, me, me. It's too much for me.

Money pressures? Yeah, that's America. But we also have a problem finding people to marry. Most of the old people here don't get married because they can't find anyone to marry.

They're not racist, they just don't feel like being with a person of another race. They're afraid they're too low for them. It's a self-imposed limitation.

You might say, 'Oh I'm going to go talk to her.' But you're so afraid and think you're too short and she's too blond and tall. You're afraid she won't love you. So instead of just going out looking for somebody they just stay at home and forget about it.

So that's my second commitment: I want to get married and build up my family and just keep my father's last name. I don't want to waste the life my mother has given me.

It doesn't matter to me if she's Laotian. I used to have this girlfriend. Everybody knows she used to call from Japan. A broken heart right now because she went back home.

I don't really care who the person is as long as she loves me and takes me as a real person and respects me and we can complete our life together peacefully.

It doesn't matter to me if she's Laotian. That's no big deal to me. I know that someday I'll get one.

Life in America is a different world to me. It's not like the jungle. When you're 18 here, you get out of the house, and when your father dies you come back to bury him and that's it.

But in our culture you should be there with him. He's looking for a wife for you. You're always connected to each other till the end of the world.

The close relationship is always there for you. Even though you're 30 or 40, if you have a problem, your father will always be there for you.

I miss that magnificent opportunity. My father died early so I don't really have that expectation of him. But I still need some warm family.

I live with my friend now, in a small room like this. You go to work in the morning, come home, sleep, go to work in the morning, come home, sleep — this is the American way."

'Yeah, It's the American Dream'

HE CAME TO THE U.S. WITH HIS FAMILY when he was 7 years old. He lives in an apartment in a 19th century brick building at the far end of Tyler Street.

His bleached hair stands out when he walks through Chinatown.

"I saw a friend of mine do it at school and I thought it was pretty cool. All you have to do is bleach it but it's kind of hard.
My mother helped me do it. She had no problem with it. My father just asked me why I did it and then he had no problem with it either.

"I have a friend in Washington and he said that almost all of the Asian kids at school do it.
But here in Boston, in my school, I'm like one among five of the kids that have it.
I'm the only Asian who has it. I just saw the look and I liked it."

When he first arrived in Boston, he says, "the biggest problem was, of course, communication skills. I didn't know that much English back then.
"The places all seemed strange. Boston seemed very big. Then I started to meet friends at school and they showed me around and it was kind of okay."

Roger is 16 years old and a student at Boston Latin School, the city's most prestigious high school.
"Boston Latin is an exam school, so the teachers expect you to know a lot and work harder than at regular schools," he says.

He says he doesn't have an opinion about the father who sued the Boston Public Schools because a racial quota prevented his white daughter from entering Latin School.
He doesn't think about racial quotas...it's not an issue for him, he says.

He says he has friends from every race. Getting along with people from other races isn't a problem.
He says he mostly hangs out with his Asian friends because he lives in Chinatown and mostly Asians live in Chinatown.

"We play basketball, we go to movies, that kind of stuff."

When he is with his friends, they speak Chinese and English — but mostly

English.

He says he never went to Chinese school to learn more Chinese.

Young people in Chinatown spend a lot of time in youth centers such as Y.E.S. and OSYC.

"People who like sports go to the Quincy School gym to play basketball...there's also a workout room in the Quincy gym, so sometimes they work out...we go to Copley and Sherry to see movies."

He says he likes living in Chinatown. "We're close to everywhere...movies are just two train stops away...the gym is one street away...phone is everywhere."

"Yeah, I listen to music, I listen to soundtracks from movies, I listen to R&B, I seldom listen to rap.

I listen to Chinese music (Hong Kong pop), I download it from my computer or buy the CDs in Chinatown."

He says, yes, he knows about that fight that recently took place at the youth center.

"I just heard that a black guy and two Cambodian people went into Y.E.S. and started making trouble.

Seven kids forced them out, then they fought and as they were going away the black guy sneaked up from behind and stabbed them. It doesn't happen every day."

Chinatown, he says, is a safe place for young people. "I think there are gangs everywhere, so it's possible that Chinatown has a gang too."

Young people join gangs probably because their friends are in gangs, he says.

"Sometimes you live in a bad part of the neighborhood and they just force you into the gangs.

I think that the gangs aren't that active in Chinatown. It's pretty safe environment for small kids."

The idea that all Asians are good students is a stereotype, though the Asians he knows don't make a big issue of it or even think much about stereotypes.

"I know that many Asians aren't doing that good in school," he says. "I think that when they say that [about Asians], they're only looking at the kids that are doing good in school and ignoring the rest."

He says he doesn't know why some students do well in school and others do poorly.

He thinks it may have something to do with their parents — maybe some parents don't care enough about education, he says.

If there's no pressure in the family to go to school, then some of them end up skipping, he says. They don't want to wake up so early in the morning.

"[My parents] give me no trouble at all," he says. "They provide financial support when I need it (laughs), and they basically let me do what I want — so I have no problem with that.

"They expect me to do good in school. So no matter what, I have to do good in school or else I can't go out. That means getting good grades and not being absent from school.

"A good grade is an A or a B — honor grades. I try. I'm like an average student B's and C's.

"After high school I plan to go to college and maybe study business or economics. I was in a business program, so I already know something about business. It looked really interesting."

"My parents won't let me date. Most of my friends' parents are like that too.

I feel that's okay. I'm still young, and even though they won't let me date they let me go out with my friends...I'm pretty much free."

He says many parents don't want their children to date because they think it will distract them from their schoolwork.

But when pressed a little further he says, of course, he goes out with girls. "They (his parents) just don't know it."

Most of the boys in Chinatown go out with Asian girls, though he says it's acceptable to go out with other girls too.

"But maybe Asian boys find it easier to date Asian girls," he says. "Maybe because they see Asian girls more often than they see girls of other races.

"But I do know a few friends who date girls of other races or boys of other races."

"It's okay with me," he says. "Girls are girls, it doesn't matter." His friends feel the same way, he says — "they're open-minded."

"I'm going to college (probably in Massachusetts) and then I'm going to get a good job and then I'm going to get a car and a house," he says. "Yeah, it's the American dream...I'm pretty sure I can do it.

To have a good life, "you need to do good in school and look for opportunities and try to make the best of them, he says.

I see myself living in Boston, but I also see myself traveling around the

States for a while."

In 1998 he was working after school at the Asian American Civic Association in Chinatown, tutoring students who needed help with English.

The student he was tutoring was originally from Macau. "I get along fine with people who just came from other countries and my friends do too," he says. "But I don't know about other people. Most of the kids in Chinatown were born here.

"I have to have a hundred community hours to graduate from high school, so I joined CAPAY (Coalition for Asian Pacific American Youth)," he says. "It's a community service program. It's run by Asian teens. I get to meet new people, I get 450 community hours [through CAPAY] during this school year.

"I find it pretty interesting...and I like the fact that I get to help people...I look back at when I was young and I didn't know any English and I really needed help then. I know these people need a lot of help and I'm glad I can provide it."

He says he doesn't think much about how to define himself. "They (my parents) just want me to think of myself as a person (not Chinese or American) in America.

"I don't need to stick to a particular race or class or anything."

'Go Straight for the Education'

HE'S A TALKATIVE, FRIENDLY 16-YEAR-OLD. He works in a small Chinatown cafe and has clear ideas about his life and future.

"I was born in China, near Guangzhou, I don't know how to pronounce it in English. I just call it dai lo.

I don't know much about China, though. I was like two years old when I came to America.

We lived in Pastoria, Ohio. We owned a house, like a pretty good house. My father worked as a cook in a restaurant but my mom wasn't working yet.

There are three kids in my family, and I'm the middle one. I have a younger brother and an older brother.

Five or six years ago we came here. We heard of the Boston Latin School and Harvard and M.I.T. The good schools were all in Boston, so we moved out here.

We moved to Allston-Brighton, but the apartment was too small and the rent was too much.

Right now I live in Chinatown, in Oak Terrace. I was around 10 when I came to Chinatown, and I'm 16 now.

Growing up, there were always bad kids and good kids. I always stayed in my park — not bad, not good.

The good kids join sports like volleyball and by the age of 16 they should have a job.

And the bad kids — they're not that bad, but bad, pretty bad — the bad kids were smoking at the age of 13 or 14, breaking into cars, just hanging out in the streets, playing games in the arcade on Washington Street.

Usually the Asian kids — the smaller ones without a group of gangsters and big guys — go down to the arcade and get robbed of their cell phone and money, usually by black kids.

I don't think the Asian gangs are any match for the black gangs because the blacks are so much bigger.

They kicked the gangs out of the arcade because there were too many fights. Some of the Asians still get pushed around down there.

Whenever there's a fight they expect their friends to back them up.

There are a few gangs but not in the area where I live. The ones in Tai Tung are just kids who hang out.

That fight at Y.E.S didn't have anything to do with gangs. An Asian was talking trash to another Asian because he was hanging with a black kid.

I'm not sure of his ethnicity but it was an Asian talking to an Asian. He got angry and then his friend came in and stabbed them.

I go to school at the Snowden International School. I couldn't make it to an exam school but my older brother did.

My parents tell me: 'Don't get a job now, just go straight for the education, and then get a job afterwards. You get at least triple the amount an hour.'

I want to study computers. I'd like to go to M.I.T. but if I can't go there I'll go down to Wentworth Institute and become a computer technician.

All my parents talk about are doctors, doctors, doctors, that's it, doctors is where the money is.

But I don't want to be a doctor. I want to be a computer technician. The money is more important to them than the job. They want me to have money because when they grew up they had no money.

My parents didn't go to college in China. The only thing they can do is work for survival and food. They can't even get a car.

As long as you can pay the rent and get food every night, that's good, but my mother wants me to have money to spend and a happy life.

My father doesn't work now. He's not really too old but he got into the habit of drinking and smoking, so he can't work now.

Working is too much for him. He used to work as a chef. Inside the kitchen it's hot and you have to do a lot of work, but he can't do the work now. He's not really too sick. He just can't take the pain of working in a restaurant.

If you haven't worked in a restaurant before, you wouldn't know how hard it is. The worst thing is the heat. There's like five fires going. The fires are this high each (spreads his hands), two feet sometimes. They just cook.

In about two minutes they probably finish cooking a meal. But the thing is when more people come in it's going to take a longer time and it's really hard at times.

My father stopped working about five years ago. He's like sixty something now. He used to work in Chinatown and in New Hampshire. He lived in New Hampshire for a while just to work in the restaurant.

People in Chinatown have to work hard because they have no education. There's no income if they don't work in the restaurants.

That's one of the places where they can work. They think it's better and convenient (to work in the Chinese restaurants) because they can speak to other Asian people. Their English isn't good.

We live on my mother's pay now. She works in an electronics factory in Brighton. But they're about to move, so pretty soon she's not going to have a job. I don't know what's going to happen then.

I have white friends and I have black friends but mostly I go with the Asians that live around here.

It's more convenient to hang out with my Asian friends, but if there were black and white friends around here I would hang out with them too.

They're, like, in Brighton, really far from here. But sometimes they come down and I hang out with them.

I think Chinatown is a very good place to live. It's convenient...there are stores and stuff around here...the restaurants are down the street.

But I don't know if I'll stay here. I'm planning to move someday. I don't want to stay in the same place.

There are a lot of differences between China and America...in the lifestyle...when it comes to girlfriends and stuff like that.

In China you're not supposed to get into that till after college.

My parents always tell me about the money problems they had. In China there's not much money.

They make you start working in the fields at 5 or 6 years old. As long as you're big enough to do work they make you do it.

My parents grew up in a Chinese village. They tell me I have a much better younger life than they had.

They had to pay for education, so they couldn't really afford that much education.

After fifth grade my mother didn't have enough money and left school.

My father left after high school because he didn't have any money.

I stopped talking to [my parents] for a while. I just go home, go to sleep. I hate talking to them because they say the same thing over and over again, for like the last 16 years, the same thing over and over again.

'Go to school, get good grades, don't do drugs, don't smoke cigarettes, don't drink beer, come home early, get a good night's rest, go back to school, finish school and become a doctor.' That's all they say.

Yeah, it's good that they say it but they're not supposed to run my life. I run my own life.

In China usually the parents take over the kid's life. Even when they're 20 something they still have to report to their mom when they'll be home and stuff.

When you're 18 in America you usually do whatever you want. You're an adult. You get charged for what you do, not your parents.

If you want, you can move out. You don't have to go to school if you don't want to.

I don't think I would like it in China. Three years ago I went back to visit my hometown — a village in China. I was there for a month. I didn't see that many kids there.

They don't really have cars...they use motorcycles... more like motor scooters. They play basketball.

It's hot there and very few places have AC, mostly just fans. If they're rich they buy a mattress, if not they just buy a wooden thing to sleep on."

INVISIBLE LIFE

A GAME OF NO RULE

無法無天

十惡不赦 天地不容！

Shots on the Street

WALKING DOWN TYLER STREET...toward the center of Chinatown...a warm summer night...close to dinnertime.

What is that sound...maybe firecrackers...people are always setting off firecrackers in Chinatown.

Maybe the opening of a shop...a wedding...a celebration of some kind in one of the restaurants.

But, no, that popping sound isn't fast enough...isn't loud enough...there's no smoke...just one sharp pop followed by another.

It sounds like gunfire but it doesn't seem possible...not at this time of day.

I look around. I don't see anything as I approach the light at Kneeland Street.

Suddenly, a group of men come streaming out of a storefront near Carl's Pagoda Restaurant, just below the abandoned headquarters of the old Chin Family Association.

The men are rushing out of an employment service that provides under-the-table jobs for the undocumented and others.

I look carefully at the people flying through the door and out to the street. I see only one man clearly.

He's tall, slender with a bony, chiseled face, he's wearing a white shirt and dark sport coat. Other men follow but I can't see them clearly.

The tall one seems older...the leader of the group. He's yelling, waving to the others to get out of there fast.

Almost instantly they are gone, disappearing into the parking lot between Tyler Street and Harrison Avenue.

Moments later a police officer arrives at the storefront — it's the Chinese-American officer who often patrols the neighborhood on a bicycle. He tries to enter the storefront but he can't get inside.

A man standing on the street says someone drove by and sprayed the front of the building with gunfire.

I stand on the street for a while to see what develops but nothing does.

For the moment that's the end of it. Few people even know it happened. The police look into it but nothing happens.

In 1990 five men were shot to death one night in a storefront gambling house at the other end of Tyler Street, but it took a long time to identify and arrest the killers.

The gangster underworld of Boston's Chinatown remains largely hidden until the sudden eruption of gunfire on a quiet street or a murder in a tong war takes place in a storefront club.

But the sprayed gunfire wasn't the end of the story this time. One of those people who ran away from the building that night — maybe the tall one, maybe one of the other faceless men who followed him — probably wasn't so lucky the next time.

Two weeks later a Chinese-Vietnamese man is assassinated inside the same storefront by a group of unidentified men — found with his head in a toilet.

WHEN FBI DIRECTOR LOUIS FREEH addresses the annual International Asian Organized Crime Conference at a Boston hotel in 1995, he is quick to note that focusing on Asian crime isn't meant to be an insult to Asians.
"The vast majority of Asians in the United States are law-abiding," he says. "They comprise an integral part of our nation."
"Like many other ethnic groups that have made the United States their home before them, the Asian community is dedicated to family values, possesses a strong work ethic, and strives to achieve the American dream," he says.

Sgt. Detective Jim Fong of the Boston Police Department makes the same point in discussing Asian crime in Boston in a conversation in1995.
Fong has worked in Boston's Chinatown over the years and knows the darker side of the community.
But like Freeh he is quick to put the issue in perspective. "The majority of [Asians]are law-abiding families," he says. They're "hard-working" people," but "every race has its problems. We're no different."

Over the years Boston's Chinatown has been spared some of the more nefarious gangster-related problems plaguing cities such as New York, San Francisco, and Los Angeles.
But local law enforcement officials also point out that Boston still has its share of underworld criminals.
A few months before the organized Crime Conference, Stephen Tse, the

alleged boss of the Ping On crime syndicate in Boston, was extradited from Hong Kong and indicted on charges of racketeering and murder conspiracy.

Although Tse and 15 others were indicted for various gang-related crimes, law enforcement officials believed at the time that remnants of Ping On as well as a number of smaller crime groups vying to fill the underworld vacuum still existed in Boston.

The authorities say that the presence of too many smaller gangs makes it more difficult for the police to identify particular groups, investigate their activities, and prosecute them under organized crime statutes.

The Ping On was thought to have controlled the Boston Asian underworld during the 1980s, though it also had growing competition from Vietnamese gangs operating in the area.

A reduction in the number of high stakes gambling parlors operating in Chinatown in recent years has diminished the power of the crime syndicates.

Police say legalized gambling at casinos such as Foxwoods in Connecticut no longer make it necessary for Chinatown gamblers to frequent clubs run by the syndicates and run the risk of being robbed by rival gangsters.

In the past, the police often raided Chinatown gambling clubs, typically around Chinese New Year, and arrested everyone who was there.

Notices of the arrests often appeared in the daily newspaper.

One observer says the presence of fewer single men in the community and alternative entertainments such as videos and karaoke have also contributed to a decline in Chinatown gambling.

"They no longer rely on going to the gambling house for recreation," he says.

Heroin trafficking is also an issue for local law enforcement. Much of the heroin entering the U.S. originates in Southeast Asia's Golden Triangle.

"Let's just say we have evidence there is this kind of trafficking going on, not just in Boston, but in the United States," said agent Charles Hickey of the FBI's Boston office.

A year earlier a number of Asians were arrested north of Boston for possession of several pounds of China White heroin.

In the late 1980s, heroin was also found in a bean sprout washing machine destined for Boston's Chinatown.

Fong says extortion continues to be a problem within the Asian community. Business owners — particularly in Chinatown — are often threatened if they refuse to pay protection money.

A major obstacle to uprooting organized crime in the Asian community is the unwillingness of people to speak out against it or provide the police with information when a crime occurs. A code of silence continues to exist within the community. Organized crime is a largely taboo subject, even in the Asian media.

Fong says Chinatown residents and businessmen are more willing to contact the police now than they were in the past, but they're still not as open "as we'd like them to be."

He says many Chinese immigrants don't fully understand or trust the legal system because they see criminals being released on bail shortly after their arrest. Some think that criminals will seek revenge on them once they're released from jail.

In the mid-1990s, crime gangs were known to move from area to area targeting local Asian business owners in home invasions, Fong says.

"Some of these gang members are known for their violence," he says. One of these groups, known to the police as Mother Qi, is believed to have roots in the Vietnamese community of Dorchester.

Fong believes that Ping On continues to operate in the area. "Being indicted doesn't make it go away," he says. "There are gang members in Chinatown," but they're not "as visible as they were before."

Law enforcement officials also say criminal groups are active in cities such as Quincy, Lowell and Chelsea.

Fong says Boston has been spared the level of Asian organized crime that has cropped up in other cities. "From a national perspective, we're fortunate enough that our gang problem is not of the magnitude of other parts of the country," he says.

Still, Boston's Chinatown has had its bloodbaths and near disasters. At the 1995 Asian crime conference, a San Francisco police detective said a bloodbath may have been averted in Boston's China Pearl Restaurant in 1992 only because a police officer happened to be in the restaurant when a gang-related killing was about to occur.

The presence of the police officer scared off the assassins.

Earlier in the decade Boston Chinatown wasn't so lucky. Five people were murdered in a Tyler Street storefront in a gambling-related crime.

And in the summer before the conference a man was murdered in another Chinatown storefront in what police believe was a gang-related retaliation.

Young people are drawn to the gangster life by money and status, flashy clothes and cars, says one law enforcement official.

Crime gives people the chance to go from being an ordinary person "to a person of stature" in a short time," he says.

Peer pressure often leads some youths to join criminal groups. Police were seeing an increasing number of incidents in which young people were being harassed by other youths on the street.

"The kids are becoming more westernized," says Fong. "They know what is available to them.

In China the laws are stricter and the punishment more severe. Because America is a freer country, says Fong, it offers more opportunity for criminal behavior to flourish.

In the summer of 1989, an alleged high-level member of Chinatown's Ping On gang was shot and killed in an Arlington restaurant.

Michael Kwong was 30 at the time of his death and alleged to be second in command in Chinatown's Ping On gang.

Kwong had grown up near Chinatown and was often seen at the Kung Fu Restaurant on Tyler Street.

He was standing near the front counter of his family's New Dragon Chef Restaurant around closing time when an assailant shot him six times. His girlfriend was also shot in the head and in critical condition.

A police spokeswoman said "it's possible it could be another gang or it could be a rivalry from within," but several people in Chinatown speculated that a rival Vietnamese gang or an enemy of Ping On was responsible for the shooting.

After the shooting Boston Police Commissioner Francis Roache walked through the streets of Chinatown to make the police presence felt in the neighborhood. "We don't know what to expect," said Roache, standing at the corner of Beach Street and Harrison Avenue. "We want to put some resources in here till we know where things are going.

George Joe, director of the Chinatown Neighborhood Council, thought the police were overreacting. "I think you're alarming the people more," he says. "Nothing really happened in Chinatown."

Kwong and Stephen Tse, the alleged boss of Ping On, had been arrested for gambling at 32 Oxford St. in Chinatown earlier in the year.

A few days before their arrest, 25 shots were fired in a Chinatown parking lot. Police at the time said they were worried about an escalation in gang violence.

In 1994, Ping On's long run in Chinatown was interrupted in a major way. Sixteen alleged members of the gang were charged in a racketeering indictment with committing criminal acts centered in Boston's Chinatown over the previous

12 years.

Stephen Tse, formerly of Braintree but living in Hong Kong at the time, was alleged to be the leader or Dai Lo of the Ping On, a criminal organization operating in Chinatown from about 1978 to 1990.

The indictment alleged that "members of the enterprise were expected to commit criminal acts including (in the case of at least certain members of the enterprise) acts of violence, as directed." It said "the enterprise acted with the purpose of controlling, supervising, financing and otherwise participating in and deriving income from illegal operations, including gambling, loan sharking, and extortion activities."

It also alleged that "the enterprise acted to protect itself by intimidation, violence and threats of violence against other criminal groups and individuals which the enterprise perceived as a threat to its control of its territory."

"The enterprise acted to protect itself from law enforcement activity by obtaining and seeking to obtain information about such activity, particularly as such activity involved the execution of search warrants on illegal gambling businesses operated by the Enterprise in Boston's Chinatown section. The Enterprise obtained such information by engaging in multiple acts of bribery of Boston Police detectives and an assistant clerk magistrate of the Boston Municipal Court.

"The Enterprise acquired and maintained firearms to conduct its various criminal businesses, to control competition from rivals of such businesses, and to eliminate real or perceived encroachments of rival criminal groups and individuals into its territory," according to the indictment.

"Within its territory, the Enterprise attempted to maintain its control by engaging in multiple acts of intimidation and extortion on both legal and illegal businesses."

When Luck Comes It Just Comes

SHE LOVES TO GAMBLE. Every week she and her friend make a trip from Chinatown to Foxwoods Casino in Connecticut to test their luck.

Buses regularly run between Foxwoods and Chinatown. People say the neighborhood gambling houses aren't as active as they once were since the opening of Foxwoods, though you can still walk down Tyler Street and hear mah jongg tiles clicking behind the closed doors of storefront clubs.

"When I first started gambling I used to play mah jongg at home. Playing mah jongg gave me a chance to meet with friends.
Every time I played I could also bring the kids together. I have kids and my friends have kids, so the kids could play together while the mothers were playing. Sometimes I'd get lucky and win some money. This made me happy. At home I didn't lose much.
In the beginning I'd gamble about $20. It was very very small. Sometimes if I had bad luck I would lose $50 to $100 at home, but mostly I'd win or lose $50.
I like playing mah jongg because I can control it and not risk too much. If it's a small game I won't get much money but I won't lose much either. If you play a big game you can win more money but it's hard to win.

When Atlantic City opened I started to go there. I would get there by bus or by car. In the beginning I liked the slot machines, but I'd lose a lot of money in them. Most of the time I'd lose like a few hundred.
If I went to Atlantic City I'd have at least $1,000 in my pocket. Most of the time I'd lose all of it. I wouldn't leave until there wasn't even a cent left in my pocket.
Of course I would feel upset, but I couldn't control myself. I liked the fun of it. When you hit the jackpot, the money comes out of the machine and it sounds so good. If I can win the money I don't feel bored.
I love casinos! I like them because you only see people gambling, walking around and playing there.
The rooms have a lot of light. It makes me feel happy. I never know if it's dark or light, daytime or nighttime outside.
I don't have to worry about outside. Inside the casino, you see people 24 hours.

After I lost $2,000 or $3,000 at Atlantic City one night, I felt scared. After going there about seven times, I said I wouldn't go there anymore.
The trip made me feel tired because I needed to ride on the bus for seven hours. This was maybe six or seven years ago.

After that I gambled only at home. I played mah jongg. I started to play a little bit bigger then. Now I usually play a few hundred dollars a night.

I am interested in any kind of gambling. I either go somewhere in my neighborhood or to my friend's home in Cambridge, which is quiet and comfortable.

I started going to Foxwoods in 1997. I go there at least once or twice a week. In the beginning I didn't bet when I went there. Then after about the fifth or sixth time I started to bet.

Then I got crazy. I wanted to go whenever I had a chance. My friend drives me there. It's so easy to get on the bus to go, but I would rather drive because then I don't have to be controlled by the time.

It's easy to drive down there. Any time I feel like it I can just go. On Saturdays I like to go after dinner, after I settle down from everything. Most of the time I leave at about 7:30 and get there at 9 o'clock. I stay till Sunday.

When I play I don't need to sleep. I don't want to leave. I get on the Black Jack table.

First thing I do is take a look at the different tables. If there's a seat I just sit down and play. I go in with at least $500 or $1,000; if I have more I will take more. I don't set aside special money for gambling.

One time I went to Foxwoods with only $100, and I hit the jackpot! I was so happy. It was a slot machine. I just put the money in and played the slot machine — $2,500 came out.

I didn't want to sit at the Black Jack table because I had only $100. At the Black Jack table I need more than $100 to play.

Last week I got really lucky — on big games and small games, at home and at Foxwoods. I won because of the feng shui. A few weeks ago a fortuneteller told me to move the clock from the wall beside me to the back wall. Two people helped me do that. After I moved the clock I got lucky.

I went to Foxwoods on Saturday. I left home at 7 o'clock with my friend and coworker. We got there at about 9 o'clock and went to separate places to play. I went to play Black Jack.

At first I had very bad luck. I lost the money I brought — $1,000. I don't know how long I was gambling because I don't carry a watch.

After I lost I went to look for my friend. I said, 'Let me have $100,' and he gave it to me — $100 in chips.

In my purse I also had an extra $75. So I sat down and bet $25. I lost the $75 I had in my purse.

I told myself, 'I don't have luck. Why not bet one time? Because if I bet $25 I can't make money.'

So I put the whole $100 down, and I won that game. I won $100 — one to one. So then I doubled down and I won again, so I got $300. So that meant I had $400. So I doubled down again and I hit it. I had $800.

I was so happy! I said I must go. I wanted to go but I said, "No, I've got luck." So that's why I kept playing more and more. So I took back $600 and I bet $200. But I was lucky and I won more and more.

So I don't know how long I sat at that table, but I made $4,000. I don't know how much time I needed. Of course I took back $1,000 of my money so that meant I only made $3,000.

I felt so happy; I thought, 'I should go.' But I said, 'I still have luck because the dealer is so good to me. This is my lucky night.'

So that's why I kept playing. And so I kept playing and somehow I lost $1,500. And then I left. I had at least a $2,000 profit.

Then I met someone who lost all her money. I know that woman. Yeah, she's from Chinatown. She asked me, 'How did you do?' I said, 'I made some.' And she asked me to lend her $100. I said, '$100 is not enough to bet, maybe you need $200.'

And then she said, okay, she would return it to me. She said she had lost, like, $4,000. Every time I go there I see her.

I see a lot of people from Chinatown at Foxwoods. Most of the time I see the same faces. Yes, some people lose a lot of money. But for me, I can still control myself because I have a family to take care of.

I'm not really, really crazy. I'm crazy but I'm not really, really crazy. I work every day.

Some people who lose a lot sometimes lose their house or their restaurant. I know a friend who lost his restaurant. He had to run away so he wouldn't be tempted. He moved to another state because he wanted to be far away from Foxwoods. It's too easy to get to Foxwoods — only two hours. He lost everything. Even some people lose their family. I don't know why they do it. Gambling is too interesting. Gambling makes it very easy for you to do something crazy.

I like to gamble because if you get lucky you can make some easy money. If you don't get lucky you lose. That's why I don't bring my credit card. I don't bring my bank card. I only take the money I can afford to lose.

If I get lucky I will share my luck, my happiness with my family and friends. I will buy gifts for my kids. I will do something I want to do.

I like Foxwoods because at Foxwoods all the people are the same. They're all gambling people. So I don't have to worry about people saying, 'Oh, you do bad...you gamble a lot.' Because we're the same type of people.

When luck comes it just comes. When you hit the game you feel strange. Maybe if you have luck you don't have to worry about anything. You just ask for the card, and you will get a good card that fits you."

GO FOR THE EDUCATION

The Great Equalizer

EDUCATION IS AT THE CENTER OF LIFE in Chinatown. Families talk about it at home. Parents set high standards for their children.

One American-born Chinese woman points out that even if she did well in school her mother would still find something in her accomplishments to criticize.

"The family stresses very much on the next generation," says Bak Fun Wong, the principal of the Quincy Upper School in Chinatown. "We all know in our immigrant experience that the only equalizer we have in this country is the next generation."

Education, he says, has traditionally served as a means to reach that goal and help Chinese surmount obstacles imposed by prejudice and cultural isolation.

A 1992 U.S. census survey shows that 39 percent of Asians over 25 had completed four or more years of higher education, compared with 22 percent of whites.

In imperial China, education was the key to power, prestige and material well-being. To become a member of the most revered class, a student had to pursue a painstaking regime of study to pass the emperor's exam.

Reaching such heights of scholarship required discipline and perseverance, dedication and hard work.

"You'd better do the hard work in school or else you won't get a good job" is the message many Chinese American children receive at home, says Ming Chu, the father of two children. "They're demanding."

Even if the parents are themselves uneducated, he says, "they still believe that education is the best way to get a better life."

Although Chinese activists often rail against the model minority stereotype imposed on them in the past, many older Chinese have no problem being viewed as a people who respect education.

It's commonplace for people in Boston to complain about the quality of the public schools, but Chinese parents are especially attentive to the issue.

In 1996 Boston School Superintendent Thomas Payzant institutes a program to raise educational standards in the city's schools. Most Chinese parents appear to support his plan to require students to do more reading, writing, and algebra.

One of the most vocal supporters of raising standards is Robert Guen, a dentist and former member of the Boston School Committee.

Guen, a founder of the Academy of the Pacific Rim, a charter school that emphasizes Asian languages and history, says Asian parents want higher standards for the public schools. "That means getting [their children] into an educational system that challenges them."

These parents, he says, also want their children to attend one of the city's three exam schools because they know they'll be required to work harder there.

While Guen's views on education are probably the majority view, Suzanne Lee, the principal of the Baldwin Elementary School in Brighton, offers another perspective.

Lee is the founder of the Chinese Progressive Association in Chinatown and a long-time activist for progressive causes.

She agrees that schools and families should have high expectations of students but questioned the new standards' emphasis on increasing educational content. "I'd like to see more in-depth than more content," she says.

Lee believes some children are entering the school system at a disadvantage. Family and other social problems make it hard for them to concentrate on learning, which in turn makes it difficult for teachers to instruct them.

She says society needs to emphasize family and student responsibility but also provide more early childhood education. Lee also supports an eight-hour school day.

Another issue for some Chinese parents is the teaching methods and traditions of the U.S. system versus what they experienced in China.

The Chinese system tends to have an "I listen, I memorize, and I give it back to you" approach to learning, " says Lee. The American approach leaves more room for independent thinking.

Students who come to American schools from Asia generally do better at math because Asian schools teach more material at an early age.

But Chinese schools tend not to encourage independent thinking or develop the ability to discuss a broad range of ideas and opinions.

Susan Fung, a bilingual kindergarten teacher in the Boston system and an advisor to Chinese bilingual parents, agrees that the Chinese system tends to emphasize rote learning over independent thinking.

But both she and Lee believe the economy of the future will "need children with better problem-solving skills. It is a higher level of understanding," she says. "It is more than just memorizing fact."

Another drawback of the Chinese system, says Fung, is that only a select few are able to finish high school in China, never mind go on to college. Education is an elite occupation, unlike in America where a high percentage of students attend college.

Still, she says, the Chinese system has a number of undeniable strengths, foremost among them that schools and parents demand more from students.

"Those children from China happen to be successful [in U.S. Schools] because their parents and grandparents have high expectations of them," she says. "My personal point of view is if we don't expect the students to perform they will not."

Fung says the bilingual teachers — many of whom came out of the Chinese educational system — continue the Asian practice of demanding a lot from their students.

"We always have high expectations for them," she says. "That is why they can be mainstreamed within a time frame of three or four years."

Unlike some other immigrant groups, the Chinese parents generally don't want their children to remain in bilingual education too long.

Some, in fact, complain that bilingual teachers want to keep their children in bilingual programs too long, in part to protect their jobs.

Chinese parents want their children to be mainstreamed quickly, believing it will lead to more rapid progress in American society.

Fung believes that many teachers already follow the kind of regimen outlined in the new standards. Although bilingual students often lag behind their American-born peers in English-language skills, they manage to do well overall in their studies.

"They're so far behind in language, yet they can still be successful," she says. "Therefore we should not give ourselves any excuse for not setting the standards for the students."

IT'S A SPRING DAY IN 1996 and a group of Boston high school students gather around a table at the Chinatown Cafe, a popular Chinatown restaurant.

Mary Soo Hoo, the owner of the restaurant, has brought the students together to discuss their experiences in the city's public schools.

The girls — all ninth graders at exam schools — appear to agree that setting higher standards for the public schools and expecting more from students is a positive development.

Many students don't take learning seriously, they say. Lack of discipline and diligence rather than intelligence is what causes some students to perform poorly in their studies.

"I think it should be more demanding," says Helen Wong, a ninth grader at

Boston Latin School.

She says students in Japan are required to work much harder at school, but Americans tend to emphasize freedom over discipline.

In one of her classes students are not required to do homework or a research paper, she says.

Sandy Wong, also a Latin School student, agrees that American students have it too easy.

More pressure should be put on them to excel, she says. In fact, more pressure was put on her at her Chinese summer school than at Boston Latin.

She says her summer-school teachers constantly put pressure on her to do well, but some of her public school teachers don't seem to care what their students do. "How can you expect the students to care?" she says, "I think I prefer the Chinese way."

Helen Wong says Chinese students often tend to do well academically at Latin School because their families have high expectations of them.

"Their families emphasize it so much," she says. "It's not that Chinese are smarter...our families emphasize education more."

Sandy Wong attributes the success of many Chinese students to Chinese culture's traditional emphasis on education and discipline.

Academic excellence is viewed by many Chinese as a way to gain respect and standing in a society in which Chinese are a minority.

Angela Soo Hoo, a ninth grader at John D. O'Bryant High School of Mathematics and Science, takes a slightly different approach.

"It's up to the students whether they want to learn or not," she says. "Some parents are more strict, which makes them want to learn and do well."

While many Chinese parents urge their children to be disciplined and competitive students, such an approach can also be stressful for them. "There is a lot of pressure but it depends on how you deal with it," says Sandy Wong.

One of the girls recalls how a friend's parents threatened to take her back to China if she failed to do well in her studies.

They said "the education there is better" and students in the U.S. were out of control and wasted a lot of time.

She says her friends' parents held high positions in China but were forced to accept lower ones here.

They told their daughter they had sacrificed a lot for her and that she should repay them by doing well in school.

While parental emphasis on education often produces children with high aspirations, Chinese children often find that non-Asian students tend to make an issue of their academic success.

"They think we're the smart ones in the class," says Helen Wong. "But we don't really know everything. I think it's a stereotype. I don't really like it."

Many Asian students feel uncomfortable with the A-student stereotype and try to avoid drawing attention to their academic success. Some are very competitive and want to be seen as the best, but they don't want to be turned into one-dimensional nerds by their peers either.

In America, anti-intellectual attitudes sometimes work against academic achievers. Parents praise their children for getting A's but fellow students call them grinds.

"In the classroom some Asians don't speak out as much" because they "don't want to be called nerds," says Helen Wong. "Even if they know the answer, they just sit there."

At school, students tend to stay within their own racial and ethnic group. "Chinese usually hang out with Chinese," says Sandy Wong.

Chinese students are naturally drawn to each other because of their common interests and cultural background, she says. They tend to be more conservative and pay more attention to their studies than other groups.

Helen Wong says racial and ethnic groups generally tend to remain in their own group.

"They're nice to each other but they don't hang out like real friends," she says. "They feel intimidated by each other."

She says she worries that students will experience that same distance in the future and carry their "prejudices into later life."

Angela Soo Hoo observes the same phenomenon in her school, but she says she makes an effort to overcome those barriers.

"I hang out with everybody," she says. "Black people, Hispanic people, Vietnamese people."

But she says her willingness to befriend people outside her group also has drawbacks.

If she spends too much time with her non-Asian friends, the Asian students ask her why she's isn't spending more time with them.

She believes she shouldn't be pressured to spend time only with members of her own racial group.

She says she has a lot in common with some African-American students and has many African Americans as friends.

"I want to hang out with the people I have more in common with rather than just the people of my own race," she says.

AT A FAMILY LITERACY PROGRAM in Chinatown, a group of Chinese and Vietnamese parents offer their views on the education their children are receiving in the Boston Public Schools.

Education seemed to be a more serious undertaking in China, says Hui Xian Pang, the mother of a first grader in one of the city's elementary schools. The schools in China were more structured and demanded more from students, she says.
In America parents have to fill in the gaps. "When the kid goes home the parents teach them more than the schools teach them," she says.
Pang feels that public school teachers don't monitor their students closely enough or spend enough time with them.
She says the Chinese system is probably better for younger children who need more guidance, while the American system may be more appropriate for older students because it gives them more freedom to be creative and adventurous.
Pang points out that the Chinese have long valued education, and part of that tradition includes a disciplined approach to learning. Chinese schools emphasize the need for students to obey and respect teachers and parents, she says.

Chin Nang Wu, who has a son in the eighth grade, believes students learn more in Chinese schools.
Teachers in the Boston schools don't take enough responsibility for their students, she says. They are in a hurry to get home when the class day is over.
In China, the teacher-student relationship often extends beyond the classroom, with teachers and students often visiting each other at home. A personal relationship is involved in the educational process.
Wu believes teachers here fail to let parents know a child is having problems until the situation is serious. In China, teachers are constantly giving parents input on their children's progress.

Xue Ying Tom, who has two sons in the Boston Public Schools, says students here have too much freedom. They're not monitored closely enough or taught to be polite and respectful enough to teachers, she says.
A student here will pass a teacher on the street without even bothering to greet him, she says. That would never happen in China.

Phuong Nhan, who grew up in Vietnam and has two children in public elementary school in Boston, offers a different view of the American system. "I think the American schools are better than Vietnamese schools," she says.

American schools provide students with more experiences and activities, she says. They also have more equipment than Vietnamese schools.

Who Attends Boston Latin?

IN THE FALL OF 1996, there is intense public discussion over who should attend the city's three public exam schools.

To enter these special schools students must first take an entrance exam. Students with the best scores are given a place at Boston Latin School, Boston Latin Academy, or the John D. O'Bryant School of Mathematics and Science.

But there's an exception to the rule. The school department has an affirmative action plan in place that sets aside 35 percent of places at these schools for the best African American and Hispanic students.

That means that some white and Asian students are bypassed in favor of African American and Hispanic students who didn't perform as well on the exam.

This school-system affirmative-action plan is challenged by Boston attorney Michael McLaughlin, who learned that his daughter Julia didn't receive a place at the prestigious Boston Latin School despite having a higher rank than 103 African American and Hispanic students who were admitted.

McLaughlin files a suit against the Boston School Committee, charging that the current system is unconstitutional and discriminates against his daughter, who received a place at the less prestigious Boston Latin Academy.

Students can enter the exam schools — which have grades seven to 12 — in either the seventh or ninth grades.

McLaughlin demands that the current system of set-asides be abolished and that his daughter be immediately admitted to Boston Latin School.

Fearing that the current exam school admissions policy was in fact unconstitutional, U.S. District Judge W. Arthur Garrity Jr. orders school officials to admit Julia McLaughlin to Boston Latin School.

Eventually the School Committee decides to scrap the affirmative action plan — though not completely.

The committee says it will continue to take steps to ensure that African Americans and Latinos — who make up the majority of students in the system — are admitted to exam schools.

McLaughlin, meanwhile, argues that the alternative plans under discussion by the School Committee have the same shortcomings as the current system because they would once again be "using race as a method to get in rather than merit."

The results would be "racial results," he says. "They're all illegal."

McLaughlin says that whites in the American South attempted to use a poll tax to keep African Americans from voting in elections.

Although the tax applied to every voter and wasn't overtly racist, the white framers of the policy knew that many African Americans wouldn't be able to afford the tax and as a result wouldn't vote.

Although on the surface the tax was not racial, the courts ruled that it had a racial result.

McLaughlin says the only alternative plan acceptable to him would be to provide more after-school programs to "prepare the students better."

But he says those programs should also be open to all students regardless of their race.

If parents want their children to perform well on the test, then they should send them to the after-school programs. "If parents don't, then don't keep my daughter out of school because you don't like the results," he says.

McLaughlin charges that the current exam school admissions policy discriminates against Asians as much as whites because substantially more Asians would be able to enter the exam schools if the system were based strictly on merit.

He says he is disappointed that more Asians haven't spoken out publicly against the current system. "I am not hearing that kind of outcry from the Asian community," he says.

For many Chinese, exam schools should be "exam schools." If affirmative action skews the results of the admissions process, then the exam schools aren't really exam schools, they say.

Dr. Robert Guen, a graduate of Boston Latin School, is a vocal opponent of the exam-school affirmative-action policy.

"I personally feel it should be based on merit," says Guen. "I sort of like the exam schools because they give children a sense that if they try hard and work hard they get accepted. "

Guen argues that academic success often depends on family involvement and the value parents place on education.

He says Asians have been performing well in the public schools in part because families emphasize education and view it as a key to success in life, instilling in their children the need to take school seriously. "When you go to school you go there to learn," he says.

Asians make up 9 percent of the Boston public school population and 19 percent of Latin School students. In the mid-1990s, the remaining Latin School population was 22 percent African American, 49 percent white, and 11 percent Hispanic.

If a system based solely on merit were instituted for the exam schools, Asians would likely make up 25 to 30 percent of Latin School students.

"Under the straight merit system the Asian students would do much better," says Guen. "I think many Asian students are being denied seats because of the quota."

"In order to give the Asians the fairest shot at getting into Latin School it has to go by merit," he says. "The purpose of an exam school is to get there on merit and to sink or swim on merit."

He says diversity is a worthy goal but should be achieved through merit. To set different standards for African Americans and Hispanics wrongly suggests that those groups can't compete on the same level as whites and Asians, he says.

In addition to opposing affirmative action for the exam schools, Guen is also an outspoken critic of the Metropolitan Council for Educational Opportunity (METCO), an educational program that bused city minority student — mostly African Americans — to suburban high schools.

Founded in the 1960s, the program gives city minority students the chance to broaden their educational experience by attending suburban schools with largely white student bodies.

Guen complains that METCO discriminates against non-African American minorities, specifically Asians and Hispanics.

In 1994, he said only 5 percent of the program's students were Asian, Hispanic, or other minorities, even though 32 percent of Boston school children at the time belonged to those groups.

METCO director Jean McGuire responds that METCO had been trying to attract more Asian students but that many weren't interested in the program.

While Guen's views on Latin School admissions appears to be the dominant one in the Chinatown community, some Chinese are willing to support affirmative action on principle.

Andrew Leong, an attorney and assistant professor at the University of Massachusetts Boston, says a student's standing shouldn't be based strictly on tests and grades but should also take into account interviews and essays — the kind of criteria colleges take into account when determining admissions. He says diversity should be a legitimate factor in determining admissions.

Leong says people who criticize affirmative action tend to forget that family and class connections rather than merit alone have played a major role in determining who gets ahead in American life.

"They don't want to talk about these back-door scenarios which exist on a day-to-day basis," he says.

Leong says American life continues to be dominated by white males. Non-whites, he says, tend to languish on the lower rungs of the corporate ladder.

Affirmative action gives those who have traditionally been left out of the process the chance to get a foot in the door.

Leong also questioned why Asians aren't considered a minority under the current exam school admissions policy.

He and others suggest that Asians are categorized as minorities when it suits the needs of the white majority but included with whites when it doesn't.

Jean McGuire, who runs the city's METCO program, believes that a single test shouldn't be the gauge of a student's overall academic worth.

Students possess a wide range of intelligences and only a few are measured by standardized tests. Some kids are frightened by tests, she says. Some have a creative intelligence. Some are artistic. Not everyone is the same, she says.

McGuire was one of two African-American girls in her Girls Latin School class in the 1940s.

McGuire attributed the low number of African-American girls in the school to racism, which also led to many substandard public schools attended by African Americans during the same period.

McGuire questions the elitism on which a Latin School is based. "Why is it we want to keep Latin School for a privileged few?" she asked.

McGuire believes all of the city's elementary schools should be upgraded to ensure that each provides students with a high-quality education.

Why not bring all the schools up to the standards of the exam schools? she asks.

Amy Wong, a graduate of Boston Latin who grew up in Chinatown, says it's important to maintain diversity in the exam schools but questions whether setting quotas is the right approach.

"Just to accept people on their race or nationality — I'm not sure that's a good idea."

Wong also worries that whites and Asians would dominate the exam schools if the quotas were eliminated.

She points out that the majority of students in the Boston system are African

Americans and Hispanic.

"I think they should include other races," she says. "You want to give [all groups] educational opportunities, the chance to reach higher goals."

To resolve the dilemma, schools could broaden the admissions criteria to include essays or volunteer work in the community.
Like many Chinese, Wong believes a student's performance in school often depends on how strongly education is promoted at home.
"I do think Asian parents tend to stress education as a ladder to get jobs and higher status," she says.

Asian Latin School students, meanwhile, seem divided over the issue. "I really think the policy they're enforcing now is O.K.," says Alan Chan, a senior at Boston Latin School. "It could be improved in some ways."
Chan says it's important to provide equal opportunity for all groups in the society. "Out in the world it's not just one race," he says.
"Even in the working world there's a diverse group of people you have to compete with," he says. "I don't think people should be ignorant about other cultures and races.
"A lot of times misunderstanding comes from ignorance...nowadays there's a lot of violence between different ethnicities...I do see it and I don't think it should be that way because we're all trying to reach a common goal and that's happiness."

Dale You, another senior, says that Latin School is an exam school and admission should be based on grades and exam scores rather than race.
She says some of the African-American students who did well on the test feel the same way because they don't want people to think they were admitted to the school only because of the quota.

Sophomore Helen Wong says race shouldn't be a factor but believes the criteria for admission should be expanded to include teacher recommendations and essays.
Basing admission to the schools on race hurts African American and Hispanic students because it unfairly suggests they need special treatment to get into the school.
"In a way it's an insult to them," she says. "Latin School should be equal opportunity."
Wong says students from every racial and ethnic group have the potential to do well academically if they work hard at it. "Not one race is smarter," she says, adding that many minority students would have been admitted to the school

even without the quotas.

"Actually I think everyone in there (at Latin School) is capable of doing" well academically, she says.

Wong believes Asian students are more or less evenly divided over the issue. "Some of them feel that affirmative action is necessary," she says. "Others feel that the quota for the Spanish group and African Americans should be gone."

But, she adds, most students don't think much about it. "We don't really want to talk about it because it might offend someone," she says. "I think the public just makes a big deal about it."

IN THE FALL OF 1996, the Exam School Assignment Task Force holds a public hearing in Chinatown to hear community views of the exam school policy.

The Task Force was appointed by the Boston School Committee to study the issue.

Many members of the Chinatown community show up for the hearing and one by one step up to the microphone to offer their opinions.

Wilson Lee, a Chinatown businessman and president of the Chinese Consolidated Benevolent Association, says many Asian parents view education and attending Latin School "as a way to achieve economic and social mobility."

Many Asian children must overcome language and cultural obstacles when they arrive in the U.S. as immigrants, he says, adding that he should know because he was one of those children.

Lee says he came to the U.S. from Hong Kong when he was 8 years old and had difficulty communicating during his first few years at school. But one of his elementary school teachers took a special interest in him and taught him how to read English.

In 1971, he was accepted to Boston Latin School and later graduated from Tufts University.

He says he recognizes the importance of increasing diversity in the public schools but believes that maintaining excellence is also important. Students "should be able to compete and get into the school based on merit, not on their race."

Henry Yee, a resident of Tai Tung Village in Chinatown whose son graduated from Boston Latin School, says students who work hard should have the opportunity to attend the city's best public schools.

If there's a quota system, some students may not have to work as hard as others to attend the best schools. The quota system is unfair to students who work hard, he says.

If students are accepted to exam schools on the basis of a quota there will be more students in the schools who cannot perform at the highest academic level.

He says the United States needs people of talent, particularly people who can develop high technology.

Only through a merit system can these skills be cultivated. A school is not a charity, he says. The primary purpose of a school is to educate students.

Lisa Tang says she has two children in Boston public schools who will one day want to attend a school like Boston Latin. "This is a highly competitive school," she says. "Without competition there would be no progress."

The goal of education is to develop people of talent, and the best schools should emphasize the acquisition of the highest academic skills. A system is unfair if those who perform well are unable to move forward as quickly as those who do not perform as well.

Basing admission to the exam schools on race is unfair. "Those who study hard can pass the examination," she says.

Robert Guen has three children in the Boston public schools. "I would like to state clearly that I believe the only admissions policy for Boston's examination schools that will ensure both excellence and fairness is one that selects students on the basis of merit," he says.

Guen says he wants his children to have the opportunity to attend an exam school but believes they should "be accepted or rejected ... solely on the basis of their ability and performance in the classroom."

He says Asians are not being treated fairly under the current admissions criteria.

"Although Asians are courted as 'other minorities' when it comes to being assigned to public schools in general, we are considered 'white' when it comes to being admitted to Boston's exam schools.

"While blacks, Hispanics, and other minorities can compete for 100 percent of the available seats in the three schools, Asians are only allowed to compete for 65 percent of them. That's not fair."

Guen says basing exam-school admissions on each racial group's percentage in the schools or in the city would also be unfair.

"Just because Asians as a group make up a small percentage of the students in the city, individual Asian students who demonstrate their ability and performance shouldn't be penalized."

He says Asians are often the "silent minority." They don't complain, he says, they play by the rules and let their performance speak for them.

"But under the current admissions policy and the ones proposed, our ability to perform is being used against us," he says.

He says the schools should prepare students to take the exam to ensure fairness.

"If not, prepare yourselves to learn a lesson: Asian parents can sue, too, and we will if the opportunity for a quality education is taken away from us and if the admissions policy you adopt for Boston's examination schools in not fair to Asian students," he says.

After the Chinese parents speak, several African American and Hispanic teachers in the Boston Public Schools step up to the microphone to offer their views.

Karen Kane says 85 percent of the children in the Boston Public Schools are children of color.

Why can't all of the schools in the public school system be considered high-quality schools? she asks. Why can't every school in the system be a Latin School?

Diane Stafford says that African American and Hispanic students who attend the exam schools all passed the entrance exam. She says those students also excelled and worked hard to get where they were today.

She says many African American parents are also "pushing their kids to get into the schools" and argued that all public school students should have access to quality schools such as Boston Latin.

She says some public school teachers discriminate against African American students through "demoralizing talk" that implies they aren't capable of doing the work.

Such attitudes can have a negative effect on students, she says.

The last person to step up to the microphone is an Hispanic teacher in a Mattapan school who says he was the beneficiary of affirmative action programs.

Testing, he says, is not always the best gauge of a person's overall abilities. Some students will perform well on one kind of test but do poorly on another.

Discrimination in society makes the current admissions policy necessary, he says.

If the set aside for African Americans and Hispanics is found to be unconstitutional, the school committee should find another way to ensure diversity in the exam schools.

Members of the Chinatown community attending the hearing overwhelmingly call for an end to the 35 percent exam schools quota for African Americans and Hispanics, arguing that admission should be based on merit rather than a quota.

Following the hearings, the task force recommends that the bulk of admissions be based on merit and a limited number be based on the percentage of that minority group applying to the schools.

Perfecting the Individual

BAK FUN WONG IS PRINCIPAL of the Quincy Upper School, an experimental new public middle school in Chinatown.

For many years, Wong was principle of the nearby Josiah Quincy Elementary School, which gained a reputation for academic excellence under his tenure.

In the late 1990s, Wong was appointed deputy superintendent of the Boston Public Schools but eventually left that post to work again in Chinatown.

"I was born in China, in a village of Toisan, in 1951. My kindergarten education was in Guangzhou, but my elementary school education was in Hong Kong.

I went to Hong Kong Baptist College knowing that I eventually wanted to come to America to study in a different school system. I graduated from that school and became a teacher.

My father and my sisters were all teachers, so I got inspired early that this was a really noble and worthwhile profession to be in.

I loved teaching. In my family we talked a lot about education. The focus was on getting a good education and passing the Form 5 exam.

I think that in Chinese history, educated people — particularly people who were scholars — ranked the highest. In people's minds there was also the idea that when you're rich you could get educated.

In history, scholars came first, then farmers, then workers, then business people.

I think that for ordinary people, education is the best social ladder they can climb. They can see that it's the best equalizer. It's not going to make you rich, but it's going to make your livelihood stable.

My sister was in Boston and my brother came here to go to M.I.T. I came to Boston on January 24, 1978 — one week before the big, big blizzard — to go to Boston University for my master's degree.

I started in the Boston Public School system as a paraprofessional, substituting as a teacher, going around to different schools. Then I became permanent and was hired to be a language specialist in the central office to do testing and construct tests for the school system. Eventually I became the bilingual coordinator.

I had the opportunity to become assistant principal of the Josiah Quincy School in Chinatown, but went instead to be assistant principal of the Harvard Kent School in Charlestown. I wanted to be away from Chinatown so I could learn what other principals were doing.

Then the principal position at the Quincy School opened in '86, '87. I was appointed principal and was there for 13 years. About 65 percent of the children at the Quincy School are Chinese.

About 20 years ago people saw the U.S. as a land of opportunity. They said, 'We're new immigrants, let's get the best of it.' They were very happy to have the opportunity they had at the Quincy School because we had a bilingual program.

Their children would not be totally out of the Chinese language and cultural component in their education. The location was also good. It's right here in Chinatown. I was the first Chinese principal appointed for the Quincy School in its history.

At that time, the goal of the parents was to have their children get a good education, take the Independent School Entrance Exam, and do well. Their goal was to get them into one of the exam schools and then move on to college.

Our success rate was high and we always had about 40 or 50 students getting into the exam schools. The majority would get into Latin School.

But attitudes have changed a little bit. Now, the second or third member of the family is going to the exam schools and the parents have been here for a little while.

In the past few years, I've been hearing parents say to me, yes, go to an exam school...because they know they can do that academically...they know that's good and that getting into a good college is good.

But now they also say, we need more than that. We need a very balanced education. We need to make sure that they know how to deal with non-Chinese people. They need to know how to socialize. They need to know how to get into ballgames. They need to play, they need to have fun.

I think that the mentality of parents, when they first came here, was different, particularly when you also had grandparents involved.

They had gone through the First World War, Second World War, Korean War, and Vietnam War, right? When they come to this country, survival, security, longevity is the main goal.

But after 20 years of training or living, people might start to realize that, okay, our next generation needs more than that now.

They need to live in this country. They need to live like other people but have their own dignity and their own culture and their own ways to become really Asian Americans or Chinese Americans.

That's what they want to be able to do now. So they're not going to give up the educational part of it but they want to get the other things too.

So in our conversations with a lot of Chinese parents lately — in the past few years — they say, 'Yes, Mr. Wong, I want you to create a school that does not just emphasize academic interests. We're not going to give that up because it has become a habit, but we've got to have choices.

So I'd like you to be able to give the students the chance to have music, to have art, to have sports, to have good people skills, so they really can take advantage of this country.'

They start with the advantage — the opportunity provided by the education — but now they want to move on to enjoy what is provided to them as citizens of this country. That to me is a big, big jump. Before they said to me, 'Don't talk to me about after-school music — just math.'

Now, the new immigrants still have that mentality. They still want longevity, opportunity, and security. Circumstances have forced them to go in that direction.

You have nothing, so education is all you need at that point. Don't talk about the fun thing.

But a lot of time you see that second-generation students start to lose that and might not be the best, cutthroat, topnotch students, though they will be happier students and become more themselves. I think that's how I see the evolution of the Chinese.

The ones who have been here for about 10 or 20 years will often say to me after their children have graduated from college: 'My son has a good job, but he stays home, he has no friends.'

They start to see the bigger society a little bit more. If you want to move forward, if you want to get ahead, you also have to know the ocean your boat is in. They start to experience other opportunities.

They can drive to another country — to Canada. They can enjoy vacation time. Before vacation meant spending money, but now they see it's probably needed.

The second generation is not going to live the same way as the first generation. The first generation is hard working. They will give money, provide everything for the second generation.

But the second generation will start to enjoy it. You can see it around here. The second generation is driving the best cars.

Why is the older generation still driving the beat up cars? It's the worry, the insecurity. But with time it lessens and you can look a little bit.

I think this is a very opportune time because they start to understand the American world and want to have both worlds together.

They need to understand the structure and how things work. You have to look at it through both lenses.

It's the point I made in my commencement speech at Wheelock College. The Chinese emphasize the perfection of the individual but the Americans always have the perfection of the structure.

That's why Americans always restructure, restructure, restructure. But for Chinese, you have to be good, though there is a lack of structure in there.

That's why when Chinese people communicate and have trade, they do it over dinner. But maybe someone here in the U.S. wants to bring in the lawyers — bring in the seals.

But you need to have both ways. I think this is a time when you can see that we still have the Asian — the Chinese culture and values — and then the American structure.

But there should be a balance between the two. That's what I would like to be able to provide the students in this school (Quincy Upper School).

In this community, people say to me, 'We were kind of sad when you left and became a deputy superintendent (of the Boston Public Schools), but now you have come back. We trust you. We will bring our kids in here now.'

Now I could have changed but they look at the individual and say, 'I trust you.' So it's the individual that matters here. They perfect me. They want me to be the one.

But on the other hand, look at the structure. You can see it in the schools. When schools are not doing right, what do they do? They restructure, instead of saying, 'Let's make the individuals better.' Those are the kinds of things I think are important to think about.

The Chinese will put people over structure, even over law. But this country emphasizes the structure. You can see it with companies. If something doesn't work well they will restructure but keep the same people in there. But that isn't good.

The Chinese will go to the other extreme sometimes. They will say, 'We have good people. Whatever you say — even though you ignore the rules — is good.' But this is not true; this isn't good either. You need to have a more balanced way of looking at it.

What I've noticed through experience is that we tend to separate people. We say this is from one culture, this is from another; this is black, this is white; this is Hispanic, this is Asian or Chinese.

But what I've been trying to do is focus on their commonality. All the kids love to dance; all the kids love to have fun; all the kids are lovely; all the kids love to read.

There might be other things that distract them from all those things, but they all like to have joy and a good day. And we affirm that.

The key is to tap commonalities first and then the differences will be a plus. If you do it the other way around — if you talk about the differences first — they're never going to come together. They'll just go away.

So what I have to do is create a platform to express these commonalities.

All the white, the black, the Chinese, and the Hispanic students dance together. So we let the parents also know, 'Hey, they dance. That's acceptance...acceptance of other cultures.'

There's nothing better in terms of people seeking acceptance. It's not just food. We see Chinese students dancing in the African-American dance group. Hey, that's good! Culture is so good and neutral.

The kids are the ones who can educate the parents and the teachers and myself. They say, 'We are the same.'

And by doing that you don't see that much difference in the students. Maybe their background is a little different, but you can accept them a little bit more.

Hey, students are successful! They can be successful in a two-family home, a single-family home, or a no-parent home.

People from every background say they want to be successful. Our approach is not to categorize them and divide them up and say some kids are not good.

Scott Peck has a book called World Waiting to be Born. There's a very good statement in there.

It says that to be healthy is not to get rid of the disease but to maintain the optimal healing process in the body. It means you don't fight that...because I'm not ever able to resolve those things.

I want to empower my students and tell them that the ultimate healing process of the body is to score strong in school. So I emphasize that part first. Reading programs. I want to get all the kids to read.

Let them be successful. That's why the scores show the success of the students. But we still have to work on other things.

I think the standards are there. You set the standards. I think the most important question is how do you get the students to reach that standard.

For me that's a more important question than whether we have standards or not. The students are here. Do we have the commitment to make sure that the students reach that standard?

It's not lowering, fluctuating the standard to meet our needs. I go for the standard but we also try to help every student meet that standard. I think that's where the system fails.

But the American school system divides — it screens out the haves and the have-nots.

There's no commitment to make sure that every student is going to be there.

There's a competition for resources. I think it comes down to the fundamental belief that every child deserves the same opportunity.

This system is time-consuming, resource-consuming, and I think it's philosophically divided.

Public education is the best equalizer in this country, but you can see there are so many things they want to take away from public education. Even within public education you see the inequities.

Inner cities have more needs but suburban schools have more resources. That is a challenge — a challenge for the individual and a challenge for the system.

If parents emphasize education more, then students will get more. There's no question about that.

But the danger of this statement is that you're going to say that some parents don't value education.

Now this is the approach that I use. I have to believe that all the parents want the best for their children. How can we make and help those parents do this? There are obstacles. New immigrants like to do this, but they work 12, 14, 18 hours a day. They don't have time to do it.

And you see the Asian parents and the Asian families are disintegrating too — slowly but surely. They do have disintegrating families.

Now, how do we take that? Does it mean that they don't value education anymore? That's where the programs, the supporting programs have to be put in.

I think that the school days have to be a little bit longer in order to do all the things that schools need to do. This means there has to be academics and also other things like art, music, and language.

That's why the Quincy Upper School is two hours longer every day. That way we can put in a full day. It's not just for studying but to provide something they would not get otherwise from school.

When would they be able to learn how to make bread? When are they going to learn fantasy baseball? When are they going to be able to learn African-American dance, Asian American dance? When are they going to be able to learn tai chi? We have those as electives for students, and they stay after school to learn them.

Now I think equity is a good concept, but when you don't have a lot of resources it's hard.

I think that when parents are put in a situation where there's only so many seats and so many choices, they, of course, will say they're afraid that if I don't [oppose affirmative action] my kid is not going to be able to have something.

Equity has to come with resources and more opportunities. How many choices do we have [in the Boston Public Schools]? Latin School, Latin Academy, O'Bryant (the exam schools). Are there any other choices?

Maybe I know my child cannot get into one of those exam schools because he or she is not as good as the other students, but at least I have a chance of going there if there isn't another criteria — say race or gender.

It's not that they don't like it (affirmative action). If it gives them another opportunity they would say, 'Great. I'd like to have that too, I'd like to have a different scenario.'

It's not that they don't believe in those things (affirmative action), but they are not put in a situation to talk about equity.

They're talking really about fear of losing the opportunity. It's the opportunity that they're afraid to lose.

When people are put in a situation where there are only three [exam] schools to choose from, obviously we will try to create another choice. This is the K-12 situation in the Boston Public Schools.

Now, parents can choose to be with us here (in the Quincy Upper School). This school is not meant to compete with the exam schools but offers another choice that emphasizes academics as well as a holistic approach to education.

It's not an exam school. There's no need for another Latin School, Latin Academy, or O'Bryant. We want to offer another kind of school.

I think our students are 60 to 65 percent Chinese, 10 percent white, 23-25 percent black, and 5 or 6 percent Hispanic. Most of the Chinese are from Chinatown.

Reform is important but I don't think reform can help us too much. I use a parable from the Bible: You cannot put new wine into old leather skins right? Because every time the new wine goes in there it stretches the bottle. And one year you pour the new wine in but it's so strong it cracks the bottle.

I think that for American education and education in this state the bottle is cracked, but we don't recognize it. We say that the wine isn't any good.
But the wine is as good as any other wine, as good as any other generation. It's not that this generation is not good.
What we fail to recognize is that the leather skin isn't good enough to contain the wine.

I have visited many schools: parochial, out-of-state, private, suburban schools. I see the same thing in those schools. They're talking about reform. We're talking about that too. All the schools have issues.

So what kind of schools do we want to give them now? What kind of schools do we want to build so the students can stay?
No matter where the students come from — an immigrant family, a broken family, a happy family — they need to know how to review themselves, refine themselves, respect themselves, love themselves, so that they'll be able to love other people. If people hate themselves they will hate other people as well.
Maybe some student will say, 'Oh, I am poor, I don't have a car, a home, I don't have all these nice fancy things.'
But they have themselves. For the adults it's the same thing — we have to find ourselves too.

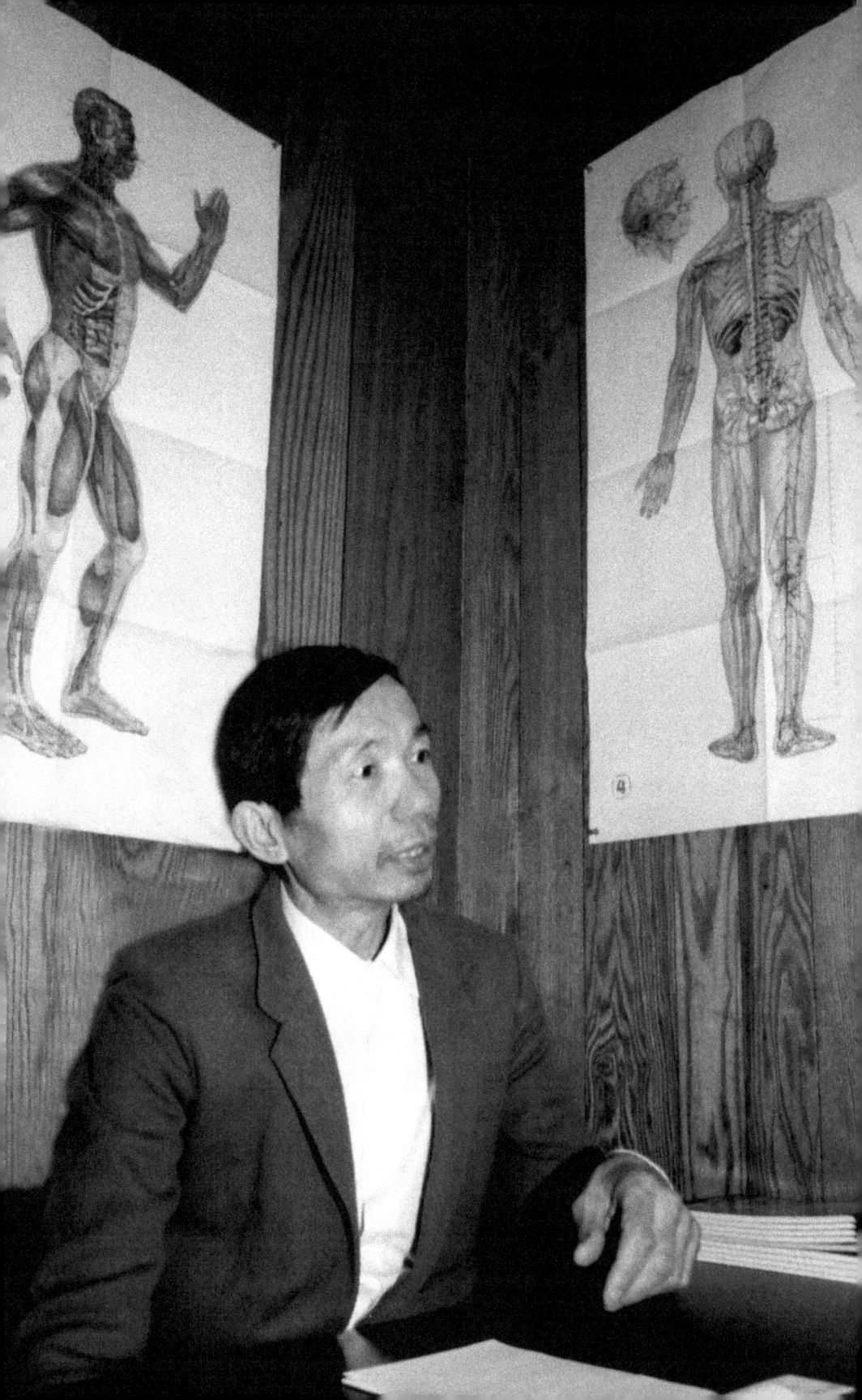

HEALING TRADITIONS

Surviving Time, Crossing an Ocean

IN A NARROW ROOM IN A CHINATOWN office building, Chinese traditional doctor Charles Lee inserts acupuncture needles into points on a middle-aged woman's back.

For 20 years the woman has been suffering from lower back pain, but she has only recently resorted to acupuncture for help.

On this day in 1997, she will receive her second treatment, says Lee, a licensed acupuncturist and herbalist. Lee says the treatments have reduced his patient's pain by about 20 percent.

In his cramped second floor space on Kneeland Street, Lee practices a traditional Chinese healing technique that has proved effective in controlling pain and treating a wide range of physical disorders, including asthma, diabetes, infertility, substance abuse, and high blood pressure.

To treat a patient, Lee inserts six to 10 needles in specific points of the patient's body. Each of the estimated 360 acupoints is associated with specific ailments.

According to traditional Chinese medical theory, the body contains 14 channels or meridians that serve as the pathways of the blood and qi — the natural energy of the body. If the blood or qi becomes blocked disease will develop.

Inserting needles into points along the meridians helps the qi and blood move more normally, says Lee, who also uses Chinese herbal treatments along with acupuncture to treat his patients.

Lee says his American patients in the past were reluctant to take herbal treatments in conjunction with acupuncture, but now they are more willing to use them.

Traditional Chinese medicine has always been popular with Chinese immigrants, but acupuncture and herbal medicine are also becoming attractive to other Americans when mainstream medicine can't solve their problems.

In the past, acupuncturists were generally found only in Chinatown or within Chinese communities, but over the years many non-Chinese have also become licensed. Many hospitals are now using acupuncture to supplement traditional Western treatments for pain.

Practitioners of traditional Chinese medicine say that acupuncture and herbal medicine can be used to supplement rather than replace Western-style medicine.

Even Chinese immigrants use traditional medicine in conjunction with Western medicine.

Both forms of medicine have strengths and weaknesses. Western medicine is most effective in treating life-threatening conditions such as cancer and heart disease, while Chinese medicine is effective at treating chronic conditions that could lead to more serious diseases over time.

The acceptance of Chinese traditional medicine by mainstream medicine has not come easily, says Weidong Lu, a licensed acupuncturist and herbalist, and the chairman of the Department of Herbal Medicine at the New England School of Acupuncture.

A Chinese traditional doctor was allowed to practice as a medical doctor in Nevada in the 19th century, but that was an exception.

Mainstream curiosity about acupuncture was piqued after President Richard Nixon's trip to China and the opening of China to the West in the 1970s.

But acupuncture was still viewed with suspicion by mainstream medicine. A 1970s American Medical Association report suggested that acupuncture was only suitable for Chinese people, says Lu.

Traditional Chinese medicine made its entry into mainstream American life largely through the American counterculture movement of the 1960s and '70s.

Young people seeking new ideas and approaches to living turned to Eastern philosophies and alternative medicines for guidance.

Some of these young Americans eventually went to Hong Kong or Taiwan to study further before returning to the U.S. to use their knowledge to treat people.

Traditional Chinese doctors who had immigrated to the U.S. also started teaching acupuncture and herbal medicine here.

The New England School of Acupuncture, for example, was started by James Tin Yao So, a Hong Kong traditional doctor who immigrated to the U.S. and started his school in the basement of his home in the 1970s.

As interest in acupuncture grew, local governments began to develop standards for licensing acupuncturists, and mainstream scientists and doctors began to study the procedures.

Lu says acupuncture is the first wave of traditional Chinese medicine to enter mainstream American medicine, explaining that it's easier to study than herbal medicine, which requires a great deal of memorization. "It's like a fast food," he says of acupuncture.

Herbal medicine requires a deeper understanding of the principles of Chinese philosophy and tends to be more intimidating to Westerners because of its complicated preparation process and bitter taste.

Chinese herbal medicine is based on the same principles as acupuncture. "The meridian theory, known in western countries for its role of integrating all acupuncture points into a channel system, is also one of the cornerstones of Chinese herbal medicine," says Shiqi Liu, a licensed acupuncturist and herbalist who practices near Boston.

"Every herb has its own attributive meridian (some may have a secondary attributive meridian) indicating what internal organ or functionality this herb acts on or applies to.

On the other hand, Chinese herbal medicine's fundamental theory is heavily or exclusively used (in mainland China) in acupuncture diagnosis and treatment."

Both acupuncture and herbal medicine posit the existence of qi, the natural energy believed to circulate throughout the body.

Other important principles of Chinese medical theory are the concepts of yin and yang. Yin refers to substances and forces in nature that are cool, calm, and inactive, while yang refers to those that are hot, active, bright, and upward moving.

Everything in existence is composed of these opposite qualities and forces, including the human body, which needs to balance internal yin and yang to remain healthy.

In Chinese herbal medicine, yin substances reduce the body's heat while yang substances increase it. The ultimate goal is to return the body to a state of balance.

IN A SMALL ROOM AT THE SOUTH COVE Community Health Center in Chinatown, Robert Tang provides patients with traditional Asian massage therapy two days a week.

Tang's specialty is working on the muscles. His practice, he says, has been influenced by Japanese, Chinese, and Western massage techniques.

Each of these approaches has its strengths. Swedish massage is effective in promoting relaxation, while Japanese acupressure or Shiatsu is more intense and powerful in reducing pain, he says.

The Japanese method is meant to increases a person's energy level by clearing up blockages in the qi. In this approach, pressure is exerted on body points to relieve aches and stimulate the internal organs.

These pressure points are basically the same as those of acupuncture and can be stimulated to influence specific organs, Tang says.

He also uses Chinese qigong on the pressure points, though using qigong requires a great deal of concentration. "I feel the Chinese [massage] is more intense," he says.

An American technique is to work on the area of the body where the pain is

located, but the Chinese method focuses on pressure points that are distant from the source of the pain.

Tang says he may have to work on an arm to relieve a headache.

"I feel the Chinese therapy is more powerful," he says, but each of the techniques has its particular strength and specialty.

The kinds of health problems he treats are often due to lack of exercise and more obscure causes such as not drinking enough water.

Personal characteristics also play a major role in health. Over sensitivity and nervousness as well as sitting, standing, eating and sleeping habits are also factors.

"What I've been finding out is that the daily bad habits will create all of the pain and symptoms," he says.

Tang says many chiropractors and hospitals use massage now, and insurance companies are also beginning to recognize it as a treatment. "It's been gradually expanding," he says. "It's just a matter of time."

Tang says he has been studying and practicing massage for four years. "It's a challenging job," he says.

The Healing Power of Nature

TIGER BONE. BIRD'S NEST. HORNED TOAD. DEER ANTLER. DRIED INSECT. GINSENG ROOT.

For thousands of years, in villages across China, people have been using plant, animal and insect substances to cure their ailments.

"The Chinese people are very complicated," says traditional doctor Li bang Zhao. "The Chinese can make everything into a medicine."

It's a fall day in 1988 and a steady stream of patients have been coming to see Zhao, who prescribes medicine from a tiny room at the back of the Vinh-Kan Ginseng Co. in Chinatown.

The late afternoon rush has begun. Behind the counter, pharmacists carefully remove herbs and other substances from wooden drawers and place them on sheets of brown paper spread across the counter.

The doctor says he seldom prescribes a single substance to treat an illness, explaining that a variety of ingredients are usually mixed in time-tested formulas to cure specific ailments.

Many of the herbs are now available in pill or capsule form, but most

Asians still prefer to take them in the traditional form of a soup, he says.

"Most of the patients just come here for long-term sicknesses," says Zhao, who graduated from medical school and was a licensed doctor in China before immigrating to the U.S. two years ago.

"There's a medical system in China that has lasted for a long time," he says. "And we study that to know what medicines to prescribe."

For example, tiger bone and deer antler are prescribed for strengthening the bones and treating bone ailments, he says, while the gall bladder of a chicken is prescribed for coughs.

When he diagnoses a patient he takes into account a number of factors. He first looks at a person's overall physical appearance, then smells the breath, listens to the sound of the voice, and takes the pulse rate.

Modern technology has also made inroads, he says, pointing to the blood pressure gauge hanging on the wall beside the desk.

An important principle on which Chinese medicine is based involves the concepts of hot and cold. If a patient is suffering from a "hot" ailment, it is treated with a "cold " element to bring the body into balance again.

Zhao says traditional Chinese herbal medicine wouldn't have lasted for more than 5,000 years if it hadn't been effective.

"In China, the policy is to try to bring together Chinese and Western systems so that medical students will know the Chinese way and the Western way," he says

Traditional doctor Ying Si Li says "some kinds of sicknesses can be cured by Chinese medicine and some can be cured by Western medicine."

Long-term illnesses such as kidney ailments are more successfully treated by the Chinese method, while heart problems and strokes are more effectively treated by Western medicine.

"It's hard to use the Chinese way to examine the heart, but the Western way is very good," he says.

A Lifetime Studying and Selling Herbs

At a table at the rear of the Nam Buk Hong Chinese Herbs shop in Chinatown, a traditional doctor sits at a small desk to hear a young woman describe the issue that has brought her here for a consultation.

In recent days her face has inexplicably broken out in a rash and she's desperate to find someone who can help her. The Western doctors were unable to diagnose the problem.

The traditional doctor takes her pulse, smells her breath, and inspects her skin and tongue to assess her overall health.

The doctor prescribes a traditional herbal mixture for the problem, which he believes was caused by an allergic reaction to something in the environment.

The doctor writes down the names and quantities of the herbs and the woman goes up to a glass counter to have the pharmacist fill her prescription.

WAI LONG LAU, THE OWNER OF THE HERB SHOP, watches from the end of the counter.

Every day he stands near the shop window dressed in a shirt and tie. He doesn't talk or move much when he's in the shop.

A pharmacist studies the prescription, picks up a small metal scale, then collects the herbs from the drawers lining the wall behind him.

He takes out the herbs one by one, weights them, and drops them in a pile on a piece of brown paper spread across the counter.

When he finishes selecting the herbs, he wraps up the mixture in the paper and seals it shut with a rubber band.

The woman will take the mixture home, place the herbs in boiling water, and drink the soup.

"My family was in this business in China for a few generations," says Wai Long Lau. "I was always around it and developed an interest in it. I decided I wanted to do this.

My family taught me what I know. I was 15 or 16 years old when I started to learn.

First I learned how to recognize the herbs and then I learned each herb's characteristics — their nature. I learned how to tell which ones are good and which are bad — the quality of the herbs.

You learn the herbs through practice. A lot of what you know comes from experience. You can also get a book and read it as a reference, but it was my parents who told him how to tell the difference between the different herbs.

I was born in Toisan and later moved to Guangzhou. My family had herbal shops in Toisan and Guangzhou, but after the revolution the communists confiscated the businesses.

I left China after the communists took over. In 1954, I went to Hong Kong and opened an herbal shop there. In 1982, I came to the United States and opened a shop here.

Chinese, Southeast Asians, and some Americans all come to the shop, he says. The Americans usually buy the ready-made, packaged herbal pills and the Chinese and Southeast Asians buy the individual herbs.

Some customers want to buy a supplement to make them strong. I don't know how they figure out what to buy. Maybe somebody tells them, helps them figure out what they need. Most of the time I don't have to tell them anything.

Occasionally I have to explain things. I think that most people who come here already have in mind what they want.
There's always been the same number of Americans coming in here to buy the herbs. It doesn't change. They always know what they want.

It's mostly immigrants who buy herbs — the American-born Chinese don't come here often to buy them.
The younger generation born here doesn't know or want to know much about them. The younger generation in my family doesn't want to deal with them either.

But I don't feel bad about that, I just like to let them do whatever they want to do. They can decide for themselves.
It's all right with me if they don't want to do this business. I'm not going to ask them to continue running this herbal shop.

I get the herbs from New York. A wholesale company there imports them from Asia. It's always the same herbs. They don't seem to have any new ones.
Chinese herbs are plants, natural things, but western medicines are all processed, produced by chemistry.
Both the Western and Chinese medicine have some good things about them. For a clinical disease Chinese herbs are better, but for emergency care western medicine is better.
I'm very fascinated by the Chinese herbs' ability to enhance your body's strength and make you strong and healthy.
Chinese herbs are good for maintaining your health. Of course, I take the herbs myself."

The Mystery of Qi, the Quest for Balance

DE-GUANG HE IS A MASTER OF MEDICAL QIGONG, a licensed acupuncturist, and a herbalist.
He and his wife Zhenzhen Zhang, who is also a traditional doctor, sell their line of pre-packaged herbs in Nam Buk Hong Chinese Herbs in Chinatown.
They also run Acupuncture & Herbal Health Care/Beijing House in a Boston suburb. On a fall day in 1997, He spoke in Chinatown about his life as a traditional doctor.

"I grew up in the countryside in Anhui Province. My village was very beautiful. The farmers there grew mostly rice, but also crops such as potatoes and wheat.

I was the sixth of seven children. When I was a child there weren't many doctors. The countryside people usually used traditional Chinese medicine.

When I caught a cold or had a fever my mother would always cook a soup for me. It was very effective.

When my mother was a child and had a cold, my grandmother would also have her drink some soup. It's a practice that is passed down from generation to generation. My mother knows a little about Chinese medicine, but she is not a doctor.

If my mother's soup wasn't effective she would bring me to a traditional doctor, who would usually give me some herbs, which we would cook to make a drink.

The doctors would choose from several hundred herbs. Their choice depended on the disease they were trying to cure.

In Western medicine there may be one kind of remedy — such as aspirin — for a cold, but traditional medicine is different.

If you have a cold. the choice of medicine could depend, for example, on whether you have or don't have a fever.

In the Chinese countryside there was little Western medicine. The traditional medicine is usually passed from generation to generation, but Western medicine is learned in a school.

When I was a child I knew about the traditional medicine and also the Western medicine.

When I was in my third year of high school, before I took the test to go to college, I didn't feel very well. It turned out that I had a disease.

When I was a child I really liked sports — badminton and wushu — and I thought my health was very good. But I got this disease — an inflammation of my skin.

In the countryside no one knew what the disease was, and I was also worried. I didn't know what was wrong with me.

Now I know I got that disease because sanitation in the village was not that good.

I had to go to the hospital to have an operation. After that experience I thought I would become a doctor, because in the countryside there weren't many doctors. Doctors are really needed there.

I took the test to go to the university and eventually went to the Anhui College of Traditional Chinese Medicine. Only two of the 30 to 40 students in my high school class went to university, and I was one of them.

Why did I choose traditional medicine? When I was sick as a child I would usually drink the herbal soup. I thought it was a good way to be cured.

The Western-style medicine required an operation or an injection. I thought an operation would not be so good and I was also a little afraid of it. I thought traditional medicine was cleaner.

At the school, we studied all the traditional Chinese therapies, including acupuncture, herbal medicine, and massage. We also gained a general knowledge of Western medicine.

Traditional Chinese medicine looks at the whole body, not just at one part of it. For instance, if you have a headache, the traditional doctor doesn't just think about the headache.

Maybe the cause of the headache is a problem with your blood. Maybe the fluid is not so good, so you get a headache. Or maybe you get a headache because you have a cold.

In Chinese medicine there's something called qi. Maybe the qi is not flowing so well, so you get a headache. Or maybe you have some psychological problem — a family or workplace problem — that is causing the headache. So we think about all the possible causes before deciding on the disease and the treatment. We don't just think about the headache.

If it's a blood problem, acupuncture or herbal medicine could be used to make the blood flow better.

In Chinese medicine we also have what are called meridians, or jing luo. In Western medicine you have nerves, but meridians are different from nerves.

For instance, if you have pain in your teeth, I can insert an acupuncture needle in another part of the body that is connected to the teeth by the meridian. The whole body is connected by the meridians.

For some diseases traditional Chinese medicine is better than Western medicine, but for others Western medicine is better. I think having two kinds of medicine is better than having just one kind.

Traditional Chinese medicine is usually good for chronic diseases that require long-term treatment. It also has fewer side effects than Western medicine. You can almost say it has no side effects, so I think that's good.

When I first went to the college in 1979 I didn't know anything about qigong. At that time there were some qigong experiments taking place in Shanghai. They found that qigong could stop pain. I read a qigong magazine and soon became interested.

When we study traditional medicine we have to study the qi, the blood, and the water or fluid in the body. The blood we can see and the fluid we can see, but the qi we can't see. I thought qigong was curious because you could feel it but not see it.

I started to practice qigong and found that if I did the exercises I could feel the qi just as I could feel the effects of acupuncture. It's the same idea. In college I practiced qigong on my own.

After five years of study I passed another test to enter the Chinese Academy of Traditional Chinese Medicine in Beijing, which specializes in qigong and acupuncture. I practiced by doing qigong exercises and also studied many books about qigong.

At that time qigong was new. I was one of the first people to get a master's degree in qigong and acupuncture. The Chinese health news wrote a story about this.

After I graduated I worked at the Academy of Traditional Chinese Medicine. I collected books and articles on qigong and did some teaching.

I also did experiments on the physiological changes that take place as a result of qigong practice.

We found that electrical changes occur in the body during practice. We also did some experiments with qigong and the kind of lung disease found in coal miners. We found it's effective in treating this kind of disease.

Qigong combines three kinds of methods. One involves sitting like this (in meditation). You don't move. It involves concentration of the mind and attention to the posture.

Another kind of qigong involves movement. Usually the movement is like the movement of some animal.

A third method involves deep breathing or stopping the breath and concentrating. This is the most difficult method. You don't think anything; you just concentrate on your abdomen or some special thing.

I practice tiao yang zang fu gong (a practice to balance and strengthen the organs), but many people do other types of qigong. Tiao yang zang fu gong involves exercises, breathing, and concentration.

There are Daoists and Buddhists who do qigong. I can't say I believe in Daoism or Buddhism, but some Daoist theory is good. In traditional medicine many theories come from Daoism.

Daoists and Buddhists use qigong for their own purposes, but I use qigong for treatment and for long life – to prevent disease.

Qigong treatment, for example, can be effective in treating diabetics. I teach the patient qigong so they can do it everyday. After three weeks, they should feel an effect.

Using the term 'qigong' to describe these methods only began in the 1950s. For thousands of years before that it had a different name but the method was the same. Qigong perhaps originated 4,000 years ago as a method that used movement to treat disease.

Wushu is a martial art, but wushu that uses qi is also a kind of qigong.

I practice every day, usually for one hour. If I have more time I do more. When I do qigong I feel very relaxed. My mind is very quiet. I also feel the qi flow in my body; I feel warm. Usually when you do qigong you feel something is different.

You could feel goose bumps. When you feel very cold or feel very nervous you get goose bumps. But you can't control them.

I can control them and make them come out when I want. (He sits still in his chair and goose bumps come out of his arm.) I move my qi. When you do qigong you feel something different. It's interesting.

I became more and more interested in qigong, and eventually went to Tokyo to study in Tokyo University's psychosomatic department. I also studied about qigong and the goose bump phenomenon.

No one I know can make goose bumps come out of their skin at will. I did an experiment on the kind of changes that takes place in the body by practicing qigong. Usually goose bumps are controlled by the sympathetic nervous system. You can't control them because they happen naturally.

But when you do qigong you can control some part of the sympathetic nervous system. I think I move my body's qi to make the goose bumps come out.

I don't know exactly when I realized I could do that. I just did the exercise everyday and some days I felt so good, so comfortable. Usually I would close my eyes and lie down. I was so comfortable and suddenly I saw these goose bumps.

In Japan I had many qigong students. Most of them were housewives who weren't too busy and had time to think about their health.

In Japan and China everybody knows about qigong, but in America not so many people know about it. They know about tai chi or meditation but they don't know about qigong. There aren't so many qigong teachers here.

In Japan I taught people how to use qigong to lose weight. It's very effective. I usually have 12 sessions over a six-week period. Several hundred people took the course.

In that six-week period, people could usually lose about 10 pounds. That's the average. The highest weight loss was about 20 pounds.

To lose weight you practice internal qigong, which means you do it by yourself. There is also external qigong in which the qigong master moves qi through his hand to the patient.

Qigong can keep the body balanced. Chinese always think that the body will become diseased when it is out of balance. When the body is in balance you will have no health problem.

For instance, if your body temperature is normal it's okay, but if the temperature is too high you will get a fever.

Qigong helps people keep the balance. When the qi is weak the balance is broken; if the qi is strong the body will maintain its balance.

A person who always wants to eat will never feel full. They are always hungry. People who feel full and don't feel hungry have a different problem because that's not normal either.

It's normal to feel a little hungry. Some people may want to eat because the balance is broken. Qigong can keep the balance and suppress the appetite to some degree.

Some people gain weight because they don't move enough. That's also a problem. People don't move either because they have no time or don't enjoy doing it. I teach people some simple movements.

Why do Americans have a problem with weight? One reason is they don't move enough. They go everywhere by car and don't have an opportunity to exercise.

Another problem is food. The food here is not very good. People eat too much meat or fat and not enough vegetables. Chinese food has many vegetables. So I think the American diet leads to imbalance.

Sometimes when I am walking on the street I see people eating and drinking. I don't know if they are eating lunch or not. Maybe some people eat four or five times a day instead of just three times. I don't know why they do that.

One problem involves the availability of food. There's too much food available here. When you see it or smell it you want to eat it.

Still another problem may be stress. America is a very competitive society. When people feel stress they have to do something to relax. Some people like to exercise so that's good. But some people don't have any time, and it's difficult, so they eat and drink to feel comfortable.

Although this may be changing now, the Chinese government in the past usually gave everybody a job, so a person could always keep the same job. Both the hard worker and the lazy worker would get the same salary, so it wasn't so competitive.

But in America it's different. If you don't work hard, or keep learning, you could lose your job, so it's very competitive.

I think Americans may be healthier than rural Chinese, but I believe urban Chinese are healthier than Americans.
Many people in the Chinese countryside don't get enough nutrition, which is why many have short life spans. They're weak but they have to do hard work.
Also, when they have a disease they don't have enough money to drink medicine. There also aren't enough doctors available in the countryside and the people haven't health insurance. I know this because I am from the countryside.
But I think conditions are much better in Chinese cities. For one thing, city people have some health insurance. Also, if you went to China you would also see many people going to the park every morning to exercise.

Chinese food is also more healthful than American food because it contains many vegetables and not so much meat and eggs.
In China you don't see people who are very fat. If people are too fat, it's easy for them to get high blood pressure, diabetes, and many other diseases.
I think people who eat too much maybe will die earlier than those who eat normally.
I usually eat Chinese food. I don't like American food, though sometimes I have eaten a hamburger or Kentucky Fried Chicken.
At home the main dish is, of course, rice, along with vegetables, doufu, and eggs or meat.
My food contains many vegetables but little meat. I think this is the best way to eat.

I recently came to the United States. I like the United States and think the American system is a good one. If you have ability here you can do what you want, but in China there's not so much freedom.
I don't find it difficult adjusting to American life. Of course, there are differences. In Chinese culture people don't talk too much about themselves, but here people tend to say they can do anything.
'I can do that, I can do that,' they say. So it's more competitive. It's a little difficult, but I think it's better.

Before I came here I lived in Japan for six years. Japanese culture is very similar to Chinese culture, but the Japanese still keep some traditions — the old Chinese traditions, I think (he laughs).
For instance, people on the top and those on the bottom have different behaviors. In Japan, a person has to listen to his boss and obey him in everything. Even if the boss is wrong, you still have to obey him.
Japanese have the longest life span. I think their food is very healthy. They

eat many vegetables and fish, but not so much meat.

There are more people with pot bellies in Japan than in China, but fewer than you see in America. This condition will develop if you eat too much and don't move enough.

Having four seasons is also good. I think a climate that is too cold or too hot isn't good for health.

If the weather is good you feel comfortable, but if it's too cold it's difficult to do things and you don't feel comfortable or relaxed. Also, if you are working in a climate that is too hot you will get tired easily.

The health care system in Japan is much better than the one in China. Japan is a developed country and China is a developing country.

In Japan, they have much medical equipment, in some instances maybe more than the Americans. And in Japan everyone has health insurance (national health insurance).

The Japanese also use a futon rather than a bed. Every day when they get up they have to pick up the futon and put it in a cabinet.

This involves one kind of movement (bending over to exercise the back). They also have to remove the futon from the cabinet and place it on the floor.

People who sleep on beds have more lower back pain than people who sleep on futons.

Also, when the Japanese say hello they do this (bows). I think this is another kind of movement. So every day when you first meet Japanese, they will do this four or five times. So I think this is a good exercise.

The Japanese usually don't lose their temper. If a boss says something unpleasant to them, they always have to agree; they always say: 'hie hie (yes, yes).'

You can't be angry or you'll lose your job. If you feel angry it's not good for your body.

Depression is also not good for your body. I think it's better for your health if you don't feel angry about little things. Anger is not so good.

It's hard to say what qi is. Translated into English qi means energy. When I make some movement the energy I use is qi. Where does the energy come from? It's hard to say.

If someone asked me to show them that energy I wouldn't be able to give it to them, but you would understand that I have energy.

Let's say that today my energy is not so good. I feel tired. But the next day I have more energy. You can say this energy is qi, which comes from food, breath, and movement. That's the body's qi.

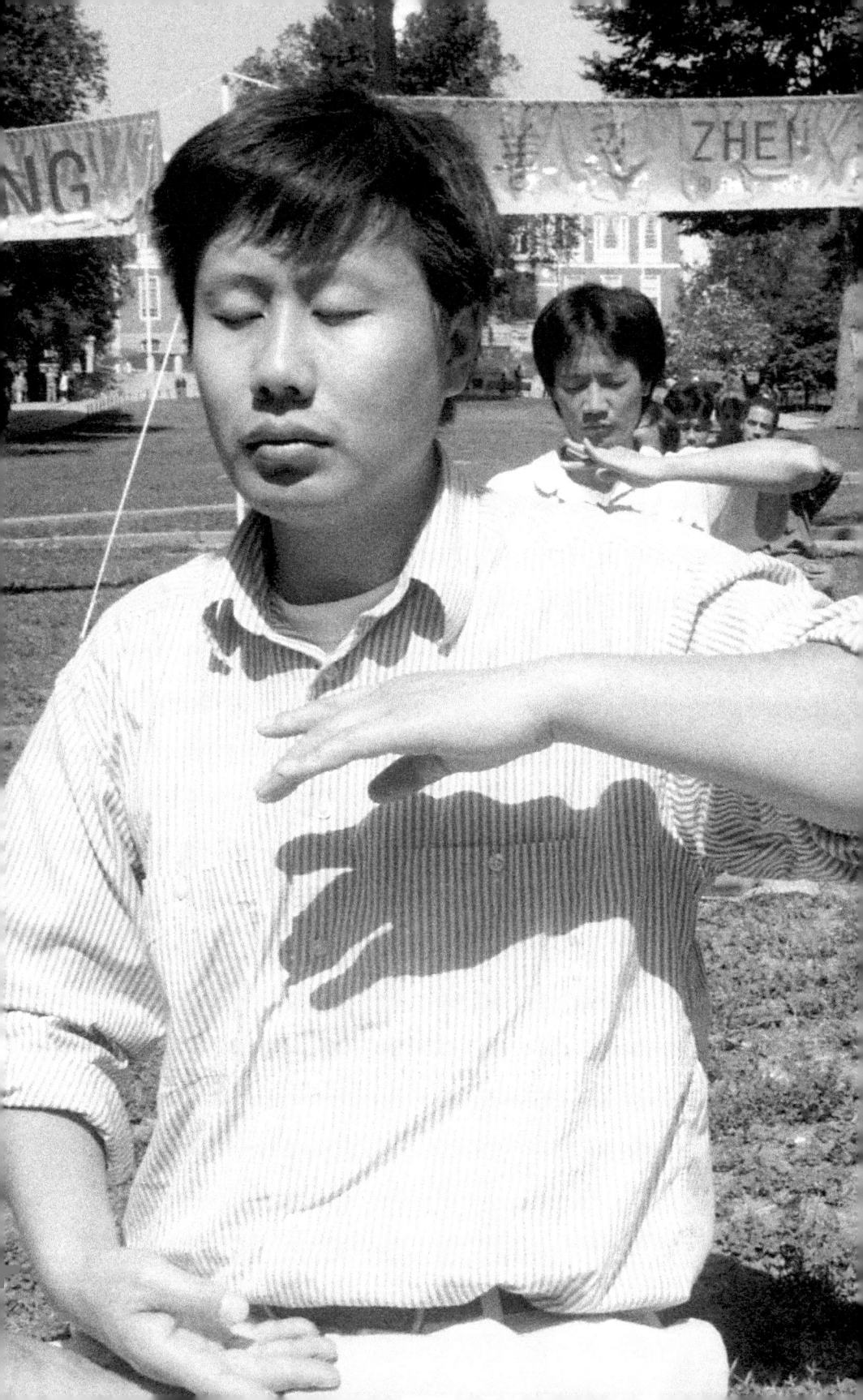

Science is starting to study it, but it's difficult, because maybe the instruments are not so good.

In China many scientists are starting to do experiments to study qi. When you do qigong, for example, you feel some movement, but what is it?"

Tai Chi Rising

ON A RAINY SPRING DAY IN 2001, tai chi chuan master Bow Sim Mark practices tai chi in her Chinatown studio with long-time student Jean Lukitsh.

Tai chi chuan is an ancient Chinese martial art that is also a form of exercise. Elderly Chinatown residents can often be seen practicing tai chi movements at the break of dawn on nearby Boston Common.

Tai chi is characterized by slow graceful movements of the hands, legs and torso. People who perform these movements with skill and grace seem to float above the ground, becoming more spirit than body.

For years Bow Sim Mark has been practicing and teaching martial arts in Chinatown.

Well known in the world of martical arts, she promotes tai chi as a performing art as well as a martial art and exercise.

"I came to the United States in the spring of 1975. I had been traveling with a kung fu performance troupe. We traveled all over America to perform. One of the performers in the troupe was [Mr. Han,] who had made a movie with Bruce Lee.

After a month I was invited to go to Europe, so I had the chance to compare different countries and cities.

At the last minute I decided to live in Boston. First I lived in my husband's family's house in Brighton. After that I wanted to live independently and moved into Chinatown for two years. In 1975 I started my school.

Even before I started teaching, people in Chinatown knew me because I had been a performer in Hong Kong. I was here only one week and they were already inviting me to join their team.

The wushu masters here said: 'Oh, Bow-Sim Mark has come to America.' I was only here one week when they started asking me to perform. Everything was still on the ship. I had only one sword with me. After I performed, a lot of people came to learn from me.

When I first came to Chinatown, there were many kung-fu schools here, but now there are even more. When Chinese people come to America they like to run restaurants and teach kung fu.

They may know just a few forms, but they'll still open a kung fu school (laughs). Maybe Bruce Lee didn't even know kung fu!

I remember when I first came here, everybody knew about kung-fu but nobody used wushu or the [kandan school]. I am the first to use wushu.

'Kung fu' means technique or skill. When you are a very good cook, then your 'cooking' gung fu is good. And if your teaching is good, then your 'teaching' kung fu is good.

Wushu is the correct name for martial arts — kung-fu is not the correct name. Wushu is a traditional Chinese sport and includes many styles — tai-chi chuan, chan chuan, and nan chuan are all wushu styles. There is also internal wushu and external wushu.

I learned wushu in China. When I was in elementary school in Canton (Guangzhou), I was interested in many different sports. I was always interested in performing. In school, my teacher always chose me to represent the school in entertainments. Little by little I became more involved. Then I joined the Canton Wushu Arts Association to learn from professional teachers. At the school they taught many different styles.

Wushu comes from combat. A long time ago they used wushu for fighting. Every movement has a self-defense application. But times have changed and now wushu is also a sport, a form of exercise (for health), and a performing art.

Today you don't need wushu for fighting. Many people in the world have guns now. Today it's more beneficial to use wushu as a sport and to promote health. Every movement, every step, is important.

In my school, I try to teach students to be very gentle. I teach it as a sport, a health exercise, an art, beautiful and powerful.

Tai Chi is one part of wushu. With tai chi, the movement is from inside to outside. It's very simple (demonstrates a circular tai chi movement with her hands).

You can feel the energy reach to the fingertips. You can feel the chest empty and the qi sink down to the abdomen and the groin.

If you keep doing it you will feel the energy flow through the whole body. If you do it throughout your life you will feel very healthy.

Chinese people still come to learn from me, but most of my students now are American. The people in Chinatown know about tai chi. They're interested in it but many are new immigrants and they work very, very hard. They are in a

hurry to make money. Even though they know tai chi is good for their health, they don't have the time or money to put into it.

When people first think of martial arts, they think of gung-fu, maybe Bruce Lee. Some young people like it for fighting, but later they find that tai chi is also good for sport and health. They compare it to other sports. If they can feel it and get a benefit from it, they're interested.

I've been teaching at Boston University for 15 years. The people there are young. I ask them why they come to my class. 'Oh,' they say, 'tai chi can make me feel more calm, more relaxed, more energetic.' That's why they like it.

When people are younger they like to do very excited kung-fu exercises. But later they may get hurt fighting or get some problem with their knee or their back. They come here because they find that tai chi is preferable to fighting. They need a more soft power. They no longer need the forceful power.

It's interesting to see this. I have one student who practiced kung-fu for 14 years, but he hurt himself and had an operation. He couldn't do anything. He had to take eight pills a day to control the pain. He couldn't do anything because of the pills.

But then he came here to learn tai chi. First he learned from my student, then, when he found out about me, he came to learn from me in a private class. Then little by little he started to think differently. He wanted to relax. He wanted to get rid of the pills.

Three years ago he stopped taking the pills. After he stopped, he continued to feel the pain, but by good patience he continued to learn, learn, learn, until now he no longer feels any pain.

He studies tai chi and tai chi performing art. He is also a part-time teacher. Now I'm training him to perform as the king in the wushu theater.

Tai chi has so many different movements: long-short, short-hard, pushing hands like this (she and her student perform the pushing hands movement). The movements are very, very rich. Tai chi and wudong are more internal.

Even if you spend your lifetime doing tai chi you still cannot know all of the movements. For me it's a lifetime's work.

Some people think tai-chi is just for the weak, for old people, but that's because they only see the beginning level, the first level.

The second level is not just for older, weaker people. It's also for stronger people, younger people. They're more interested in this level. The kicking spirit is part of basic wushu training. The young people like the harder movement.

The character of the tai chi movements is circular, relaxed, calm, contained, intent, focused. It's a circle. Like water. No fighting. Very gentle. Tai chi is very scientific.

I have written two books that tell in more detail about wushu and tai chi.

Tai chi is based on yin and yang. One side is working, one side is relaxed. One side is calm, one side is moving.

From the outside, yin and yang look very simple. You see up and down, yin and yang. There are always these opposites.

But inside there's also yin and yang. My hand is calm. It doesn't move. Yin doesn't move. It's calm.

But if it's moving it's yang. Now there's a movement (quick movement of the hand), that's the yang.

It looks slow, but it's fast (demonstrates tai chi movement).

That's why the spiral can be very relaxed but still be powerful. Relaxed but powerful.

Now I'm making the new form, seven movements, the essence of tai chi (she performs a series of movements and talks).

Wait for him like a club. Four turns. One, two, three, four. Where the first tail will come. Welcome spring. That's one thing. You see the character, slow then fast.

If you're very fat, tai chi will improve your shape and tighten your muscles. If you're too skinny and the circulation isn't good it will make you feel healthier. You can eat more and build yourself up more. It improves the circulation. It helps you stay young.

If the circulation is good and the inside is clean, then the outside will also become clean and flexible. After practicing, your skin and eyes will feel different. The movements can improve the circulation.

But you don't use force to do it. With tai chi, if you use more energy you can get more energy, just as you can get more money sometimes by using more money.

Americans make time to run very fast. The heart is thump thumping all the time. They want to do everything quickly, quickly.

But patience is very important. They say, 'Okay, maybe I need a few months to do this.'

So they hurry to do, to do, to do. They want to do it fast. But the heart also beats very fast, fast.

With tai chi, you gain new energy but don't feel this (huffing and puffing).

American people have this interest in wushu and tai-chi because it helps them control problems they have a hard time controlling.

I think that little by little they are beginning to know wushu especially tai chi. Tai chi is used in some hospitals now. They find that tai chi is good for some patients, for the heart, for balance.

I want my members to feel more healthy and feel more young. This is a benefit of tai chi. I don't think other hard-style sports can do that for you.

Many young people do the hard-style sports all the time but they're thinking. 'Oh, my knees hurt, my back hurts.'

In my lifetime I have trained a few people who have gotten awards. One of my students now lives in Pennsylvania. He has power. He travels to other countries to join the wushu meetings and to be a leader. He is good. He has almost 200 students.

Some parents send their children here to learn martial arts and Chinese culture. They know that my way is to lead them to understand that wushu is one part of Chinese culture.

I have about 20 young students — teenagers, seven-year-olds, ten-year-olds. They were born here and can't speak Chinese well. Twenty years ago some of their parents were my students.

I trained my daughter since she was four years old. When she was six years old she was in the class and doing very well. Both my daughter and my son did very well. They used to practice very hard.

My daughter used to practice here for a few hours by herself. If I went out do something — to buy something — she would still be playing when I came back.

When she was 12 years she still performed very well, but after that she no longer liked it. My daughter is like an American. She has her ideas.

I trained my son Donny Yen since he was 9 years old. When we went to Hong Kong I would teach him every morning in the park. He learned from me and helped me teach some of the students the higher level tai chi. He knew all of it.

He has the power to learn anything. He is very smart. He is a movie star now, a director and producer. He does kung-fu movies and works in Hollywood (including in Star Wars).

His first movie was a tai chi movie in Hong Kong. I let him join that movie because the director was the director of wushu for the movie "Crouching Tiger Hidden Dragon." He is my friend.

Over 20 years ago I worked with him. He knows my tai chi is special. When his sister came to America she took back a copy of my book "Combined Tai-Chi

Chuan" in Chinese.

When he made the tai-chi movie the next year, he gave my son a major role. Donny was about 19 years old. So my way is not just for wushu. It's also for art, for the movies.

It's a style that helped my son work in movies. Some of my other students — John and Michael and Stephen — have also worked in movies.

Sometimes I feel very happy that my wushu is used for art, is used in films. The filmmakers like using tai-chi in this way.

When I do the wushu theater I still follow the wushu techniques. Wushu theater is still wushu, not just theater and entertainment.

When I play Wang Zhau Jun, you can still see the root martial art technique in the movements.

If I do the sword I still do the root sword technique. When I did wushu theater in China, they thought my way was the right way.

Why do I go this way (wushu theater)? Everybody goes the other way. Why doesn't anybody want to go the more beautiful, more powerful way?

Wushu as theater can get more people interested in wushu. And if more people are interested in it more people will come to learn it. That will improve wushu.

With my background I really like to perform. I started to think: Why not let wushu focus on art, on theater? Why not use the movement to tell a story?

The last time I was in China — in Shanghai — the wushu students were really very, very good.

But the people in the wushu department there said my wushu theater was way ahead of theirs. They said they want to learn from me.

When I first came to America, the new language made me feel different. But little by little I stopped feeling this difference. I found that the people here are also interested in wushu — in tai chi.

Now I know Chinese and Americans come here for the same thing. I too am an American now (laughs). You see American people and Chinese people are together more now than before. We're no different. We (pointing to her American student sitting nearby) are like sisters.

I have been here 25 years. I find that in American culture, everything goes fast. But in Chinese culture everything is longer, older, more traditional, more closed. The American and other western styles are more open. These two styles are different.

But over time the eastern and western styles have become more friendly and open to each other.

Now younger Chinese people know and follow the western style. They're not different. The difference now depends on other things, on where you're living and on your background.

Right now I'm doing the wushu theater, performing Wang Zhau Jun to carry the Chinese culture to the western culture. The two cultures help each other.

My way of thinking is that I have come from China to here. I bring my culture here. I use it here.

But then I also learn a different culture from here. So we help each other out. From here (America) I have learned to be very free, very open. Here the science is very good and the people are very true.

But when I was in China a long time ago (I know it's more open now), the people were more closed. They were sometimes afraid to talk. They weren't free.

But I like it here now. Five years after immigrating I became an American citizen. If you work hard in this country you can get what you want. If you work hard and don't lie to people, if you are honest, then you can make a very nice living here. I like it here. I like this country.

I used to always be in Chinatown because I was teaching seven days a week. Even if I didn't have a class I would still do my own thing.

I wrote my books. I had my school in Chinatown for 20 years, but I still felt outside when it came to talking to people about certain things. Whenever people invite me to perform I always go, but after that I come back to my school.

During those 25 years in Chinatown there would often be some family or community conflict, but I didn't pay much attention to them. I thought it was very nice being together with people in Chinatown, but these other things didn't interest me.

When I taught at the Kwong Kow Chinese School I only focused on my sport and the students.

It doesn't matter to me what people say or do. I don't mind. Both sides are my friends. They invite me to perform.

When I was in China, the political life there was very unhappy. I came here to find freedom and a happy life. I wanted to learn how to do things. I wanted to help the people. What I know I want to give to my friends and students. That's my purpose. I don't want to know who is the leader. I'm not interested.

Clysler, my husband, is the editor of the (Chinese language) newspaper (Sing Tao), so every week, every month, I am invited to some party. But I'm not interested in going. One thing is, I don't have time (though sometimes I contribute money). When they go to a restaurant or go to a meeting or go to some entertainment, I'm teaching.

That's why 25 years after I arrived here they know me and I know them but we are not the same in certain ways. It's the tai-chi way. The tai-chi way is not like that.

I only can say that every time I do some research, I only think about how I can make the wushu, the tai-chi rise to a higher level. That's my way — a very peaceful way."

Practice, Practice, Practice

OVER THE YEARS THERE HAVE BEEN many martial arts teachers in Chinatown. Chinese who arrived in America with a few martial arts moves could often parley their limited knowledge into the martial arts business.

For some of these teachers, studying the martial arts wasn't a life-long calling but a way to earn money in America.

Some less than stellar teachers could make a living with their limited skills because students associated martial arts with an Asian face.

The popularity of kung-fu performers such as Bruce Lee in the 1970s drew many non-Chinese to study martial arts. In fact, most martial arts students in Chinatown today are not Chinese.

When Chinatown holds a lion dance for a special occasion, the performers are as likely to be white or African American as Chinese.

Chinese immigrants don't have the time to study the martial arts and most don't want to spend the money on lessons.

Second generation Chinese also tend to shun the martial arts because Chinese have often been stereotyped as experts in kung-fu. Many want to disassociate themselves from any old world associations.

But many of those early non-Chinese students of kung-fu were serious students. They took the martial arts seriously and turned it into a life-long endeavor.

One of them was kung-fu master (sifu) Bob Rosen, the first non-Chinese sifu in Boston Chinatown.

Every day Rosen arrives at the Wah Lum Kung-Fu Athletic Association on Edinboro Street to begin a day of teaching.

The club's room is at the top of a dark stairway in an old Chinatown building. The stairway may be dark but the Wah Lum studio is bright and orderly. A collection of swords stands against the wall and a traditional ancestral altar has been set up nearby. Lion heads and photos decorate the walls.

On a summer day in 2001, Rosen's students arrive late in the afternoon — two young Chinese men are the first to appear followed by a middle-aged white man.

Rosen prides himself on the diversity of his students. He says he wants to make everyone feel welcomed at the club.

As a non-Chinese martial arts master, he says it took him a while to gain acceptance in the Chinatown community.

"My interest piqued about 30 years ago through watching various shows and movies. Every kid started to get interested in kung fu and Bruce Lee.

I came across an American guy who was a black belt in karate. I started to take some lessons from him and before I knew it I really liked it. That was around 1972.

I enjoyed it. I liked the physical changes. I liked the fact that there was culture and science behind it. The philosophy we studied was more Chinese than Japanese. It was hard and soft, so it concentrated more on the self-defense aspects.

Then I got hungry for more knowledge and came across Grand Master Chan at his North Station School.

I didn't know him. I never saw him. I didn't know much about Wah Lum. I knew there was kung fu but I didn't know there were so many different styles of kung fu. I went in to meet him and talked to him about signing up. That was 1976.

Master Chan had left Chinatown in 1972 and moved to a nice big space near the Boston Garden. He had his own school and a lot of students that were starting to develop into instructors. I got involved in the regular program, just to try it out and see if I liked it.

The results were terrific for me. I got more flexible. I lost weight. I thought I had known a lot about martial arts from my previous training but once I started that program I found in just six months that there was so much more to learn.

He taught me a different aspect of it. It became more artistic than just a fighting art. There were so many different things to learn, such as weapons and stretching, flexibility and more Chinese culture.

But that really wasn't my main interest — it wasn't so much the Chinese culture but the philosophy that interested me. The philosophy came through the work we did.

By studying with him I learned more about the traditional aspects of kung fu — why we do certain things, why there are certain ceremonies and how important they are to upholding the traditions.

I got into his instructor program and graduated in 1979. Shortly after I joined the school, I became a professional student. I liked it so much that I trained with him every day and worked in restaurants at night.

In 1979 I was a member of Grand Master Chan's first sifu group. There were approximately 13 of us, but as of today I am the only sifu from that group left in the organization.

In 1980, Grand Master Chan moved to Orlando, Florida, to open up his Wah Lum Temple, which is the main headquarters for the Wah Lum school now. During that process, he left the school in New England to other instructors.

In 1984, Grand Master Chan decided to bring the Boston headquarters back to Chinatown. There was a senior group of students who were interested in helping him re-establish the headquarters.

My job was to operate the school and to run the classes and keep the tradition going. That was 16 years ago and I've been doing that every day now through the long cold winters and the long hot summers.

Through that process I got more and more involved with the Chinatown community. It was not the easiest position to be in. There was a lot of competition.

There were all these senior kung-fu masters here when I opened up. There was master Roman Yu, a seven star preying mantis master. There was Sifu Konti Fu, Calvin Chin's instructor, who was right down the street over the Dynasty Restaurant. And there were two other martial arts schools as well as Bow Sim Mark.

Not being Chinese made it even tougher for me. I had to actually be here every minute, every day. I just had to keep the doors open and let people come in. People were a little disgruntled when they found out I wasn't Chinese, but once they started and trained they understood that the training was the same. It was traditional and hardworking.

Our style was very elite to other styles. It was very physical and acrobatic. I had proven my skills with my sifu and he had put me in this position to prove myself even more.

But you had to get accepted by the Chinese community if you were here. Nobody knows you, nobody respects you because you're not Chinese.

But over the years I helped out in all types of community events – Chinese New Year, Dragon Boat Festival, August Moon Festival, 10-10 Parade. And each year my team comes out stronger and more sociable.

We're a very large group. We've also become more and more traditional. We do dragon dancing and lion dancing and continue to put on kung-fu demonstrations at these events. Chinatown is constantly asking us to be part of that.

So it took a lot of years, and after it happens one year you got to do it the next year. And each year you have to do it a little bit better. It just doesn't get easier. It gets a little bit harder because in kung-fu you're supposed to get wiser and stronger as time goes on.

You might get a little less adequate in the physical department but you're supposed to have a lot more knowledge and patience.

For a while the only type of students we got were working class people, adults who worked in the general area. They came here and were looking for almost the same thing I was looking for when I started martial arts: something different.

They wanted to get more involved in martial arts. They wanted more self defense and things like that.

And at first we didn't have much in the children's department or that many Chinese members, but as the years went on we've got more Asians. We're a very diverse group now, and that's because our door has always been open to everybody.

People come to Chinatown to look for the best instruction. That's what they're really looking for — the best instruction — not necessarily a Chinese teacher. The schools in Chinatown are generally rated as good schools.

But you still have to keep that door open. You have to keep working at it to get that reputation.

People are looking for an alternative to going to the health club and running on the treadmill and riding the bicycles. And they're looking at kung fu because they see it in the movies and television shows that come out today. Every single thing has martial arts in it now.

The Chinese who study are more short term now. They get a little bit of the knowledge. They exercise and get routines but then they're off to school or looking for a career. They're not really interested in it as a career — not too many people are nowadays.

That's one of the differences between the 90s and the 2000s compared to the 60s and the 70s. Back then you had a real influx of people who were really gung ho. They wanted to learn it for different reasons than they do today.

Back then there was more concentration on fighting and learning the secrets and things like that. Today it's advertised as tai go or aerobic kick-boxing. Every health club has some type of martial fitness program. That's what it has become today — kind of like a fitness program.

And we treat it that way too in the sense that we have to let people understand that kung fu is about hard work. They're going to find out that it's not what they see on TV. There's a lot of work to get to that.

Even a lot of kids who walk through the door won't last very long because they're expecting they're going to do all these flips and flops and everything. When they find out that they have to do stances and basic fundamentals first, they don't last very long.

You try to influence them that the benefits of martial arts are self-discipline, good physical fitness, and philosophy.

The Wah Lum style is a northern style of kung-fu. It comes from Shantong Province, China. The praying mantis style was developed over 300 years ago and this is just one branch of it.

Wah Lum is a long-range style of fighting. It emphasizes the praying mantis techniques — a lot of jumping and a lot of low-ground techniques. The full name is Wah Lum Tom Toy northern praying mantis kung-fu.

It's a combined style of the Wah Lum praying mantis and the family style of Tom Toy, which is a seeking-life style — a kicking style. It has a vast array of different weapons that keeps people interested. It's such a strong system that it takes many, many years to develop the skills.

It's not a passive style. It's a self-defense style. Over the altar it says 'Geng Long,' which means excellent fighting hall. This means that our style is developed to defend ourselves through self-defense, self-preservation.

But the most important thing is on the side of the altar. It says "Ju Zhou, Zu Si, Ju Gou," which means 'respect the grand master, respect the sifu, respect the teacher.'

So right away the first thing people learn is how to respect each other. On the left side is 'Hai Kurn, Hai Ki, Hai Kung-Fu.' That's 'Learn humility, learn fellowship, learn the hard work.' The translation of 'kung-fu' is 'hard work.'

And that's finally what we try to profess to people and show them. We give them that philosophy through practice.

Also on the altar are four ji dou zher, which is the sign for fire upside down. That means 'patience and control.' We teach people how to control their anxiety, their stress, their anger and so on, and that's through the hard work.

Hopefully they can defend themselves after a number of years of training. We teach them how to use it, but the object is basically to preserve themselves and enjoy their lives, not to go out picking fights and so on.

I try to avoid a lot of Chinese expressions. That's really not my personality. My personality is to come in every day and do my routine. I practice hard, I work hard, I just kind of live the life that suits me. It's kind of a cross between a Daoist and a Buddhist philosophy. It's passive but it's always changing.

We have a lot of different people that will come in. Some are competitive-minded. They want to get more involved in competition and have a whole different mindset. You have to work with those people in a different way. They have a hard-working attitude and want to win. I prepare them more for battle than for just going home or going to work with less stress after they leave here.

In China, kung-fu was taught more as a survival technique. You didn't just learn it for the art but for the skills to help you protect yourself. And when you learned a weapon you learned it very tediously; you had to do every single thing properly.

When Master Chan came to America and started teaching, there wasn't

such a long process. In America, everybody is like, 'Hurry up. I want to learn. I want to learn.' That's the American way. They're in a hurry to get it going.

The Chinese are more patient, but it also depends on where they're from and what they're doing. There are people who have been living in this country a long time and watch all the TV and all the commercials and they're the same as every other American — they have no patience whatsoever.

The parents will send them here and hope they can learn more patience through kung-fu. You'd be surprised. Parents want the discipline. They want the philosophy of this school.

I have my own routine. I come into work every day. I have private students during the daytime. It's important for me to get my daily exercise in. I need that. I need my meditation. I need my quiet time. My idea of meditation is just being here by myself and focusing on some work or sitting in the chair or coming out and doing some tai chi at midday. Or I might just be working on some specific project. I might be developing a routine for a demonstration.

Right now we're preparing a team to go to China at the end of August. It's a competition team, so we've been focusing on that type of material. I've been to China four times. We're there for personal training, competition, and just personal development. This year we'll spend 20 days there, travel to Beijing, and then go down to Hong Kong.

In between we're stopping in Junzhou for the Shaolin International Tournament. We'll probably be introduced to some different masters and do some different training, so we're exposed to other styles, not just Wah Lum instructors.

I've gotten close to some people in Chinatown, some of the older men in the Chinatown Business Association. I help them out. They ask us to participate in events.

I really stay away from politics. It's not my business. I don't stick my nose where it doesn't belong. I know the area around here. Probably more people know me than I know.

I've been involved in the Chinatown Freemasons. They're just kind of a businessman's group and they pretty much help direct the activities in Chinatown. They're all from old Chinese families.

But Chinatown is a very closed place. You can walk down the street and see someone you know and they'll walk right by you and not even recognize you.

They would do it to Grand Master Chan too, when he was here. He said it used to make him mad. One minute they'd call him sifu, the next minute they won't even say hello. That's the way they are. There's nothing you can do about that part.

But in most cases, when I see some of the big shots, or whatever, they're,

'Hello Bob. How are you?' or 'Hello sifu.' It's really nice when I walk in some of the restaurants and they're, 'Hey sifu, how are you?' You know they respect you.

I've gotten older. You get injuries. You get worn out parts. And these things start to catch up with you. But that's why you try to continue to develop people who can help you and work for you. That's what gung-fu is about.

There's an aspect that makes it hard physically but then there's another part that challenges you to keep doing it. And if you can't be as physical, there's another part of it that allows you to be more soft, more pliable.

So it's kind of like a continuing cycle. You're always changing. It's the yin-yang. There's hard and soft. You're never just one way. You can have a real hard physical day, a challenging day, and you can have a real smooth soft day the day after. It's always going up and down, up and down.

But one thing I feel — I'm not in search of the answer. A lot of people are, because there's always a new question. Every day there's a new one. You just learned something and you ask a question. The question is, how does this work? The answer I got when I was a student was — no answer, you got no answer, you got a look and then a walk away.

What you were expected to do was practice and through that the answer would be there for you. And it's always nice to have someone there to explain every little detail to you, but if we explain the detail to you that doesn't mean you're going to get the answer.

You really have to focus on the physical aspects of it for a long time. You have to look into it. You have to feel it and be sensitive to it and that's when the answers come. So just because someone tells you the answer doesn't mean you know it — your body doesn't know it.

The Chinese way is that practice will bring you success. That's about the last cliché I have. That's what I was always told. Just practice. It's there. I've been practicing for 30 years and it's true. You know the secret — the secret is practice. There is no secret — no ancient Chinese secret.

Someone may have a secret form — something that they've been holding back. Something that they know but haven't taught to a student yet. But that's the only kind of secret. There are no secrets.

The secret to success is to keep practicing. I mean you have the qi, but it's already there. How does one control it? How does one develop it? It comes through constant practice and research over time. You can't research it in a day.

You could read all the books you want on it, okay. You could have all this theory but if you don't practice that theory over a period of time, you can't feel what you read. You've got to feel what's going on. You have to feel the power, you have to feel the energy.

There's no one answer and there's no quick fix. You just have to work for it."

WORDS SONGS PICTURES

A Bridge to Chinese Culture

IT'S A COMPLAINT OFTEN HEARD in Chinatown — that community leaders and residents don't pay much attention to the arts.

Controlled largely by the neighborhood's business community, Chinatown has primarily been a destination for people in search of Chinese restaurants and markets.

People interested in Chinese language and arts turn first to local universities, museums, and concert halls.

If Chinatown's business leaders got involved in anything beyond business it's generally Boston politics.

In the 1990s, some owners of culture-related businesses in Chinatown complained publicly about the state of the arts in the neighborhorhood.

"I think Chinatown puts too much emphasis on food," says Peter Chan, the founder of the Chinese Language Institute in Chinatown. "Many people complain about this, but no one can change it."

He says the most logical place to absorb Chinese culture should be the area's largest Asian neighborhood.

Chan's friend Man Chun Kit has opened bookstores, art galleries, and gift shops in Chinatown over the years and shares his view about culture in Chinatown.

"I want American people to come here and have the impression that Chinatown is a clean community — a cultural community," he says. "Boston is known as a cultural city," but Chinatown hasn't contributed much Chinese culture to the city, he says.

Chan and Man say it hasn't been easy selling culture in Chinatown. They both run culture-related businesses in the neighborhood, but they are just getting by.

Chinatown's choice rental spaces are too expensive for cultural enterprises like theirs. Also, many people don't recognize the value of cultural activities and need to be informed.

"I don't think we can just see it as a business; we also have to educate people," says Man.

"Art is a good bridge to get people to come to know Chinese culture," says Chan.

One of the earliest promoters of the arts in Chinatown has been Doris Chu, founder of the Chinese Culture Institute, an exhibition space for contemporary Chinese art.

In the late 1990s she embarked on a new and challenging course by transforming the Culture Institute to also serve as the area's first Asian American theater.

The theater opened with the production of a play written by Chu based on the life story of Boston's first Chinese resident.

"When I came to the States (from Taiwan) in the 70s I studied art history," she says. "I started at the University of Pittsburgh, and then I got a Mellon Fellowship to do research at Harvard University.

All these years I've been involved in different areas of the arts. In recent years I have been writing plays, and before that I published short stories and wrote novels.

I was very interested in creative writing, but my published works were mostly research projects.

When we started the visual arts work in the 80s there were no other galleries, no other efforts to promote Chinese visual arts, except for the museums.

But the museums were mostly doing historical rather than contemporary art. I remember one time Mr. Wu Tong — now the curator of the Museum of Fine Arts but then a research member — said CCI was doing a very good job by complementing what the museum was doing.

The museum would show artwork before the 20th century, while we mostly showed contemporary work. At that time no art galleries were showing Chinese contemporary art, so we felt it was very important for us to be doing it.

Years ago there was no effort put into the arts in Chinatown, but now clearly you see different things going on — art galleries, book stores — you know many things are going on.

Therefore I feel we don't need to duplicate the effort. I feel there are so many things in the arts that need to be done, and we shouldn't all be doing the same thing.

For instance, we were doing music concerts and dance presentations, but in the past 10 years others have started to do that as well.

So we gradually shifted our efforts more toward things no one was doing. And the theater was definitely something that nobody was doing. Not just in the Chinese community, but also in the Asian community.

I thought theater was a very important link in a culture, and since no one was paying attention to that I thought we should take it up.

We helped establish an organization called Asia On Stage, which is affiliated with CCI. In the last few years we produced one major main stage drama plus two or three or four smaller productions. The smaller ones were staged at CCI, but we had to rent auditoriums for the major ones.

And renting an auditorium was sometimes very difficult. One time we almost had to cancel our show because the theater management double booked.

We thought if we could have our own facility it would solve our problems and also allow us to do more dramatic projects as well as music and dance performances.

So over a year ago we began to plan the theater project. It was awfully difficult. Certainly money was a big issue. People warned me not to get into it but I was very stubborn, just like I was when I started CCI in 1980.

At that time I was still doing my dissertation and my friends said not to do it because it would be very labor intensive and not rewarding to me. They said it would cost me my career.

But I was very stubborn and overcame every difficulty. I have always been very stubborn: if I set my mind on something I don't give up, I never give up.

So although I knew it would be a tremendous effort and that we didn't have any money I went ahead.

We did raise some money — from several foundations and the trustees and private contributions — but it's not enough. It's going to be a problem. Right now if you ask me how I'm going to complete the project, my answer will be that I really don't know how.

Once the space is renovated it's still going to be CCI, but it will include the theater. The theater will have its own name but it will be under the Chinese Culture Institute.

We thought about the name, and we're tentatively going to use the name Tremont because it's located on Tremont Street and it's a name that people will easily remember.

We're not going to use the theater space all year round because we won't have the capability of producing drama every day.

So part of the time we will let other small theater groups use it for a small rental charge, which will be used to help support our theater projects. The theater will use the space in the evening and the art gallery will use it during the day. As you can see, all the wall space can be used for artwork.

Our own productions will be focused first, on Chinese subjects, and second, on other Asians subjects. They will include new works by Asian American playwrights and translations or adaptations of existing Asian drama and dramatic masterpieces.

We'll focus on subjects that reflect the history and culture of an Asian nation, or the history and contemporary life of Asian Americans. These will be our own production subjects.

Other theater groups can do whatever they want, but of course within certain limits.

This will be the first Asian theater in New England. In New York there is a Pan Asian Theater with 25 years of history, but that is the only Asian theater in the eastern part of the United States.

I think we will produce four dramas a year. Right now there is one theater company — a Russian theater company called the Chekov Theater and Film — that plans to come in perhaps as a resident company. They are in Boston but do not have their own theater; they have been using different places for their productions.

They asked me, Will the Chinese community object? I said no. We will not object. We are in America. We will be friends with every group in Boston. Even though Russia and China historically had conflicts, here we have no conflicts because we are ethnic groups in America.

Acting was part of my extracurricular activities in school but I never thought I would write a play. I had no training in it, and it was totally different from writing short stories or novels.

A few years ago I wanted to produce a Chinese play but I couldn't find a good English script. So I started to adapt this very well known Chinese play into English.

I didn't translate it because it was too long; I adapted it. I kept the story intact but rewrote it. And that was the beginning of my playwriting career.

At first I had absolutely no confidence in it, but a few people told me they liked the script.

One person was a playwright himself, another one was an actress from Hollywood who said it was a good play, with good writing. She knew the original Chinese play but this was an English version.

She happened to be in town and saw it. She said it was a very good adaptation, so that gave me confidence to do a second play, which was an original work. After that I did another one and another one.

One of the plays I wrote will be produced in April when the theater opens. It tells the story of a Chinese merchant who lived in Boston from the 1850s to the 1870s.

He came here, got married, had a very successful business, but in the end he gave up everything and went back to China, because that was where he came from.

I have two possible titles for the play: "That Gentleman From China" and "Return to the Roots." There is a Chinese phrase: "Falling leaves return to the roots."

The play reviews a chapter of American history and allows the audience to contrast 19th century America to late 20th century America.

People still complain about discrimination, prejudice, and unfair treatment and all that, but if we compare today with 150 years ago, the difference between the two periods is like day and night.

Chinese people went through hell during that time. In this play we are just reviewing some of it; we are not complaining about it or criticizing anybody; we're just looking back at history to see more clearly what life is like today.

After the production in April, we intend to have a discussion between the actors and the audience. Race and ethnicity will be two of the issues we'll want to discuss.

The gentleman on whom the play is based was not only accepted, but also respected. He was wealthy and generous, a big philanthropist and a naturalized US citizen; he was baptized as a Christian and was even accepted and welcomed by the Masons.

But what did all that mean? It meant that he had to give up himself. He had to give up his name when he adopted an American name.

He didn't have a religion because Chinese were not a religious people. He was a Confucianist and a Confucianist was not a religious person but an ethical person.

He had to become a Christian, a religious person, in order to fit into the society. He also had to become a citizen. This was a tremendous privilege because he was the first Chinese to become a citizen of the United States.

So he was the first Chinese to marry a white woman, become a citizen, and become a Christian. He was a pioneer on all these fronts, but in the play he says: But I am still a foreigner, although I am respected, I'm still a foreigner.

He told his son — who was half Chinese, half American — not to go to China with him because in China he would be a foreigner forever; he would not be accepted. So this really tells of his deep down feeling.

In a way, it also tells about how we feel even today. I never feel I am an American. I never do. I've been here for 20 years but I still don't feel I am American.

I've heard of many Chinese Americans who were born and raised here who have this identity crisis because they do not feel like other Americans — because of their look, their skin color.

But they cannot identify with the Chinese either because they know nothing about China. They have no cultural or linguistic knowledge.

When they travel to China they cannot communicate. They don't speak the language. So this identity crisis is with them.

But because I came here after college I don't have that feeling. I always think of myself as a Chinese living in America.

And I don't feel I'm out of place here either; I feel like I'm a guest here. If you treat me very well I thank you, but if you don't, well, this is not my place.

At the same time, I feel very very comfortable here. I don't feel this is my country but I feel very comfortable.

Last year an actress, a Chinese American, felt very offended when someone in downtown Boston asked her how long she has been here and whether she could speak the language."

If people ask me, Do you speak English? I don't feel insulted at all.

On the Right Side of History

WHEN PEOPLE IN CHINA THINK OF America they often think of it as a place to earn money — a place to buy things, a place to live out modern materialistic dreams. America is Gold Mountain

It's also a place that imposes pressures on immigrants because they often don't know the language or the culture. The struggle to earn money and survive becomes the essential reality.

In Chinatown, art and culture tends to fall by the wayside, though scattered among the restaurants and markets are people who continue to make art.

The Chinese-born poet Meng Lang is one of them. Working at the Chinese Culture Institute in Chinatown, Meng came to the U.S. to escape harassment from Chinese authorities in the years following the Tiananmen Square crackdown of 1989.

He says he came to the U.S. because he thought he could freely practice his art here. He didn't come here to climb Gold Mountain.

He expresses curiosity about the American writers Walt Whitman and Henry David Thoreau. He's curious about an America even many Americans have forgotten.

"My parents were really opposed to my going into literature, especially my father," he says. "My class advisor in high school was also against it.

Even though he taught Chinese, he had suffered a lot during the Cultural Revolution and was against my choosing literature as a career.

But I was 16 and buckled under the pressure. In October '78 I joined the college for mechanics in Shanghai.

For four years I studied optical instrumentation, though I spent most of my free time in the library reading up on literature, philosophy and history.

I feel that those four years in college really formed the way I write and were important for my growth as a poet.

At the time Chinese society was just beginning to open up. New ideas were arriving from the West. I spent a lot of time reading up on Western literature in magazines and books.

It was also the time when the Democracy Wall movement was going on in China. I was very interested in this movement and often went to People's Square in the middle of Shanghai to read the posters expounding on democracy.

My ideas at the time inclined toward democracy — I was sympathetic to democracy.

But in 1980, the authorities suppressed all those democracy movements and all the political magazines that came out in '78 and '79 were banned. Any unauthorized publication at the time became a very dangerous activity.

There was a policy handed down from the central government banning all unauthorized organizations and publications.

Between 78 and 80 when I really started writing seriously, I mostly wrote modern poetry in Chinese, although sometimes I still wrote old-style classical Chinese poems.

Although my writing at the time was still influenced by traditional Chinese literature, I also was very influenced by French literature and American literature starting from the latter half of the 1800s.

Free-verse writing in modern Chinese — in colloquial Chinese — really only started after 1919, so at the time it was only 60 or 70 years old.

It was really a young medium. So I tried to learn how to use this very young medium to express ideas and explore different ways of styling the poems.

At the time, I published a magazine called MN with two friends from high school. MN is an acronym for the two syllables in the word 'modern.'

I thought at the time that Chinese society was in such huge transition and that we were the generation to bury certain things.

The question was mainly literary and aesthetic because I thought the old ideas of aesthetics were going to be buried. But in a way it was also political.

The magazine came out in the spring of '81, and the print run was only 60. The magazine was distributed to college friends devoted to literary matters.

In the next three or four years we published six or seven issues of this magazine. Through the publication and exchange of these magazines, I got to know a lot of leading figures in the underground literary movement in Shanghai and beyond.

In the mid '80s we formed two literary groups in Shanghai. One was called Seaside, and the other was called Everyday. These culture groups were all formed spontaneously by young intellectuals and college students. We had art exhibits, literary salons and poetry readings.

At the time, people were also publishing underground poetry in other Chinese cities. By exchanging our publications we gradually formed this network. Through the 1980s this network of underground publishers and writers of poetry almost formed a kind of unofficial secret society.

The aesthetic ideas we had were on the edge of Chinese society because they were so avant-garde. They could not be accepted by the mainstream. The ideas we had challenged both the political reality of the time and popular tastes.

It was really quite interesting, because we didn't necessarily know each other personally. If someone in the circle wanted to go somewhere and I had a friend there, I would introduce him to the other person by writing a note. Then he would be warmly welcomed by that friend. The same thing would also happen to me if I wanted to go to another city.

A common feeling among the poets was a total antipathy toward oppression and control over thoughts and literature. Although everyone had his own political views, I don't think we actually got involved in political activities as such.

Through the medium of the arts we were trying to express ourselves, trying to express our individuality.

Because we formed our own organization and had our own publications it made the authorities very nervous. From the very start they tried to stop what we were doing because it was a challenge to the political reality.

In 1990 we had a meeting of all the poets in China and we joked about it. We said if alternative parties were allowed in China we could form a poet's party.

We would be one of the most mature, most well-organized organizations, though I have to stress that poets are also very individualistic.

At the time of the Tiananmen protest, I was working as an editor and reporter for Shenzhen University's Editing and Reporting Center. Shenzhen is just across the border from Hong Kong.

I was reporting on the movement, but also actively participating in it by advising the students. After the movement was over I was questioned a few times by the Shenzhen Police.

Some poets were more active in the 1989 events. A few poets in Szechwan Province wrote poetry and made videos of the movement. In 1990, they were

arrested and sentenced for their activity.

I think more than 90 percent of the modern poets in China at the time were on the side of the students. They were fighting for democracy.

Chinese society makes it very difficult for anyone to express his feelings, his thoughts, his views freely. Because of this I think most of them just kept quiet.

In Shanghai we were under the surveillance of a special branch of the police for political activities.

In April '92 I was secretly detained by the political security branch of the Shanghai Police along with another prominent figure in Shanghai poetry circles. We were detained in a hospital within a police compound.

I was totally isolated and didn't know that my friend was also there. I was in a hospital room with three beds.

I slept in the middle bed and two policemen specially trained in boxing slept in the beds to my left and right. Shifts would change three times a day but two people were always there.

For the entire period I was detained, I didn't go out at all and didn't see sunshine. During the day, the political police would come and interrogate me.

They wanted to know about a publication called Modern Chinese Poetry, which was organized by others and me in 1990.

My detention aroused an outcry from international poetry societies, Pen International, and international media. Because of that pressure the police let me go.

The excuse they gave for my detention was my receipt of some money from an overseas democracy group. The money was donated to support Liu Xiaobo, Wang Dan, and Zhou Duo, prominent figures in the Tiananmen Square demonstrations.

This money, which was for them and their families, was given to me because I knew Zhou Duo. I was supposed to give them the money. So the police said this was a political activity to overthrow the government.

They gave this as the reason for my arrest, but that was only the excuse. There was another reason. During the interrogation I learned they had detained me because they thought I could tell them something they wanted to know.

While I was detained, I spent 90 percent of my time being interrogated. They asked me about my literary activities.

When the police interrogated me, I always told them my views. I would tell them that China should have a multiparty government and that the ban on publications and party formation should be lifted. The police said my thoughts were really problematic.

They said, 'These thoughts are sick, and that is why we are here interrogating you. Your art is in your politics and your politics is in your art.'

But these people didn't have any training in aesthetics. They didn't really understand beauty. They didn't even understand my poems. That's why the only thing they could think about was politics.

I was detained in April '92 and released in May '92. Between that time and September '95 — when I came to the States — I was frequently questioned and harassed by the police. I was constantly put under surveillance.

So during that period there were two or three months when the police would come to question me twice a week. It really turned my life upside-down.

If I wanted to work for a magazine as a journalist they would talk to the magazine, so the magazine wouldn't hire me because I was on a black list.

If I wanted to travel outside of Shanghai I also had to report to them. So this really caused me a lot of difficulties. I had very little personal freedom at the time.

It was around this time that I received an invitation from Brown University's Freedom to Write Program to become a visiting scholar. When Brown gave me the invitation I applied to go abroad.

I was taken by the police to this tourist resort outside of Shanghai. They needed seven policemen and two cars. They talked to me for three nights and two days, trying to figure our why I wanted to go abroad.

I guess I was already on their list of troublemakers. Some months after that talk, they finally gave me the passport.

My experience in the U.S. has largely been positive. But even though I am here in the U.S., I still feel I am underground, mainly because I'm studying Chinese literature and Chinese poetry. I also publish a magazine called Tendency Quarterly.

Poetry is such a precious thing. It's something that survives despite the pervasiveness of consumerism and capitalism throughout the world.

The pursuit of the human spirit and the aesthetic ideal is very precious in this world.

I observe and question and criticize capitalism. My main political views now are based on equality, justice, and democracy.

I think I have a tendency to be on the left, but I'm not a supporter of communism.

Communism is the same as the totalitarian regime that I hate.

Coming to the U.S. has changed me in several ways. I have more freedom and have become more individualistic. Because I am in a new environment, I see many new things. The subject of my thought and poetry has become much broader here.

My poetry focuses more on the pursuit of a universal experience for all of humankind rather than on the experience of a specific group. I feel that humankind as a whole has a common destiny, a common fate. So when I write now I want to write for the entire humankind, not just for the people of one country.

Humankind is at the gates of the third millennium, but is still experiencing a lot of difficulties. It's a time of crisis. There are problems associated with nuclear weapons, the environment, energy, and over-population.

I think America sets a trend for the hogging of energy and space, but unfortunately everyone is involved in this now. Even China is being swept into this trend.

But I feel that humankind shouldn't just pay attention to what we have now. We should also show some responsibility for the environment and for the future.

Unfortunately, as a poet, I can only watch this trend sweeping along without being able to do much about it.

My conscience tells me I should focus on these questions in the interest of humankind. So my basic standpoint as a poet is to struggle against the evil in man, which is a manifestation of his endless pursuit, his endless greed.

But by saying that I don't want to come across sounding like a guru or a spiritual leader either, because in my writing I view this from the standpoint of aesthetics.

I work here now and get what I need to get by. Of course, I feel related to Chinatown. It's like a miniature China, in a way. I can get a lot of groceries and foods and eat in nice restaurants here. I like this.

But I think Chinatown has its limitations — mainly because of the composition of the population.

In a way, I feel it's disconnected from mainstream American culture. It's becoming a tourist spot. In a way, I think it's become a huge restaurant.

Of course, people like me have feelings for Chinatown. If there were more people like me who spend time looking at culture, Chinatown would change — there could be a cultural revival.

I'm not saying the population here only works in restaurants because I know they do other things as well. There are many Chinese in greater Boston who work with computers and do other things.

But I feel the people here are oblivious to modern arts and people like me who practice modern arts.

In the U.S. most artists are modern artists. So if we could introduce modern arts to the Chinese population here, they could maybe become more accepting and have a broader mind. It might bring them closer to mainstream American culture.

But it's not just modern poetry that's hard for people to accept. Anything that's avant-garde will be hard to accept.

In the case of, say, a novel, at least it has a story and a framework people can understand, but poetry is more spiritual, more intuitive.

It takes a lot of psychological preparation and requires readers to have years of training. I really didn't think the readership in China had that.

And it's not just poetry either. If they looked at Western art, dancing, movies — they would find that hard to accept as well.

I have a handicap in the English language, so I can only read poetry when it's translated.

I have talked to American poets. I guess my understanding relies more on intuition, but I read the poetry of Emerson and Thoreau and Poe.

In my humble opinion, contemporary poetry in the U.S. seems to be fairly light. It's not substantial enough.

In the last 10 or 20 years American society has been very placid, very calm. I think the poets here maybe have too much nutrition, too much nourishment. They're not like the Chinese poets who have lived during upheavals and felt the anxiety and anger.

Although my wish is to be able to go back to China tomorrow, my return has as a condition my ability to live a peaceful life there.

My ideal life would be to go back to China to write and live a peaceful life, but at this point I can't really predict when that will happen.

I am in fact more optimistic than many of my friends, who say I should be prepared to stay here for a long, long time. When I came to the U.S. I received political asylum, so I rely on the protection of the United States to live and think and write peacefully.

I don't want to go back to a life in which my thoughts and my every movement are under surveillance.

At this point, when I talk about my writing, I often have to repeat my life story, the experiences I've just related to you.

But I really want people to know me as a poet, to know my thoughts, to know my views on aesthetics and poetry.

I think I feel a need to communicate with people about human nature, to communicate through the heart and through poetry. I would like that to be my means of communication.

At the same time, I think it's necessary to politicize my views. In October '97, when Jiang Zemin came to Cambridge, I was in the protesting group. I was one of the dissenting voices.

And when Premier Zhu Rongji comes to Boston next week, I will be there again. I do this to express myself. I am not against him personally, but I'm against the system he stands for.

To use the words of President Clinton: They were in the wrong of history and I want to be in the right!

A Unique Musical Tradition

THE AUDITORIUM OF THE CHINESE CULTURAL Center is packed on this Saturday afternoon in 1996.

Members of Chinatown's Performing Artists Salon are tuning their instruments. Today's concert offers Chinatown a rare opportunity to hear the traditional music of China.

Few of the musicians performing today are able to work as professional musicians in this country, but many were trained as musicians and worked as performers and teachers in China.

They play the native instruments that give Chinese music its distinctive sound — the erhu (a two-stringed Chinese fiddle), the yangqin (a hammered dulcimer), the pipa (a pear-shaped lute), and the ti (a side-blown bamboo or ivory flute).

Klysler Yen, who plays the erhu, says — unlike much Western music, which tends to excite the emotions and senses — Chinese music tends to have a calming effect on both musician and listener.

Catherine Chan, who produces concerts for the Performing Arts Salon, says Chinese music induces in listeners "a sense of tranquility, meditation...Asian music tends to give you more room to think, to imagine."

In China, music was a component of Confucian education, says Yen. "There were six main courses for education, and one was music. Music was used as a tool of education to develop manners and cultivate the spirit."

Chinese music relies on a five-tone pentatonic scale, but Western music has seven notes plus five half tones, says Yen.

Chinese traditional music is simpler than classical Western music, with each instrument of an ensemble playing the same musical line. In Western

compositions, different instruments often play different musical lines.

The erhu is like a violin, says Yen. It has two strings and is played with a bow. It's an instrument with a quiet sound, almost "like somebody's voice." You might describe it as "very beautiful and a little sad."

"When we perform, the western people are very interested," says Yen, who believes that in the future Chinese and western music will have a greater influence on each other.

An editor and reporter for Sing Tao, an international Chinese daily newspaper, Yen played violin professionally in Guangzhou before immigrating to the U.S.

Chan says boundaries between musical traditions are breaking down as musicians from different parts of the world have more contact with each other.

Chinese musicians living in this country no longer feel they have to be pigeon-holed as either eastern or western. The two musical traditions are "melting into each other, " **says Chan.**

Hybrids are acceptable now. "More and more, they feel this is a world music," she says. In the past, Chinese musicians may have been unsure about what tradition to follow, but now they absorb everything and use it.

Yang Yong, a composer and teacher at the New England Conservatory in Boston and a graduate of the Central Conservatory of Music in Beijing, says the music he composes now has both western and Chinese elements. "Something Chinese always comes out naturally from my mind," he says.

Eastern music is "non-linear and doesn't follow a step-by-step progression" as does western music, he says. Two musical events may follow each other but "are not necessarily connected."

Some Westerners may have difficulty appreciating Chinese music because of its meditative quality — because it doesn't make grand gestures and movements.

"The line doesn't develop, so to some people this kind of music...doesn't have any climax," Yang says.

The excitement is experienced through subtle changes in tone and other effects, he says.

This meditative quality has its origins in Taoism, which views life in terms of opposites — yin and yang, high and low, hot and cold. "The balance doesn't go anywhere," he says. "It just stays in-between."

But Yang worries that western forms may be altering Chinese traditional music. The music played by the salon, he says, shows many western influences.

"I think we are losing our traditions," he says.

From Chinatown to the Boston Symphony

"WHEN I PLAY MUSIC I FORGET EVERYTHING," says Wu Man, a virtuoso pipa player who occasionally plays with the Salon. "I'm totally concentrated on the music."

The pipa is a four-stringed, lute-like instrument that originated in Central Asia and traveled along the Silk Road to China.

Unlike the guitar, the pipa is held straight up like a large bass and played with the fingernails rather than a pick. The strings are also strummed in the opposite direction.

What distinguishes the pipa from the guitar is the quality of the sound, says Wu. The pipa has a penetrating sound that seems to carry over long distances.

Wu started playing the pipa when she was nine years old — during the Cultural Revolution in China. "At that time every parent wanted their children to learn something to keep them at home," she says.

In those days, there was fighting on the streets of some cities. Her parents had to leave home often to attend political meetings and wanted to keep her busy while they were away.

Her father — a traditional Chinese painter — was drawn to the pipa because of its association with poetry and culture, she says.

He found a friend to teach her how to play the instrument and two years later, at the age of 11, she applied for admission to the prestigious Central Conservatory of Music in Beijing.

"I took the exams," she says. "They were very, very difficult...you have to pass three different examinations."

Wu was accepted by the school and took a 22-hour train ride from Nanjing to the school in Beijing.

"The first year I was so upset," she says. "We didn't have a telephone. We could only write letters to our parents."

But over time she adjusted to her new life and the school became her second home. "Three years later I didn't want to go home," she says. "I wanted to stay at school."

She stayed in that school for 13 years, attending high school, college and graduate school there. She even taught there from 1987 to 1990.

Mastering her art in her early years required painstaking effort. In middle school she played her instrument up to 12 hours a day.

"Right now I don't have to pay attention to the technique," she says. Now it's the emotion and artistry of the performance that she strives to perfect.

Wu says she decided to leave China after the 1989 student demonstrations in Tiananmen Square. "After that I just wanted to go out to see what kind of life musicians had outside," she says.

She also found that the opening of China to the outside world during the 1980s was slowly altering the musical tastes of the Chinese. Traditional Chinese music was gradually being eclipsed by a surge of interest in rock and pop music.

When she arrived in New York in the early 1990s, she didn't think she could continue her career as a musician but looked for any opportunity to continue performing.

"I found Chinatown had a music ensemble," she says. "So I joined them and played each weekend."

Her break, she says, came when she played a concert by a classical composer at Merkin Hall that eventually led to a commission to perform a pipa concerto.

She says one experience led to another, and soon she was living in Boston and by the late 1990s regularly performing with the Kronos Quartet, a well-regarded string quartet.

Now she regularly performs in Europe and Mexico and has recorded a number of CDs. In Boston, she has played with the Boston Symphony Orchestra.

Much of her performances now are pieces by contemporary composers who want to include the pipa in their work, she says.

Wu is confident that she can find a place for her instrument in western-style music.

Audiences respond to the pipa enthusiastically when played in concert with western instruments. "That's the way to show the pipa to the western world," she says.

She also plans to return to China to perform with a western string quartet and show Chinese audiences how the instrument can be played with western music.

The pipa is flexible, she says. It can be played with both Chinese and western music.

This is the idea that inspires her now. "I think if I stayed in China I couldn't have had such a wonderful musical career," she says.

Art to Calm the Spirit

MAKING A LIVING IS OFTEN A STRUGGLE for Chinese painters living in the U.S.

Over the years, many artists have worked in Chinese restaurants and done other odd jobs to make ends meet. A lucky few find work in design firms and in art-related fields.

"I'm lucky because I have an art gallery," says Michael Mei, a painter who opened a gallery in Chinatown in the 1990s.

To support himself now, Mei sells his landscapes and calligraphy, paints murals for Chinese restaurants, mounts and frames pictures, and runs his gallery.

He spends 50 to 60 percent of his time working in art-related jobs, but he still works as a waiter in a Chinese restaurant two days a week to support himself.

He says many Chinese artists come to the U.S. with highly developed skills. "They have very good training in China," he says. "Their basic knowledge is better than the western artists."

Qing Xiong Ma, a painter, did whatever job he could find when he first arrived here from Beijing in 1991.

He was a babysitter and a dishwasher; he worked for a while in a Chinese take-out restaurant.

The man serving a carton of fast Chinese food on a rainy night in the 1990s could have been a highly skilled painter like Ma. What sustained him through that period was a belief in his art, he says. He knew he had this talent to paint no matter how others saw him.

In time he started to exhibit his landscape paintings and soon found jobs teaching brush painting around Boston. He says piecing together a living still remains difficult, but his life has improved significantly since his early days here.

Ma continues to do traditional painting but also experiments with western materials such as acrylics.

But even when he uses acrylics, he says, he continues to use a Chinese brush because it allows him to paint more subtle shading.

The Chinese brush, he says, has a pointed end and is made of animal hair. The one he uses now is made of goat and pig hair.

And while museums and collectors have long been interested in Chinese art of an earlier era, "they don't pay much attention to contemporary work," **he says.**

Some western artists have been incorporating traditional Chinese painting techniques into their work, Ma says.

The late-painter Roy Lichtenstein used his distinctive style to paint a series of Chinese-style landscapes, while one of Ma's students has been producing abstract paintings in a style influenced by Chinese art.

The difference between Chinese and western painting is rooted in the materials as well as the theory and spirit behind the two traditions.

Chinese brush painters use special inks and paint on rice paper. Colored inks were used in Chinese paintings hundreds of years ago, but more recent Chinese art has favored a monochromatic style.

Now Chinese brush painters have again begun to experiment with color and innovative painting techniques, in part due to the influence of western painting styles and materials.

Monochromatic ink paintings, says Mei, tend to have a calming effect on viewers. Western-style paintings tend to generate more excitement through the use of color and realistic detail.

An ideal of Chinese culture is to create art that calms and soothes the spirit and senses, says Mei.

Chinese brush painters have traditionally chosen subjects — landscapes and bird and flower scenes — that have a calming effect on the spirit.

Calligraphy, or the painting of Chinese characters, often has the same effect, he says.

The style and temper of the brush stroke reflects the inner spirit of the painter. A painter puts his life experiences into his painting to create a distinct feeling, he says. The viewer will "feel your knowledge, feel your experience," he says.

Chinese painting can be loosely divided into a "fine style" in which the outline of leaves and other objects are drawn with the brush, and a "free style" in which an object is painted rather than drawn with a brush stroke.

"I use the free style...because it makes my spirit feel better," says Mei.

Chinese art also tends to be more abstract than Western painting. Western art strives for a more realistic three-dimensional effect, but Chinese art has more empty space so that viewers have more room to imagine, says Mei.

Chinese writing has traditionally used pictures to communicate ideas and feelings. The Chinese character for bright combines the visually suggestive characters for sun and moon.

The same ink, brushes, and paper are used to paint landscapes and write Chinese characters.

In Chinese language, painters say they "write" the painting rather than paint or draw it, says Ma.

Nature plays a central role in the Chinese art tradition. Chinese ideas about nature are generally rooted in Daoist and Buddhist beliefs in the value of simplicity and living in harmony with nature.

Both philosophies have as an ideal the ability to maintain a calm and balanced mind and spirit.

Unlike Western painters, Chinese painters often include a poem in their painting that provides commentary on the image, says Mei. In his painting of an old house, the accompanying characters call on the spirit of spring to endure.

Mei says he wants viewers to feel the beauty of the house and season rather than the dilapidation of the house.

If he paints a picture of a wealthy person's mansion, he'll strive to communicate a similar feeling. His goal is to neutralize the extremes of wealth and poverty so that the simple beauty of being is more important than wealth or social status.

It's an idea rooted in Daoism, a principle at the heart of Chinese culture.

CHRISTIAN I BUDDHIST

'The Spirit Was with Me'

THE STAGE AT THE BOSTON CHINESE Evangelical Church in Chinatown is crowded with young people dressed in blue jeans and white T shirts.

They raise their hands high above their heads, they hold each other's hands, they cross their arms to draw the spirit inside them.

Drums, electric guitars, and spiritual songs accompany their movements.

It's a Christmas event for youth that's part performance and part preaching.

The performance is high-spirited and contemporary but with an unmistakable religious fervor.

With its mix of skits, hymns and sermons, the night's activities are a far cry from the kind of Christmas services the church's founders would have participated in when it opened in the early 1970s.

Services in a traditional Chinese-language church tend to be formal and subdued, but tonight's event is informal and spirited.

The spirituality of this new generation of English-speaking Chinese Americans differs markedly in language and style from that of their Asian-born elders.

Rev. Thomas Lee says the Evangelical Church wants to place the universal message of Christian brotherhood in a context that speaks directly to Asian Americans.

The church, he says, must appeal to two distinct groups: the first generation Asian-born members who attend services in Chinese, and the American-born generation who attend services in English.

Lee's focus is developing programs and services for the English side of the church.

Chinese Americans may be drawn to the Christian idea of brotherhood and relationship in part because they sometimes feel like outsiders in America, says Lee.

American-born Chinese are still drawn to ethnic churches like this one because they find people there who share their experiences. "They still resonate with people who are more like themselves," he says.

Although the Chinese ministers place the Christian message in an Asian context, the message remains the same.

"The Christianity that will survive is the Christianity that has the vital relationship with God," says Rev. Lee.

The church shouldn't be viewed as a kind of Chinese school for conveying

Chinese culture or language to the next generation, says Lee. Instead, it's a place where young people can satisfy their spiritual needs in a context they understand.

"I came to church to find God," says Lee, adding that young people want to be engaged, they "don't like it when they're treated like the kids."

Many Chinese ethnic churches in the U.S. grew out of Bible study groups formed at local universities by students from Hong Kong and Taiwan, says the Rev. Tsu-Tung Chuang of the Chinese Bible Church of Greater Boston.

One study in the 1990s showed that 5 to 8 percent of first generation Chinese Americans are Christian, and more than 60 percent of the Chinese churches in the U.S. are nondenominational.

About 70 percent of Chinese Christians belong to these nondenominational churches.

Lee says today's American-born Asian Christian community is in flux and can't be easily analyzed.

It's unclear whether American-born Christians will continue to seek out Chinese churches as their "spiritual home," opt for mainline churches, or reject Christianity altogether, he says.

Several area churches are beginning to experiment with pan-Asian churches and multiracial churches.

While the idea of multiethnic and multiracial churches is appealing and in keeping with the Christian message of brotherhood, Lee says the "flavor" of a church tends to reflect the culture and sensibility of its dominant group.

Many Asian Americans may still want to continue attending an Asian-American church because it addresses concerns specific to them.

Chinese churches in the U.S. grew at a phenomenal rate in the 1990s, but some studies suggest that many second generation Asian Americans have been quietly leaving their ethnic churches to enter mainline churches or rejecting Christianity altogether.

Nancy Wong says a college friend introduced her to Christianity. She says she was moved by the emotional expressiveness of the practice.

Her spiritual transformation came about one night while she was singing in a church service.

"I felt the spirit was with me," she says. "Asians don't really express their love that much," she says, but Christianity emphasizes the importance of such expression.

She says her Buddhist mother was initially opposed to her decision to be baptized, though she also thought Christians were "good people."

Pauline Leung, a volunteer at the Intervarsity Christian Fellowship's Asian American chapter at Boston University had a similar experience.

She says her parents' spiritual life involved honoring ancestors. Many Asian-born Chinese families have small ancestral shrines in their homes.

But Leung says her parents accepted her and her sister's decision to become Christians because they believed the Christian teachings had a positive effect on them.

There are differences between her and her parents' idea of spirituality, she says. While she tends to be concerned about the next life, her parents are guided by a Confucian belief in hard work as the key to a good life in the here and now.

"What I believe is that there is more than this life," she says. "Chinese people don't talk about it (spiritual subjects and life after death) that much in the family."

Leung says some Asians may resist Christianity because it often requires them to reject their parents' beliefs.

If young people were to accept a belief contrary to that of their parents, they would be admitting that their parents were wrong.

"It's hard because that's not what their parents believe," she says. "For some it is an issue."

Addressing the spiritual needs of Asian Americans requires focusing on issues relevant to their cultural experiences. Issues that strike a chord with Caucasians may not have the same effect on Asian Americans.

For example, many Asian young people often find themselves dealing with the issue of parental authority. "I think for Asians that is a more prevalent issue," she says.

Traditional beliefs, meanwhile, continue to be a factor, particularly for the older generation.

There are Confucian beliefs and Daoist beliefs, Buddhist and ancestral beliefs.

Rev. Frank Chan, the pastor of Chinatown's Chinese Baptist Church of Greater Boston, says many new immigrants may initially be drawn to churches by the social services and ESL classes offered to them during their period of transition.

But "once people settle down, they won't come back to the church," he says

Chan says that Buddhism is becoming a powerful force in Hong Kong and Taiwan and believes its influence will eventually be felt here as well.

The growing influence of Buddhism in the local Asian community can already be seen in the founding in the 1990s of the Thousand Buddha Temple in nearby Quincy.

Traditional Buddhist beliefs still exert a strong influence on people who may be drawn to Christianity, says Chan.

He recalls how one woman's husband wouldn't allow her to attend church services because he had made a vow to the Buddha.

The husband believed that switching allegiance to another deity could jeopardize the good luck they had so far experienced in the U.S. "That still has a kind of power," he says.

Chan believes that second or third generation Chinese Americans tend to leave the ethnic churches, which differ in style and tone from the American churches.

"Chinese sing very solemnly," he says, but the "Americans go with the rhythm."

THE REV. THOMAS LEE SAYS his first encounter with a church occurred when he was a boy in Toronto.

He was in a church but he wasn't really there to worship: "There was a gym in it," says Lee, whose only exposure to religion up to that point was his parents' ancestral worship.

When Lee moved with his family to Boston, he was still playing basketball, this time in a multiracial neighborhood of Jamaica Plain.

He always felt a little outside while growing up in the city. "I was kind of the only kid who was Asian," he says.

But that feeling changed when friends introduced him to the Boston Chinese Evangelical Church.

"That was my first encounter with God," he says. "I really felt I belonged."

Lee had enjoyed math and science in high school and studied chemical engineering at Tufts University.

But he soon discovered it "wasn't something I had a fire for...I really didn't enjoy chemical engineering that much when I was in school," he says. "I thought it was a secure profession."

He says his parents repeatedly reminded him that he had "to earn a living to survive in America."

Lee worked as an engineer for a few years, but remained dissatisfied. He made a career change and took a job working with computers in the Boston

Public Schools.

He found that job more satisfying though not because he was especially drawn to computers. "I enjoyed the people part more than the technical part," he says.

Meanwhile, his interest in religion continued to grow — so much so that he decided to attend a Bible college in Chicago for a year, though at that point he still didn't feel "called."

"When I got there I was so humbled," he says. "Up to that point I thought I was very spiritual."

He was especially impressed by students whose focus on the material life was secondary to their religious work. He was especially struck by a Chinese couple who had given up medical careers to become ministers.

He knew he was being drawn deeper into a spiritual life, but he still resisted giving himself over to it completely.

"I was still holding on to the Asian American dream that my parents held so close to their heart," he says.

Lee says his father was shaped by his experiences. He lived through the difficult war years in China. He came to North America with nothing. His father had memories of working a day in the fields in China for a day's worth of food.

When his father first arrived in North America he worked first in the laundry business, then moved on to restaurants. Eventually he owned his own place in Braintree.

He worked hard to ensure that his children were educated, says Lee, he did well for himself here and "his dream was that we would do even greater."

When Lee returned to Boston he found himself struggling with the same conflict between "the Asian-American dream" and his own spiritual quest.

Which would he choose? Always there are choices. How are you going to live your life? Which way will you turn?

He decided to travel the less predictable road and take a leap into the unknown and not make his material life his primary focus. "Somehow I would be able to survive," he says.

In 1986 he began working at the church and soon was studying theology at a North Shore Seminary.

"I had never seriously considered the ministry because that's not the kind of secure career my parents envisioned," he says.

But it soon became apparent to him that he would have to let his parents know about his plans. "I was trying to honor him (his father) by being truthful," he says.

But his father didn't see it the way he did. "He basically hit the roof," says Lee.

How could his son give up the American dream for a religious life? He couldn't understand how someone could take such a cut in pay.
He kept asking himself how he could "raise a son who was so stupid," he says.

"For him it was a very keen issue that his children would be able to provide for themselves and have some cushion," he says. "He never really was a very spiritual person. The things that are concrete are what mattered to him."
But over time his parents came round to accepting who he was and the career he had chosen. His mother even became a Christian.

His decision to follow his own path became a rite of passage. "I had to prove to him (his father) that I was old enough to make my own decisions," Lee says.
Guided by the idea that "working for God, working for the church was sufficient," he accepted that he wouldn't be living the "Asian American dream" and that he and his wife and two children "wouldn't have the biggest house in the biggest suburb."

He wouldn't be letting his life be guided by the demands of money and status — by appearances rather than the real thing.

In 1996, Lee became a minister who spent most of his time working with young people in Chinatown.
Over the years he has also become an activist in the Chinatown community, attending neighborhood meetings and participating in community decision-making.
Lee says he wants the church to be a place where young people can feel "unconditionally" accepted. "We're all God's children," he says. "That's why we should be respected, loved and cared for."
He worries that many young people in the Asian community don't receive enough attention from their parents, who often work long hours and have limited time to be with them.
"Families are supposed to be a paradigm of how God cares for us," he says, but in America, he adds, the family is under stress.
The church's job is more difficult now, he says. There are more divorces,

more single-parent families, more teenage pregnancies in the Asian community and among church members. "The rates have increased tremendously," he says. "The traditional family is in trouble."

Lee says much of the trouble in American life is the result of selfishness. People are unwilling to act altruistically. They act if there's something to be gained but there's no higher goal, no ideal, he says.

People are operating on the same principle in their marriages, but a marriage should be "based on commitment and trust."

There are other stresses in the society as well. Both men and women are working and raising children.

The stress can be reduced if working parents have extended families to help with childcare. In his family, he feels lucky to have his wife's parents helping out with child rearing.

Many Americans raised in an individualistic society have only their nuclear families for support. They have no one to turn to when the pressure builds up.

Lee finds it ironic that parents are working day and night and sacrificing family stability to give their children the material comforts of life. "Our materialism is cheating us," he says.

He believes Asian Americans are yearning for something to fill a void in their lives. "Most of us fill it with the Asian American dream, with careers and success," he says.

"Chinese are spiritual people but that spirituality has always been focused around a Confucian ethic, and that Confucian ethic has been focused on the here and now," he says.

Lee says a high percentage of young people involved in religion on college campuses today are Asian.

The church in Chinatown has also been growing, he says, noting that its English service has grown so much that closed-circuit television has to be used as a temporary solution to a seating shortage.

About 1,200 people were attending the Cantonese, Mandarin, and English services on Sunday in the late 1990s.

"I would like to think it's growing because God is using us to help fill a spiritual void in people's lives," says Lee.

Lee says his spiritual life is rooted in his experiences. "For me it's a personal expression of receiving love and forgiveness from God and from Jesus."

His gratitude for this, he says, is what inspires him to share that experience with others.

Pure Land in Boston

DRESSED IN GRAY AND BLACK garments, she stands out when she walks through the streets of Chinatown.

In 1996 the Rev. Sik Kuan Yin converted a former banquet hall and restaurant to create a large Buddhist temple in the Boston suburb of Quincy.

Many people from Boston Chinatown and other Greater Boston communities worship at the temple now.

Inside the temple, 1,000 small golden Buddhas line the walls of the main hall. Outside, a large stone Kuan Yin — the Buddha of compassion — stands in the courtyard.

"In 1988, when I came to Boston for a visit I found that a lot of Chinese people wished they had a Buddhist temple here.

Even when I went to the Chinese supermarket (in Chinatown) people said, 'Oh, I will donate money to help you. I will support you. We want to have a temple here.'

When people drove me around they saw that I was a nun and said hello to me. Once when I was in the Buddhist temple in New York City someone called the temple. I by chance picked up the phone and spoke to that woman.

She was from Boston and she was very sad. She said she wanted to have a place in Boston where she could go to release her trouble and pray but there wasn't such a place here; she said she had to go to New York. I spoke to that woman for a half hour.

Always I heard the same story from people. When I traveled between New York and Hong Kong, people on the airplane often told me that they had to go to New York to visit a Buddhist temple. Why don't we have one in Boston so we don't have to go so far away?

There are a few Christians among the Chinese immigrants here, but the majority of the Chinese are Buddhists, especially the people from Vietnam, Taiwan, and Hong Kong. The people from Mainland China also practice Buddhism.

More and more of the Chinese immigrants are Buddhists. Some may not formally join the temple or call themselves Buddhists, but they have a strong Buddhist influence from their Chinese culture.

This is especially true of the new wave of immigrants who came here after China opened its doors and changed its economy. Even if they don't practice regularly, they still like to have a temple they can go to.

So I decided to open a temple here. There were already a group of

Buddhists in this area, and they helped me buy a house in the Wollaston section of Quincy.

I moved into that house and we started to practice Buddhism together. Gradually more and more people were attracted to the temple — people who used to go to the New York temple.

After we opened the temple in Wollaston we realized we would have to find another place. The first temple was located on a residential street in Wollaston. The people coming and going to the temple created a lot of traffic. It was unsafe for the children who lived on the street.

The neighbors thought we should move to a commercial area where there would be more parking. So we started to work on it.

It took us almost three years to find this new location. We received a lot of support from the local Buddhists who helped us find this place and build the temple.

The formal Pure Land worship involves a ceremony. You have to be here to watch it — to understand what it is. I can't really describe it.

It's a ceremony and a formal practice. This temple has enough room to hold a formal ceremony. Some temples are more crowded — like a residential house.

There's a difference between chanting and the formal Pure Land ceremony. The chanting is actually a reading from a Buddhist text (the Lotus Sutra).

Chanting is like reading a book. After you read it many times, its meaning seeps into your mind and consciousness. Once its meaning gets inside you it can guide you through your daily life.

In the ceremony you kowtow before the Buddha. You put yourself in a lower position. In this way you can better control your ego because once you put your head down and lower your body you cannot have that kind of ego.

This is a way to help people control their sense of self-importance and their ego.

I'm confident about the future of Buddhism in this country. I believe that Buddhist teachings are good for individuals and for the society as a whole.

Many Americans have an understanding of Buddhism and practice Buddhism now. I can only reach out to them in a limited way because I don't speak English. I cannot really go into the society.

All I can do is make available more English books for those who don't know Chinese. Americans who are interested in Buddhism can take those books and study on their own.

I know there are different Buddhist groups in this area; there are several Zen centers where Americans go to practice and study Buddhism.

There are also three or four other Asian Buddhist temples in the area, including a Chinese temple in Lexington and a Vietnamese temple in Boston.

Buddhism's teachings really help people purify their hearts and souls and bodies. When people are confronted by problems in their lives they need a place to go to purify their minds.

Once they become calm and purified they can find a solution to the problem. For this reason many people like to practice Buddhism.

Buddhist teachings are the same for all people, no matter what form of Buddhism they practice. The goal of the teachings is to purify your mind and your heart.

There are different ways to practice, and Pure Land — the form we practice here — is one of them.

This is the way I prefer to practice, but there are other monks and nuns who come to this temple who teach other ways of practicing Buddhism.

People from other schools also come here to teach their way of practice. The Zen practice emphasizes meditation, but in Pure Land we do chanting.

All Buddhists have the same goals, the same theories. So it's just a question of preference. The Buddhist teachings are all the same.

In Buddhism there are a few basic rules to guide you. The rules are meant to lead you in the right direction, to help you purify your heart and soul.

If you follow these rules you're unlikely to get into trouble; if you have a problem and keep your heart quiet and pure, you will more easily find a solution to your problem.

First, you should abstain from evil acts; second, you should always be kind to others and promote the good of society; third, you should keep your mind pure and know your own intentions.

Sometimes people do things without thinking or being aware of why they are doing them.

In the basic Buddhist practice, there are also five prohibitions.

First, it's wrong to kill any living being because killing in any form shows a lack of compassion. If you have compassion for all the sentient beings, you should not kill any of them.

Second, it is wrong to commit adultery because adultery breaks up the family and leads to much suffering in society. Adultery causes pain for yourself and other families.

Third, you should not drink alcohol because alcohol can confuse your mind and make you lose control of yourself.

Fourth, it's wrong to be greedy. Greed can lead to much trouble in society. It can lead to stealing and other wrong actions. Even the thought of desiring too

much isn't good for yourself or the society.

Fifth, it's wrong to lie or insult others. Lying and insulting others leads to more suffering.

If you follow these basic rules you will be following the Buddhist way.

As a Buddhist you should always have compassion. To live the Buddhist life you must have the capacity to tolerate and forgive others."

Who They Are, Who They Can Be

FOR YEARS THE 19TH CENTURY BRICK building next to the old Quincy School on Tyler Street was the home of the Maryknoll Sisters Center. In the 1990s the last Maryknoll nun returned to Canada to care for her ailing mother and the building reverted to the Archdiocese of Boston.

The building was renamed the Chinese Catholic Pastoral Center, and the Rev. Denis Como, a Jesuit priest who had lived in the Middle East and China, became its director.

Father Como counseled Catholics who came to the center for visits and taught elderly Chinese English.

He also allowed a Russian Center to operate out of the same building.

"I try to make people realize who they are and how they can know who they are, to be happy with who they are and then be able to give themselves to other people.

I'm dealing with new people who have come to this country. They may feel disconnected because they're not in a place that's familiar to them. So I try to make them realize what they bring and who they are and how they can contribute and how things here can contribute to who they are.

They don't have to stop growing just because they're out of their usual flower box, so to speak. I think that living in Boston can do that to them.

They're coming from a different society — a family society, a group society — and it's hard for them sometimes to access what is here because they've never had to do that in their own country.

A lot of their information, their culture, their values come from the big group they're probably immersed in. This could be Chinese culture or any new people's culture.

In American society everybody kind of picks and chooses who they are and what they want to be as an American. They're very eclectic.

For new people, it's very difficult for them to go into a place and plug into something that is different. They can do it, but they need someone to lead them

— almost like a family situation, like a father or a mother — to lead them to a new experience.

I think a lot of the language programs provide it when they take somebody to the market or to the bank and show people how to make use of very practical things.

If you get a service bill and you've already paid it, what do you do? That gives them a certain amount of self-confidence.

On a deeper level it's a little more difficult with things like culture, music, art, even American values, because there's no pressure to do that. It's not like a bill.

Some values here would be the same values you'd find in China, but they're dressed up in different colors and sizes and shapes so they may not be instantly recognizable.

In the United States there's a value for the community. I think Americans do have ways to express their interest in the community and in getting involved.

We have the reputation of being very individualistic, but there's another side to us that is not — that is very much turned on to the community.

But that may not be understood by someone coming out of a very homogeneous society like China, where everybody is from the same tribe. Pointing out those things for them makes them feel more at ease and that we're not all individuals.

Although Americans are very individualistic, they will come together for a cause. I'm not so sure that Chinese society or even Arab society, where I spent 10 years, will come together for a cause.

It's more difficult to move them out of the known into the unknown. Whereas here if somebody wanted to have a walk for hunger or a walk for this or that it wouldn't take long to get a group of Americans interested and get many people involved, if it's a good cause.

I don't think it's strictly Christian, because you get all kinds of people with different religious backgrounds joining in. America is known for its volunteerism, but volunteering is not common in many other cultures where people only ask their tribe or clan to help. I don't even think they have to ask. It's expected.

But Americans are individualistic. Maybe only half the family originally came on the boat or families were broken up once they hit the shore here, so we have to kind of create the clan through volunteerism.

I think that's shown here by the causes, whether it's the March of Dimes or whatever. There are hundreds of ways. And we're not linked by blood but we're doing it and kind of living by blood.

I think the Chinese are like the Arabs. It's blood, clan, family, whereas with Americans you sense that term being used in a different way. Let's say someone goes every night to the Pine Street Inn. The councilors and other people go there every night too. They become family to this person. That person doesn't mind calling those people their family.

But it would be terrible for people from other countries to say that this is my family. In a lot of these families they won't adopt a child because the blood is not theirs, nor would they give up their child for adoption because part of their blood is going somewhere else.

So their concept of family has a more physical basis than ours. I think ours is a bonding, a concern, a cause.

I think something similar happens on an elevator. In an American elevator nobody talks. But if the elevator gets stuck, then people get very annoyed with the situation; they get annoyed maybe with a crying baby; they get annoyed with the fact that somebody doesn't seem to mind; they get annoyed with the person who minds a lot, and blah blah blah.

And for a while there's a lot of tension but after a while when they hear a voice that says, 'Things will be okay, we're working on it,' then people will kind of look around and say, well it's not the end of the world.

We will soon move and then we hear the thump thump of the cap or whatever it is on the top.

And then there's a bond because they're all in the same situation; they're all in the elevator and there's almost a sense of, 'Oh, I see you on this elevator a lot; you know I always wanted to ask you where you got that thing you're wearing' or something like that.

And then there's this sharing back and forth so that when the elevator starts again there's that feeling of should we go back to being quiet again or should we be annoyed that the elevator is working and we'll never talk to these people again.

There's that kind of dynamic that goes on in United States life, depending on what happens in the elevator and if it does stop.

And American life stops sometimes. People feel insecure. Things that are familiar aren't working. Everybody is going to get angry at everybody else.

But as soon as you say, 'Well, it's never going to work again,' then you stop and say, 'Well, if it's not going to work again, let's sit down and have a coke, enjoy one another while we're waiting for something to get fixed.' I think the only way to solve it is to make people very aware that it's always going to be like this.

If they were born in a period when not so many people were coming into their neighborhood and they thought it was going to be like that forever — I'd say that's not true. It's just going to keep changing colors and shapes and ideas and smells of food.

Some of the things that get people really upset is they grew up in a neighborhood where they always smelled Italian food and all of a sudden they smell Korean food and they think it's the end of the world.

Oh maybe before you die it will be Brazilian food. So you help them see that it's OK that things change because you basically are the same. These things are going to affect you but not disembowel you.

I think it was a lot more difficult in other countries where you had the value of tribe all of a sudden being brought into question because somebody thought something different. I think they just throw that person out of the tribe.

In the United States you have individuals, so it shouldn't be strange that one individual has different values than the other.

Yet, even though American society loves individualism — I'm my own boss and all the rest — there is also a concept somewhere left from the tribal days that there's only one American way to do it, and it must be my way since that's the one I'm happy with. So how dare these people...

And yet when we reflect on it, we find it's not even just a different face coming up with a different value, but we have different values than our parents and grandparents, which would be unheard of in most world societies.

And if you did have a different opinion than your father, you would never voice it because it would be an insult to your parents and that's going against a supreme value that you're a chip off the old block and if you're not then there's something wrong with you.

I don't want to impose my values on someone else but I'd say the basic value that I would like to see maintained everywhere, at all times, in all generations, is that the other does have value — even if I don't understand it and can't see it — I wouldn't want to have that go.

Because if I believe that the other person also has value then I'm always open to being able to allow that person to walk into my life and hopefully that person will allow me to walk into his or her life.

You have to keep on redefining, re-positing your response to faith in different ways. Generations and times and ethnic and racial groups have to see it differently. Otherwise they're not true to who they are.

Faith is not coming out of some compartment that has no relation to a person's personal life. It has to come from the person.

Basically a person's prayer life or vision of life has to be colored by the person, so the more it is that way the more confusing it is going to be to other people who look around and find out one person's got a drum and one's got a bugle and one's got a violin and one's got nothing.

I mean the variety must be there. It can't be uniform. But the basic uniformity and vision would be that there is a God or a supreme being and that God has an impact on my life and that I matter to that God.

But how that works itself out and how it expresses itself in each person's life and in each community's life is unique. Some things that are part of the spirituality of other people aren't going to affect me at all.

My own experience, my own background and what I was locked by most while growing up was being in the Middle East and listening and seeing how the Arabs get so excited about listening to other people's stories — and I think I've picked that up.

I really find that a kind of spiritual experience — to hear another person's story. Not a whole life's story but at least part of it or how they see something and they're excited.

The most exciting thing is to meet a person who is like 89 years old and is still excited by living.

I think that's wonderful. But anybody's story about actively attempting to live more fully is really exciting. That is a real God experience!

THE BENEVOLENTS

Trouble Brewing on Tyler Street

THE NAMES OF CHINATOWN organizations are often long and complicated. People tend to shorten the English versions of names by using acronyms.

There's the CCBA and CEDC, ACDC and AACA, AARW and CPA — an endless jumble of upper case letters that makes your head spin when printed on the page of a newspaper.

From the start the name of Chinatown's most powerful organization — the Chinese Consolidated Benevolent Association — stood out.

The name contains a lot of long words that don't seem to sit well together. There's that strange word "consolidated" paired with the charitable word "benevolent."

The word "benevolent" was nested like a colorful flourish inside the name, giving the organization the flavor of an old-time charitable organization; while the word "consolidated" has a financial tone, a darker, more self-interested aspect.

The CCBA has its office in the old Quincy School building at 90 Tyler Street. In 1983, the city of Boston sold the organization the building for $1.

The building itself was famous because generations of immigrant children had been educated there. It was said to be the first public school in America to place students in different grades in separate classrooms.

The Benevolent Association needed a new location because its previous building had been destroyed several years earlier in a gas explosion in Chinatown. The organization was able to acquire the school building because it promised the city it would use the building as a community center.

The Benevolents planned to have their office in the building and lease the rest of the space to the Asian American Civic Association, Chinatown's primary social service and education center, and the Kwong Kow Chinese School, the community's Chinese language school for children.

It helped that Billy Chin was president of the CCBA at the time the organization acquired the building. Chin was one of Chinatown's most recognizable figures and at the time the owner of the China Pearl, one of city's most well-known Chinese restaurants.

He and his brother Frank were involved in city politics and made a point of supporting and befriending Boston mayors and city councilors.

For years the Benevolent Association has served as the nominal leader of the local Chinese community. It was founded about 80 years earlier as an umbrella organization for local Chinese merchants.

Although it sought to portray itself as an organization that represented the entire Chinese community, it was at heart a merchant's association and represented first and foremost the interests of the Chinese restaurant and laundry industries.

In the Chinatown immigrant community, small business owners have traditionally controlled the community's political life.

As generators of income and jobs in a community where few immigrants spoke English well enough to find work in the mainstream world, the Chinese merchant class played a critical role in the stability of the community, particularly in the first half of the last century.

Over the years, mainstream officials and organizations often turned to the Benevolent Association when it needed to communicate with the local Chinese community.

Boston's establishment — the mayors, the city councilors, the local institutions — generally knows little about what occurs inside Chinatown and tends to latch on to a few higher-profile people or organizations to gain insight into the community.

Billy and Frank Chin were adept at insinuating themselves into the power loop and pulling strings to help their faction in the community to draw benefits for the Chinese community overall.

The CCBA holds its meetings in a conference room at the back of its Tyler Street building. The meetings are held in Toisanese, the Chinese dialect spoken by the original Chinese inhabitants of Boston's Chinatown.

The organization's leaders sit at a long table at the head of the room. On the wall behind the table are framed portraits of George Washington and Dr. Sun Yet-Sen, the founder of the Republic of China.

A quotation from Sen — who visited Boston Chinatown earlier in the 20th century — is also carved into the marble base of the statue of Confucius at the front of the building.

CCBA claimed that it represented a broad swath of the Chinese community because its membership included representatives from many businesses and community organizations.

Every two years CCBA held an election to select a new president and business board members. These elections were often hotly contested by the major factions that made up Boston Chinatown.

Some said the factions developed along family lines — with the Wongs on one side and the Chins on the other.

But that didn't accurately describe the situation either because some Chins were active in the Wong faction and some Wongs were supporters of the Chin group.

Also, some Wongs in reality were Chins and some Chins were Wongs if their ancestors were paper sons — immigrants who purchased documents stating they were relatives of Chinese who were U.S. citizens.

For years the CCBA was controlled by a clique within the Chinese community led by Billy and Frank Chin.

This group's supporters generally controlled the organization's 25-member Business Council, which played a key role in the election of the organization's president every two years.

Whoever controlled the Business Council determined who would become the next president.

It was generally believed that the Chin faction controlled Chinatown politics and the CCBA. Some people referred to Billy, the most voluble of the Chin brothers, as the mayor of Chinatown.

His younger and more reserved brother, Frank, was also a visible presence in Chinatown. Frank was the owner of a gift shop on Beach Street in Chinatown and also the City of Boston's purchasing agent.

Both Billy and Frank Chin usually campaigned for mayoral candidates and generally had the ear of the mayor once elected.

They seemed to survey the field to determine who was likely to win, then throw their support behind that candidate. They had an uncanny knack for picking a winner to support in the elections.

Like any group that has power and wants to hold on to it, the Chin brothers were resented by some of their less well-connected peers.

Although the lines of battle in Chinatown weren't drawn along strictly family lines, the Wong faction had for years resented the Chin dynasty and had been struggling to topple it.

The fall for the Chins came in 1994 when Paul Wong, a former head of On Leong (The Chinese Merchants Association) was elected president of CCBA.

The Chinese Merchants Association had once been a powerful force in Chinatown but had lost standing in the Chinese community after indictments connecting it to the Chinese underworld.

The election of Paul Wong as the Benevolent Association president announced the start of a round of internal fighting in the association that would eventually spread through the entire Chinatown merchants community.

Frank Chin says tensions between the two CCBA factions grew during Wilson Lee's term as president.

He argues that Lee flouted parliamentary procedure on a number of occasions. "He does what he likes to do," he says. "He doesn't follow rules."

He says an example of this behavior was Lee's decision to call a meeting just before he left office to vote on eight new CCBA organizations. Chin and others questioned the legitimacy of at least one of the organizations.

As in the Chinatown Neighborhood Council, a small group of players try to control the outcome of elections by working behind the scenes to collect votes.

Frank Chin suggests that some people want to control the CCBA "because there's money involved," while his brother Billy argues that in general there's too much self-interest in Chinatown, especially compared to an earlier era.

Frank Chin says that past CCBA elections were competitive but respectful. The competing factions may have "banged heads" over issues and elections, "but after that we were still friends, we still talked...if I lose I walk."

He says that attitude no longer seems to be operating in today's Benevolent Association.

Wilson Lee, who has often been at odds with the Chins, claims he tries to take the same approach to his participation in community affairs. "It's good to have competition, but people should not take it personally," he says.

Lee believes Chinatown's recent factional fighting has historical causes. For many years, he says, Chinatown politics was controlled by the Chin group, which now must compete with new forces in the community.

Because the neighborhood economy is based on restaurants, people in the past feared their businesses would be affected if they rocked the boat and failed to pay allegiance to "the powers that be," says Lee.

"In the past, people were scared," he says. "They were scared of retaliation. Finally people said, 'Wait a minute!'"

Asked if Frank and Billy Chin have benefited the community over the years, he says: "I think they have, but at the same time, I think they've benefited themselves too."

The Benevolents Evict the Civic Association

NOT LONG AFTER THE BENEVOLENT Association and the Asian American Civic Association began living under the same roof at 90 Tyler Street in the mid-1980s, the two organizations began to bicker.

In the late 1980s the Civic Association began to withhold rent because it believed it was being overcharged for building maintenance costs.

The two organizations were at odds from day one. At least part of this was due to cultural and generational differences.

The AACA had many American-born Asians and non-Asians on its board and took a more mainstream approach to providing services in the community. CCBA was an old-world organization that played by old-world rules.

The key principles of that old-world behavior were Confucian: obedience was important, youth should obey and respect age.

The Benevolent Association had been ruling Chinatown for years, but the Civic Association was a younger organization with just a few years' history in the community. From the Benevolent Association's point of view, AACA should kowtow when CCBA told it to.

But the Civic Association believed CCBA had been overcharging it and it also didn't like the way the Benevolent Association handled community money.

CCBA thought it could do as it pleased – if it wanted to spend community money on a banquet it would spend the money that way.

The Civic Association, meanwhile, was pressed for money, relying on grants and government funding to support its English-language and skills-training programs, as well as the Sampan, the Asian community's only bilingual Chinese-English newspaper.

Every penny counted for the organization. Its teachers and social workers were paid minuscule wages. It was training people to function in American society but was often given little respect in Chinatown.

To members of the Civic Association board, the Benevolent Association was given control over a great deal of community property and potential resources without providing critical services to the Chinese community.

The bickering between the Benevolent Association and the Civic Association began when the Chin faction controlled the Benevolent Association, though the disputes at that time never spiraled out of control.

David Wong, a Chin ally and even-tempered owner of the Sun Sun Market, Chinatown's first Chinese supermarket, argued that the Benevolent Association wasn't always at fault.

The Civic Association was difficult to deal with, he said one winter day in the 1990s. He said he tried very hard to reason with the Civic Association but to no avail. They didn't want to compromise either, he said.

But whatever harmony that existed between the organizations changed dramatically when Paul Wong was elected CCBA's new president in 1993. One of the first actions he took after becoming president was to order the eviction of the Civic Association from the Tyler Street building.

Wong said he was evicting the organization because it hadn't paid its rent, but the Civic Association countered that it had been overcharged for maintenance costs – AACA was paying for building maintenance but the

building was poorly maintained.

AACA counter sued, saying that it had a right to stay in the building because the Benevolent Association had promised them a place in it when it acquired the building from the city for $1.

All the local media showed up in Chinatown for the announcement of the AACA suit. The TV cameras were whirring. Two Chinatown organizations fighting sounded like a good story to them.

The Civic Association argued that if it hadn't been part of the original proposal, the city would have been less likely to give the Benevolent Association the building for $1. CCBA received the building because it promised it was going to use it as a community center, AACA argued. It wasn't meant to be a benefit for the Benevolent Association alone.

As part of his effort to evict the Civic Association from the building, president Paul Wong decided to turn a broom closet into the office of the Chinese Welfare Association.

He apparently did this so he could claim that the Benevolent Association was also providing social service programs. He had the words Chinese Welfare Association painted on the closet door.

Meanwhile, the building's janitor continued to unlock the closet door to retrieve brooms and mops.

Thus began a long and bitter fight that would culminate six years later in the eviction of the Civic Association on a gray November day in 1998.

After the Benevolent Association and the Civic Association began their drawn-out court battle, the Civic Association began to look more closely at CCBA's financial affairs.

It knew, for example, that the Benevolent Association had been receiving rental income from a building it owned at 50 Herald Street.

The New England Medical Center and Tufts University — both located in Chinatown — had given the Benevolent Association that building in the 1980s as a community benefit in return for the Chinatown community's support of a Tufts University building project.

When the medical institutions needed to expand their facilities in Chinatown, they always offered a carrot to the Chinese community. Land was scarce and some groups in the community wanted it to be used for new affordable housing.

The building was the carrot and the Benevolent Association and others involved in the bargaining were eager to bite.

But CCBA was given the building on behalf of the Chinese community with the stipulation that it would be used to create new affordable housing.

For years, the Benevolent Association had been receiving rental income from the Chinese supermarket that leased the property from them, but CCBA clearly wasn't using that income to create new housing.

The Civic Association eventually figured this out and brought the matter to the attention of the state attorney general's office.

By the time Reggie Wong succeeded Paul Wong as president of CCBA in 1994, none of the rental money from the so-called Herald St. building had been spent for housing. How the money had been used was an issue of special interest to the Civic Association, which was still threatened with eviction by CCBA.

Reggie Wong, the owner of a pub on the edge of Chinatown and a member of the Chinatown Neighborhood Council, was a member of the Wong faction, but the Benevolent Association's new auditor, real estate developer Paul Chan, was an ally and close friend of the Chin brothers.

Although Reggie Wong was an ally of outgoing president Paul Wong, he didn't project the kind of animosity that was a hallmark of his predecessor's reign in Chinatown. The brother of a well-known Chinatown activist, Reggie had grown up in Chinatown and was well-liked in the community.

As soon as Chan became auditor he reviewed the Benevolent Association's books and soon discovered that the association had been using rental income and interest generated from the Herald Street building to cover its own expenses. Some of the money had been spent on banquets, some on legal fees.

The CCBA board had earlier voted to allow the use of interest from the fund to cover a shortfall in the organization's accounts, but it hadn't brought the issue before the community for approval.

In an apparent effort to embarrass Paul Wong, Chan surprisingly made a public issue of the misspent money. He contacted reporters and revealed his findings. Though the issue was written up in the Chinese newspapers, there was barely a whimper of indignation from members of the Chinese community.

The community didn't even complain when CCBA refused to provide the Asian Community Development Corporation with much needed financing to begin building its Oak Terrace affordable housing project in Chinatown.

"Obviously, the diversion has gone much beyond current interest and clearly without Council approval," wrote CCBA auditor Chan in 1994.

In the same statement, Chan noted: "There has been talks within the community, even among those who represented CCBA in the negotiation with

Tufts and NEMC, that CCBA ought to pay back the funds 'borrowed' from that account. There also has been talk of bringing CCBA to court on this if CCBA fails to do so."

Even after Chan revealed that the money had been misused, it continued to be spent at an even faster clip — doubling to a whopping $229,051 in 1995 — during Reggie Wong's term as president and Chan's term as auditor.

Chan said that while the 70-member CCBA Council apparently believes it can spend the money with impunity, no other community organizations or members had been surveyed to determine their views on the issue.

Chan said it was unclear if the CCBA Council speaks for the larger community on this issue. "It's up to the community and the Attorney General's office to decide whether they should pay back [the money]," Chan said.

After Chan's disclosure was made public, Reggie Wong vowed not to spend any more of the building's rental money on the organization's expenses and instead said he would use the money to acquire Tai Tung Village, one of the community's largest housing complexes.

The Benevolent Association had an option to purchase the building before its government-subsidized mortgage expired. The organization said it was purchasing Tai Tung Village to preserve the housing development's long-term affordability after the federal mortgage was set to expire in 2014.

A group of the building's residents sought to have CCBA buy the building because they wanted the Chinese community to maintain long-term control of it.

While the argument was that CCBA's purchase would keep the building affordable, the purchase seemed motivated largely by the self-interest of the people who lived in the building — since there appeared to be no guarantee or restriction in the deed that the affordability of the complex would be maintained after 2014.

Although using the rental money to buy an existing housing complex was contrary to the community's original intention to use the money to create "new" housing, people in the community seemed to go along with the purchase because the money was at least being used for housing.

But the Benevolent Association's poor record overseeing community resources didn't seem to affect its effort to evict the Civic Association from its Tyler Street building either.

When the Civic Association went to the Boston City Council to ask for support of a resolution supporting its right to remain in the building, City Council President James Kelly, acting on behalf of supporters in the Benevolent Association, blocked the measure.

In 1998, a superior court judge ruled in favor of the Benevolent Association, saying that the Civic Association hadn't the right to remain at 90 Tyler Street because it wasn't given that right in the original deed of the building.

CCBA's current President Wilson Lee, meanwhile, claims he will not put AACA in the street and will continue to negotiate a resolution. Discussions continue for months but negotiations fail to resolve the matter and the feud enters a new — more dangerous phase.

When Wilson Lee's term as president expires, Robert Leung, another member of the Wong faction, is elected CCBA's new president.

Leung owns a printing shop on Hudson Street and a suburban restaurant. He is also the distributor of an imported beer from mainland China, which he advertises around Chinatown.

Leung vows to carry out the eviction of the Civic Association once and for all.

Staff at the Civic Association, meanwhile, express concern about conditions in the building.

There's hardly any heat in the winter. Fuses are constantly blown, the rest rooms are never clean. No one seems to care about the condition of the building.

The Civic Association asks the city to mediate the conflict and it appears a solution will be found. Mayor Thomas Menino says he doesn't want the Civic Association to be evicted from the building.

To work out a compromise, the Civic Association agrees to pay $6,000 per month in rent, compared with the $3,500 it has been paying.

But at the last moment the agreement collapses because the Benevolent Association sends the Civic Association a license to operate rather than the agreed-upon lease.

The Civic Association's lawyers request a lease because they believe an operating license won't provide the agency with enough protection in the future.

The Benevolent Association refuses to provide a lease and says it will serve the eviction if AACA does not sign the operating license.

The Civic Association refuses and the Benevolent Association's lawyer informs the agency that the sheriff will be arriving to confiscate its property if it isn't out of the building by Nov. 11, 1999.

In a community drama that goes largely unnoticed by the local media, the Civic Association's teachers and counselors work late into the night on Nov. 10 to pack the agency's computers, books, and files.

The equipment is transported by truck to a temporary site at the edge of Chinatown where the organization will operate until a permanent site can be found.

On the day the Civic Association is packing its belongings and preparing to leave, Wilson Lee saunters into the building and asks for the key.

Former president Paul Wong also drops by to witness the spectacle. Current president Robert Leung is nowhere to be seen.

Mayor Menino did little to stop the eviction. The mayor's Chinatown liaison Sherry Dong claimed his hands were tied because the court had ruled on the case already.

The mayor had done what he could, she said. He had told the Benevolent Association that he wanted the Civic Association to remain in the building.

He had asked the Boston Redevelopment Authority to mediate the dispute, she says. He had done what he could do to stop the eviction.

"This was clearly a private dispute from the beginning," said Dong, who seemed to ignore the fact that the property in question was given to the Benevolent Association for $1 in the belief that it would be used as a community center.

SHOWDOWN OVER HOUSING

Competing Visions for Chinatown Housing

IN THE LATE 1980s, two community organizations initiate a fierce competition to develop a parcel of city-owned land in Chinatown.

The Asian Community Development Corporation (ACDC) and the Chinese Economic Development Council (CEDC) both want to build a new affordable housing development on land owned by the city on Washington Street.

The two groups represent the competing forces that often come into play in the course of Chinatown affairs.

On one side is CEDC, an older, more conservative organization; on the other, the upstart ACDC, a community development organization recently founded by progressives in the community.

CEDC has been dominated by co-founder George Pan, a Taiwanese-born businessman who was jailed for 30 days after being convicted of defrauding the U.S. government of about $105,000. The conviction came as the result of contracts between Pan's Randolph firm, Systems Architects Inc., and the U.S. government.

In the summer of 1988, competition between the two organizations is heating up. Stephen Coyle, the director of the Boston Redevelopment Authority, regularly visits Chinatown to promote the project and to gather information about both groups. The Redevelopment Authority will designate one of the two groups as developer of the project.

It's a typical Chinatown competition, with the two sides literally at war with each other and people pressured to side with one group or the other.

CEDC has the reputation of taking a more authoritarian approach to its work in the community. There are also rumors that people use the nonprofit community development organization to advance their own interests.

CEDC is burdened by a slightly tainted reputation in some quarters, but it's difficult to say whether it's deserved or not.

ACDC is largely the creation of American-born professionals in the Chinatown community. Many members have long been active in Chinatown and are dedicated to making the neighborhood more livable for its largely immigrant population.

ACDC sees itself as a more trustworthy, altruistic alternative to CEDC and believes it's rivals may be susceptible to using the organization for their own ends.

A leader of ACDC is architect Tunney Lee, chairman of the Department of Urban Studies and Planning at MIT, who grew up in Chinatown and worked on development issues for the city of Boston.

Lee at one time also worked for Buckminster Fuller and the architect I.M. Pei.

As in many Chinatown organizations, CEDC and ACDC's members are drawn largely from the suburban Chinese community. In Chinatown, most community leaders don't live in the neighborhood.

In fact, when the Chinatown Neighborhood Council holds elections, Chinese from across New England are allowed to vote and run in the election.

This may be a questionable practice for non-Chinese living in the neighborhood, but Chinese argue that Chinatown is the cultural center of the region's Chinese population — a kind of city within a city.

In the summer of 1988, the Boston Herald runs a story about Pan's past problems with the authorities.

In Chinatown there is often an unspoken pressure not to bring issues like this into the open. It's all right for people to gossip about them but putting them in a newspaper is a different story.

Pan is personable and someone who clearly enjoys being the center of attention.

In an interview in a restaurant on Beach Street, he immediately says he wasn't really in prison — at least not the kind of facility most people envision when they hear the word "prison."

In 1984, Pan was charged with over billing the government and using the money for personal expenses. He was convicted of defrauding the U.S. of about $105,000.

Pan says the government is still seeking more than $1 million in fines and restitution in a civil suit, but he says he has also sued the government and is seeking millions of dollars in five breach-of-contract suits. "I feel a little bad — sad in a sense," he says of his conflict with the government.

Pan says this was the first time he was speaking publicly about the incident. "I would never do anything to hurt anybody."

"There's no question whatsoever I was innocent," he says. "I have a clear conscience. That's why I have faith to walk into Chinatown."

Pan says the conviction was the result of an accounting problem. "I do not get involved in the accounting aspects," he says. "But I was held responsible for all the accounting issues."

He says the government came after him in retaliation for a $50 million breach-of-contract suit he filed against it. "I know a lot of minority businessmen being prosecuted for the wrong reasons," he says.

As the competition between CEDC and ACDC heats up in Chinatown, an anonymous informer starts to spread information about Pan's troubles with the government.

Someone has been passing on his court records to CEDC associates. "I don't want to accuse anybody," Pan says. "I think this should not be an issue."

Several people in Chinatown suggest that someone associated with the Benevolent Association is taking revenge on Pan for his role in the association's decision not to hire Frank Chin, Paul Chan, and Yu Sing Jung as consultants for CCBA's Waterford Place project.

Instead, the Benevolents appointed a seven-man committee and hired a consultant. Pan says the $20,000 paid to a consultant was less than the cost of the three-man team.

Consultant's fees are one way for people positioned in the right Chinatown organizations to benefit financially from non-profit projects, according to some people in the community.

Pan, however, doesn't think the Waterford Place issue is the reason for the anonymous person's efforts to discredit him.

Community activist Marilyn Lee Tom says efforts to bring up Pan's past aren't really new. She says she received such information packets on Pan when she served as the city's liaison to the Chinese community.

She says the person distributing information on Pan "has great knowledge of George's activity and CEDC's."

"I know that whoever's doing it is very sophisticated," she says. "It's very detailed."

"I think there is someone out there trying to dilute George's power in the community," says Lee-Tom, a member of the Chinatown Housing and Land Development Task Force, which supports ACDC's bid to build the new housing development.

Lee-Tom says the merits of the housing proposals should be the deciding factor in selecting a developer. "I think we don't have to take the low road," she says. "The project has to be judged on its merits."

Pan's past "is a factor, but I don't know if it's the most important factor" in the BRA's decision, she says.

"It's not an issue with me," says ACDC director Neil Chin. "We just want to be judged on our merit...We have a better plan."

"It's up to the BRA to decide if it's an issue or not," says ACDC staff member Tarry Hum. "We want the community's vote and the BRA's vote based on the merits of the proposal."

Ron Fong, who is overseeing the project for the BRA, says the BRA staff is aware of Pan's background.

"And it has been a concern," he says. "I don't know how important it's going to be to our board....As long as it's a concern of the community we'll be concerned with it."

But the revelations eventually start to take their toll on Pan. If Pan stays in his position there's a good chance CEDC won't be chosen.

Tempers continue to rise and Pan finally resigns as chairman of the CEDC board, though after he resigns he is more willing to strike back at his anonymous detractors.

He says he was already planning to resign but decided to do it now if it could help CEDC become the developer of the project.

"I don't want my family to suffer from all these attack articles," he says. "I don't want CEDC to be destroyed by the negative campaign of the new forces in Chinatown."

Pan says ACDC waged a negative campaign against him, adding that he was told by three people that a member of ACDC was responsible for circulating information about his legal problems.

"I can tell you right now there is absolutely no truth to that," says ACDC's Tarry Hum. "On the record, off the record, there is no truth to that."

Hum says Pan has apparently made enemies in the community who emerge when the opportunity arises. This won't be the first time his court records have been circulated. "In fact, it's happened before and ACDC had nothing to do with it," she says.

Although ACDC wanted to keep the debate focused on the merits of the proposals, the background of board members is a legitimate issue in choosing a developer, says Tunney Lee.

One former CEDC board member paints an uncomplimentary picture of Pan's style. "George ran the meetings like a dictator," he says, adding that board members came and went without attention paid to the bylaws.

One source says Pan would make most decisions without much discussion and dismiss "people who may have challenged him."

Pan says all of these charges are untrue. He says some of the resentment against him stems from his involvement in two development projects – the Kingston-Bedford project (eventually built as One Lincoln Street) and 125 Summer St.

A year earlier, a number of former CEDC board members requested that the Office of Attorney General investigate alleged bylaw infractions by CEDC.

Pan, however, says the bylaws were followed and that he couldn't remove people from the board so easily. "Nobody in CEDC has that much power," he says. "To dismiss somebody like a mosquito."

"If you think George Pan is a person who can determine the destiny of Chinatown you're wrong," he says.

"I don't want to give you the impression that organizations don't have

politics," he says. "I'm trying not to deny that in Chinatown a lot of things happen that involve the overall political climate of Chinatown."

He says some of the developments occurring on the perimeter of Chinatown have at times created controversy because "people wanted to take a piece of the pie."

These projects include the One Lincoln Street project — whose investors include Paul Chan and Frank and Billy Chin as part of a minority developer affirmative action program — and the 125 Summer St. project.

Pan says getting involved in community affairs always has the potential to create difficulties for participants. "I get involved," he says. "I definitely make enemies…If ACDC is successful five years down the road they're going to have the same problem."

"I don't like the trend that's taking place in Chinatown," he says. "Instead of trying to work out our problems, we're trying to declare war."

Bing Wong, the Taiwanese-born biotech entrepreneur who replaces Pan as CEDC chairman, comes to Pan's defense. "It is a tough decision for him to make," says Wong. "I admire his courage to face such a challenge. In the past he has made numerous contributions to Chinatown."

"He is unfairly targeted this time," he says. "His cases are not completely settled yet. Attacking him before the final decision is not proper. People are innocent before they're found guilty. Nobody understands the facts. I don't understand the facts myself."

Pan says that during his tenure as chairman he saved the organization from the brink of bankruptcy, developed the China Trade Center (which the organization eventually loses), and created housing at Oxford Place and 31 Beach St. He says he has never benefited financially from his involvement in CEDC.

Pan says he sold CEDC the 31 Beach St. building — which now includes housing and office space — without making a profit. "I could have made at a least a few million dollars alone on the building and I refused to do it," he says.

Coyle, meanwhile, finally makes a decision — and it's a surprise to almost everyone.

If it were another neighborhood he may have simply selected one of the groups to build the project, but Chinatown is different.

The fighting between the two groups has become so bitter that Coyle has to play Solomon and divide the land into two parcels so that each group can develop part of it.

In the 1990s ACDC develops the Oak Terrace housing complex on the site and CEDC develops Mei Wah Village, a small elderly housing project.

Eventually a new city middle school — the Quincy Upper School — is built on the rest of the original site.

THE STRUGGLE FOR LAND

Vote 'No' to a Garage on Parcel C

FOR MANY YEARS THERE WAS A COLD WAR in Chinatown over the use of available land.

On one side was the Chinatown community, on the other side the New England Medical Center and Tufts University Medical School. The two groups share the residential section of Chinatown.

In the 1980s and '90s, both the hospital and medical school had plans to expand their facilities in the neighborhood. To do this, the institutions needed to assemble the required parcels of land.

But Chinatown also wanted to expand community housing and services and have access to some of those same parcels. The flow of Asian immigrants to Boston continued to grow during the 1980s and '90s, but there wasn't enough housing for them in Chinatown.

The community's long-standing battles with the institutions reached a climax in the early 1990s when the two forces faced off over a hospital plan to build a garage on a piece of city-owned land known as Parcel C on Oak Street.

In the 1980s, hospital, city, and Chinatown leaders divided up the available land and set aside some parcels for institutional use and some for the Chinese community.

Parcel C was reserved for a future Chinatown community center and a nearby parcel was set aside for Chinatown housing (the future site of Oak Terrace).

In the 1990s, an adjacent parcel along Washington Street would become the site of new New England Medical Center buildings.

But those plans are disrupted when the recession strikes and the real estate market collapses in the early 1990s. The Boston Redevelopment Authority's plans for the community collapsed along with it, including construction of a Chinatown community center.

Further complicating the situation is the BRA director's decision to leave Boston for a more high-profile job in Washington D.C. Stephen Coyle was often in Chinatown to help push along projects, attending meetings and mingling with the neighborhood's decision makers.

With Coyle's help, Mayor Raymond Flynn kept his hand on the pulse of the neighborhood.

But the Menino administration that followed was more aloof and generally less effective on a grass-roots level. Menino visited the neighborhood often on public relations missions but he seemed to work with only a few well-chosen Chinatown allies.

His City Hall workers were often more aloof and less likely to make adjustments to satisfy the various constituencies in the neighborhood.

In its dealings with the Chinese community, the medical institutions tended to use the age-old strategy of paying off the opposition.

In the 1990s, the institutions agreed to offer the Chinatown community a series of benefits in return for community approval of their projects.

When financing dries up for the proposed community center, the New England Medical Center proposes a plan that it says would benefit both the hospital and the neighborhood.

The hospital will build a garage on the community center land and in return provide Chinatown with a 10,000 square foot community center on the same site or give the community $1.97 million to develop such a center elsewhere.

The progressives in the community oppose the plan and eventually form the Coalition to Protect Parcel C for Chinatown.

But in the spring of 1993, the Chinatown Neighborhood Council approves the plan by a 12 to 2 margin, despite opposition by the progressives. The BRA also approves the institution's plan.

To fight back, the Parcel C Coalition organizes a community referendum to give residents and others a chance to vote on the issue. The referendum is held in Chinatown in September, 1993, and the voters reject the garage by a resounding 1,692 to 42 margin.

A year later the city and the hospital pull the plug on the project after the Parcel C Coalition develops a plan to demonstrate at City Hall.

Rather than give the progressives in the community the opportunity to oversee development of new plans for the site, Mayor Menino puts the project in the hands of the Chinese Consolidated Benevolent Association.

The mayor ends up seeking guidance from a small group of well-known Chinatown business and organization leaders. Paul Chan, a real estate developer and CCBA auditor; Bill Moy, co-moderator of the Neighborhood Council and the Benevolent Association's English secretary; Reggie Wong, the Benevolent Association president; and Frank Chin, the city's purchasing agent and an advisor to the mayor on Chinatown issues, all attend a City Hall meeting in which details of the Parcel C issue are worked out.

Members of the Parcel C Coalition, which fought the garage, aren't invited to these meeting.

The city selects the Benevolent Association to oversee development of Parcel C even though it has an uneven record handling community resources in the past.

While it had successfully developed two small community housing projects in Chinatown, it had squandered almost a million dollars in revenue from a building at 50 Herald St. that was supposed to be used for new community housing.

The Benevolent Association was also embroiled in a dispute with the Asian American Civic Association — a major provider of social services in the neighborhood.

Many in the community questioned why the mayor should be giving this organization another community resource to oversee?

But Lydia Lowe, a spokesperson for the Parcel C Coalition, surprisingly argues that CCBA shouldn't be judged by its past record, noting that the organization did have experience developing housing, and the mayor was proposing housing for the site.

In the past the Benevolent Association and the progressives in the community were seldom allies, but at the height of the Parcel C battle, the Benevolent Association under president Paul Wong had joined the Parcel C Coalition, apparently to strike back at the Chin brothers and Paul Chan, who opposed the Coalition plan.

"We're pleased that the mayor decided to honor the City's commitment to Chinatown," says Lowe in a press release. "But he needs to stop dealing with only a few hand-picked representatives and closing off access for the broader community."

Although the New England Medical Center lost the garage fight, the medical institutions generally got what they wanted from Chinatown during the 1990s — i.e. the go-ahead to significantly expand their facilities in the neighborhood.

In November 1994, the Neighborhood Council approved a Tufts University Master Plan that called for the development of new medical school facilities in the neighborhood.

Parcels of land were designated for development by Tufts, while the university provided the community with significant benefits, including $2.2 million for a new South Cove YMCA.

The university also offered land at 193 Harrison Avenue and a building at 203 Harrison as part of its benefits package.

For years, the YMCA project was heavily lobbied by its director, Richard Chin, who was also a member of the Neighborhood Council.

Tufts eventually builds new facilities on the parking lot along Harrison Avenue and on Tyler Street.

Meanwhile, in a win for the community, a section of a recently closed private high school is converted to a new YMCA, with Tufts paying most of the bill.

ROUNDING UP THE VOTES

Who Controls the Neighborhood Council?

WHEN THE CHINATOWN NEIGHBORHOOD Council holds its annual election in 1996, the big winner is a slate supported by Frank and Billy Chin. All four candidates on the Chin brothers' slate are victorious in the election.

Tapping their connections to local businesses, the Chins help their slate win and bring down the slate supported by Wilson Lee, the recent president of the Chinese Consolidated Benevolent Association (CCBA) whose CCBA faction has been feuding with the Chins' group.

Billy Chin says he decided to campaign for a slate in the Neighborhood Council election after "some people" in the community told him that Wilson Lee was running on a slate called the "Dream Team."

"Why should I let them win for sure?" says Chin.

Chin says he wanted to let them know the "dream team" is not necessarily a dream team. "I want them to know that the Dream Team does not control Chinatown," he says. "Wilson Lee is not the so-called leader of Chinatown."

To beat the competition, the Chins do what they always do: they persuade businesses to send their workers to the polls to vote. "I went door-to-door in Chinatown, small stores and big stores," says Billy Chin.

He also went to three garment factories. If people didn't respect him, he says, they wouldn't be willing to follow his direction and vote for the candidates he supports.

How could he and his brother influence elections if they didn't have the respect of people in the community? he says.

"We do everything legitimate by supporting the candidate," says Frank Chin, the city's purchasing agent. "That is the American way...if we don't come out and take the leadership nobody really gives a hooey."

A key to the Chin brothers' power in Chinatown has been the connections they have developed over the years at Boston City Hall. The Chins have become especially skillful at placing allies in key City Hall positions.

Chin ally Nancy Lo was a mayoral advisor and later chairperson of the city's Licensing Board. Jason Chung, another Chin ally, served as the city's Chinatown liaison and also held a position in the city's licensing office.

Licensing is especially important to the Chinese restaurant industry because it determines who receives a liquor license and who can extend operating hours.

Although people sometimes refer to him as the mayor of Chinatown, Billy Chin says he doesn't want to control Chinatown; he just wants to speak his mind. "Because we know they do something wrong, we point it out," he says.

The Chin brothers' strategy has traditionally been used in community politics to get out the vote, but critics of the Neighborhood Council election argue that many voters in the recent election didn't know the views of the candidates for whom they were voting.

They were simply voting for candidates out of loyalty to influential people like the Chins.

Beverly Wing, coordinator of the Chinatown Coalition, says there are several ways to look at the Neighborhood Council election. "Part of me says this is how the political machinery works," she says.

In a democratic society, candidates round up as many supporters as they can to win elections, she says.

But she also believes the political process in Chinatown could be improved if the Chinese press took more time to explain each candidate's views on specific issues. "Some people don't mind being herded" to the polls to vote for a candidate supported by an acquaintance, but some people take a more thoughtful approach and want to know more about a candidate's views.

If voters know a candidate's views, it's easier for them to hold them accountable for their council votes and actions, she says. There needs to be a "higher level of accountability" from Chinatown community leaders than there is currently.

"I think the problem is machine politics has dominated Chinatown for a number of decades," says Lydia Lowe of the Chinese Progressive Association. "I think what the community really needs is a chance for real democratic participation."

"Groups of people tend to be herded into the polls by a relatively small group of community leaders and voting is done more often based on loyalty and exchanges than on informed decision-making," she says.

Similar practices can be seen in other city neighborhoods, but that doesn't make it right, she says. "Is that what we aspire to?

Lowe argues that ordinary Chinatown residents have little influence over a council dominated by business interests.

People are not being encouraged to consider broader community issues when voting in community elections, she says.

This is especially important in a neighborhood like Chinatown where "many of the people have never voted for anything. People need to learn about the process," she says.

"I think that Frank and Billy (Chin) have been key leaders in the community for a long time," she says. "I think they have a particular approach, which I see as an old-style approach to politics."

It's also an approach that "they're trying to pass on to another generation," she says.

"If people go out to vote, then they should be aware of who they vote for," says Neighborhood Council member Bill Moy, who also argues that the Chin activities are legal and that similar tactics are used in elections everywhere.

"Nobody twists anyone's arm to vote," says Moy, a council leaders and Chin ally. "Nobody forced them to go out."

The Chin brothers, he says, are simply adept at getting out the vote.

Billy Chin says the tactics he and his brother use are common strategies in most elections in the city and elsewhere.

He says 80 percent of voters know little about the candidates they're voting for and are often influenced in their choices by people they respect.

Critics of Chinatown elections say some council members have an ulterior motive for wanting to be elected.

Some members see serving as a way to protect their own interests. For example, someone who has a restaurant may want to have influence over who receives a liquor license. Another member may want to make sure his organization receives benefits from new developments planned for the area.

Kathy Chan, who was elected to the Council in 1996, is associated with the Jumbo Seafood Restaurant, which earlier went before the Council to seek support for extending its hours from 2 to 4 a.m.

In the election, she ran on the same slate as Jason Chung, who works in the city's licensing office and is a protégé of Frank Chin.

There have also been obvious conflicts of interests associated with the Council. In the 1990s, the council received some $50,000 a year from the New England Medical Center, which often had business before the board regarding its building projects in the neighborhood.

The Neighborhood Council funding, which was eventually discontinued, was used to cover Council expenses and to pay Davis Woo some $36,000 a year to serve as executive director (at first he was paid only $25,000).

"I think it's in the interest of the community as a whole to have stronger stands on issues such as conflict of interest," says Lowe.

Lowe cited a number of past instances of conflict of interest on the council, including Jason Chung serving as the council's co-moderator while working as the mayor's Chinatown liaison; or Bill Moy serving as co-moderator while

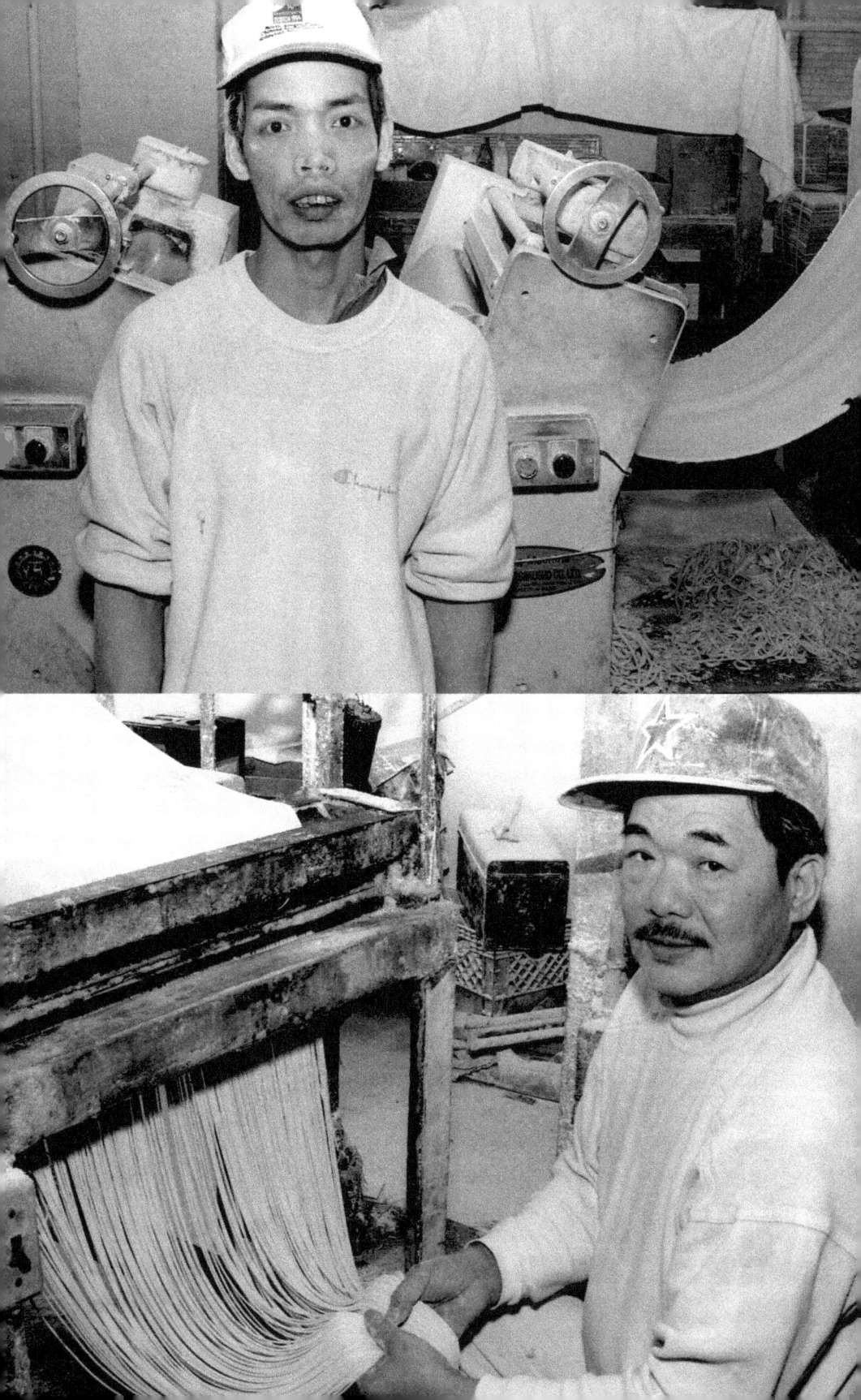

employed as the Central Artery Project's Chinatown liaison.

Both members were eventually pressured to resign as co-moderators because of the conflict. Such dual roles can be viewed as conflicts because the council often addresses issues related to city government and the Central Artery project.

"It just makes it look kind of ludicrous," says Lowe.

On the Front Line of Change in Chinatown

LYDIA LOWE SITS IN THE CROWDED OFFICE of the Chinese Progressive Association where she has worked for almost 20 years.

The office is in a building at the very center of Chinatown owned by the Union of Needletrades, Industrial and Textile Employees AFL-CIO.

She has played an important role in most of the major progressive causes in Chinatown over the last two decades.

"I was born in New York and grew up in California," she says. "I didn't come to Boston until 1981 when I was already about 20.

Both of my parents came from China when they were teenagers, during World War II. I grew up mainly with my mother.

And although I was in California, in the Los Angeles area, which people think of as having a lot of Asians, I was in the suburbs, first in Riverside, then in Venice Beach, then in Pasadena.

And there were not a lot of Asians around at that time, there were not many Chinese in particular, there were more Japanese Americans.

When I was a teenager I started to become involved in student organizing as a high school student. It was sort of the tail end of the Vietnam War. It was some antiwar stuff and some student rights issues and anti-racist issues.

The Pasadena School District started busing for desegregation shortly after Boston and there was a school board that was trying to get rid of desegregation.

I was part of a group of students that organized against the school board. We did some organizing against standardized tests.

I think through the experience of becoming active in high school and becoming really interested in politics and how society runs I became interested in finding out more about the Asian American community. Up till then I had just read about it.

I had some friends who were in the Black Panthers and then somebody gave me a book. It was called Roots: An Asian American Journal. It was like the first Asian-American studies anthology to be published.

In the book there was something about EWaiQu, an Asian-American revolutionary organization that was started in San Francisco and New York.

When I saw that, I was really interested. I thought, "Oh, this is just like the Black Panthers, but it's for Asians. I'll have to go find them."

So I moved to San Francisco where my father lived. I was looking for a stronger Asian American movement. There was a strong one in LA but I wasn't connected to it. I was in the suburbs, and it was also more Japanese American.

I think most of my childhood I didn't really think about [my background] that much and it wasn't until I got to be a teenager and went to college that it really hit me that I did have this question about my identity.

The good thing about the way my mother raised us was that she always taught us to be proud of ourselves as individuals.

I think I grew up with a lot of confidence in my abilities in a certain way, but not with any feeling of identifying with other Asian Americans around us.

I think in a way I have kind of internalized a lot of racism. I had stereotypes of what I thought Asians were — you know, which didn't include me.

So that's why when I went to San Francisco and went to San Francisco State and took Asian American Studies, it was really eye-opening because that was the first time I met a lot of other Asian Americans who were born in this country like myself and had a lot of similar experiences to me.

They were very diverse and weren't like the stereotype I had of what I thought other Asians were like. I realized that we were all in the same situation and that a lot of things I had been feeling were related to being Asian American and growing up as a minority.

I think that was how I became involved in community work because I hadn't come from Chinatown — either here or there.

All these memories came back about always being the one who was really different. I think it's just the identity thing.

You realize it's affected your whole outlook on yourself. You realize that things that you just thought were personal — like not having confidence or whatever — were related to racism and society.

Like those common experiences — like going somewhere and everybody's like, "Oh, you speak English so well."

And sometimes we would talk about more subtle situations where there's nothing explicit but you just feel that something's going on. It was like a flash to me — like, "Oh, they all experience it. So it wasn't just me."

I think my mother couldn't really understand that. In some ways, she's very Americanized because she's been here since she was a teenager. But in other ways she really identifies with being Chinese; she has that background.

So when I told her as I got older, when I talked to her about this, she was just appalled. She was like, "What do you mean, what do you mean you felt ashamed?"

She said, "I've always been proud of being Chinese; you know Chinese have the oldest civilization in the world; I've always been proud of being Chinese."

And I'm like, "Well, that's great for you," and she's, like, "You know I always told you you should be proud of being Chinese."

And I was like, "Well, it's different because I just don't feel that connected to China, I know you always told us that but somehow it wasn't enough."

And sometimes it was hard for me to distinguish whether it was being Chinese or just some other differences. When you're little you just want to fit in, so everything matters.

We never had peanut butter and jelly. It was like we always thought it was the greatest thing to have peanut butter and jelly sandwiches like everybody else. Now we laugh about it.

Sometimes our neighbors would eat cereal for dinner and we thought it was the greatest thing. And then we never ate potatoes. That's why I still love potatoes.

My father thinks it's funny because in fact our neighbors were really having a hard time because they had like eight kids and that was why they ate potatoes all the time. But we just thought they just liked to eat potatoes.

So some of it is just little stuff like that but I think that taking Asian American studies — besides bringing me in contact with other Asian Americans that I could identify with for the first time — was also really enlightening.

Learning about Asian American history and learning that there has been that history of inequality from the beginning and how that's worked really made me think about it.

It puts in a broader social and historical context why we feel this way on a personal, psychological level.

I think it was through that process of analyzing this that I really became interested in learning about the Asian community. I just started to see that my life was connected to the Chinese community.

Before I had never seen that. I just thought, "I'm myself. Don't stereotype me. I'm not like other Chinese Americans."

Like when I was little I didn't want anyone to think I spoke with an accent. I resisted learning Chinese because I didn't want to be different. I knew there were some other Chinese kids that spoke with an accent and I didn't want to be like them, which is all kind of normal stuff when you're little.

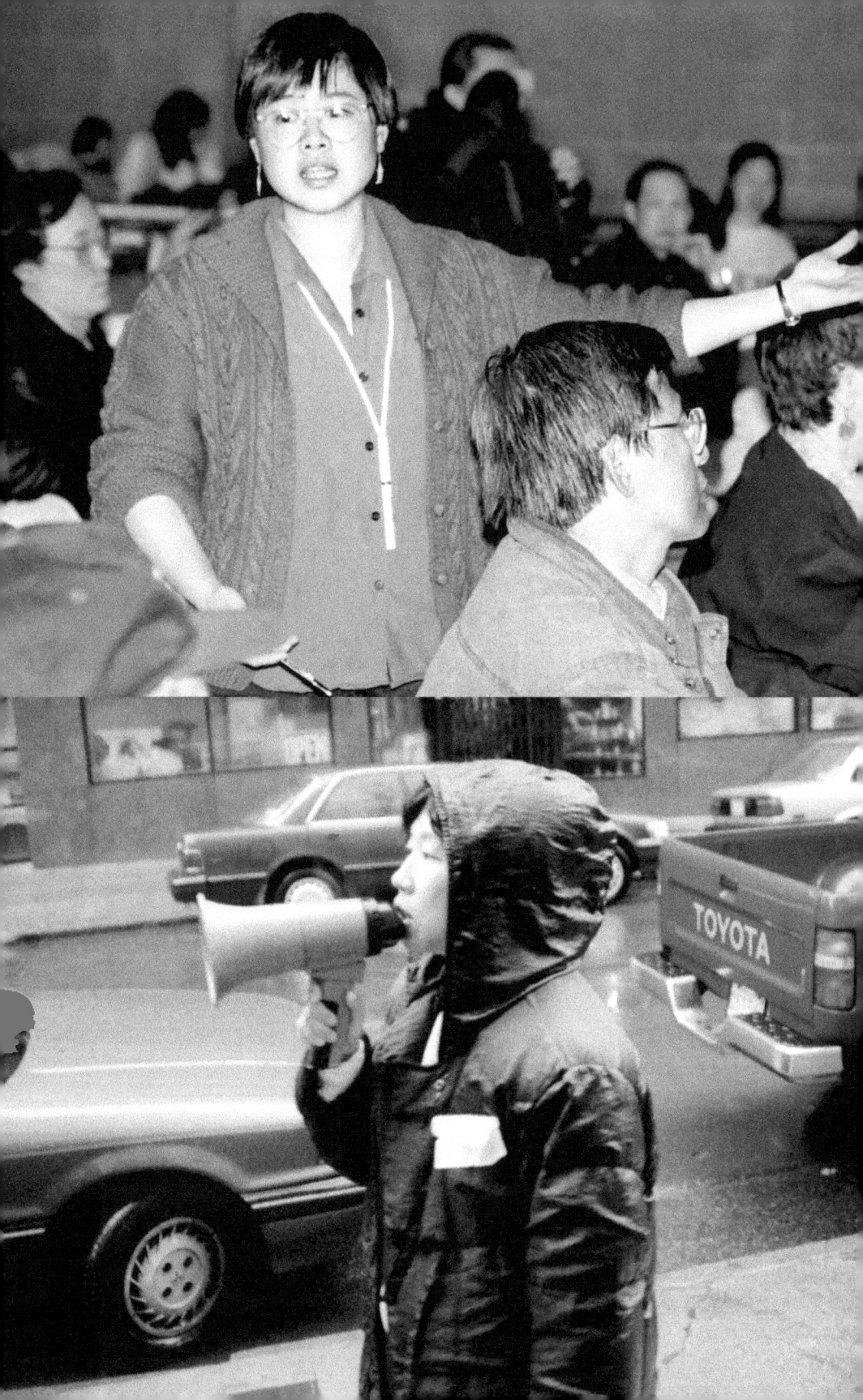

But then as an adult, as I thought about it, I realized that it's really true that no matter what, you're always connected.

If society is racist and there's still inequality and Asian Americans as a whole are looked down upon and aren't able to exercise any power in society then that's going to affect individual Asian Americans and how they're perceived and what they can rise to and how they can feel about themselves.

So I think I came around to my interest in the community that way.

I got involved in volunteering in San Francisco Chinatown. Initially there was a Chinese Progressive Association there. They're not the same organization as the one here but they've had a similar history.

At that time they were fighting the eviction of this big hotel called the International Hotel. I don't know if you've heard about it but it was like one of the last blocks of old Manila Town.

It was sort of like Chinatown and old Manila Town. It was a single-room occupancy hotel with a lot of old timers, and the landlords were trying to evict them.

I guess I got involved in '76 and then they got evicted in '77. But there was a really huge citywide movement to support the tenants. The eviction was carried out very brutally.

They rented police from throughout the area and used horses because the protesters created a human barricade around the hotel. Then they used horses to charge the barricade.

That was a very heavy experience. I think that going through an experience like that just made me feel more strongly about social change.

After that I moved to New York for a couple of years. I moved to New York, one, because I was interested in seeing the East Coast and knew I was born in New York but had never been there since I was a baby. So I wanted to see it.

And the other thing was, I had been very involved in founding the Asian Pacific Student Union on the West Coast, which is like an inter-campus network of Asian college organizations.

And the East Coast Asian Student Union, which was founded around the same time, was having a lot of problems and was kind of falling apart, so we talked about it and some people were saying, "Oh, we need more people to go to the East Coast to help pull ECASU back together."

I said, "Ok, I'll go," so I moved to New York and went to Brooklyn College for a year and then switched to City College. That was in '79. So I was there from '79 to '81.

Then I got lonely in New York so I moved to Boston in 1981 because a friend of mine had moved here.

When I came to Boston I looked up the CPA and started volunteering. I went to UMass Boston, which was where I finished college, and then I volunteered at CPA for a while.

I wasn't really that involved but I was supportive and volunteered pretty regularly. I got involved in doing campus organizing at UMass and helped start the Asian Center there.

Then I volunteered for the Sampan because I was interested in writing. That was '82, '83. Writing some articles for the Sampan was good for me because it gave me the opportunity to learn more about the community. I think I covered the SCM building issue.

I remember interviewing different people on the street. I interviewed some youth and interviewed Billy Chin — who was looking at me like, who are you?

But I think the turning point for me getting more involved was at the end of 1985 when Long Guang Huang was beaten by the police. That was just like really outrageous. I was somewhat involved in the support committee.

He was just a small elderly man and he was walking down Washington Street, which then was still the height of the Combat Zone (the adult entertainment district) — he was walking down the street and then as far as he understood it, all of a sudden this big, six-foot-something white guy just jumped on him and started beating him up, and he didn't know what was going on.

That guy was a plain-clothes police detective named Kelly, and he said that Mr. Huang had been soliciting a prostitute.

And as Mr. Huang was being beat up all the eyewitnesses said that this prostitute turned around and said, "Kelly, Kelly, you got the wrong guy, it's the wrong guy!

So apparently Kelly had some deal going with this prostitute and was helping her beat up a john but got the wrong guy.

So it was just a really outrageous incident that made people in the community really feel like — if you're not safe walking down the street in your own community, where can you be safe?

I think it was shocking for a lot of immigrants who thought that the police were supposed to protect you to see that the police were beating him up and then denying it and charging him with assault and battery on a police officer.

And I think a lot of youth were really upset too because they felt they were always being harassed by the police and it was kind of like the last straw to them.

So the community was just really angry. We used to go to the court to support Mr. Huang. Finally the court said that Mr. Huang was right, so the city had to pay him some money.

Later that year, P&L Sportswear closed. It was one of the largest garment shops in the area at the time. There was a period when all these garment shops were shutting down.

At the time it closed, 400 women were thrown out of work (at one time there were 1,000 working there). Most of the work was being sent overseas.

I got involved in the garment workers support committee to try and help them advocate for job retraining.

After the plant shut down, they wanted to get job training. One worker's son saw on TV that the Colonial Workers had experienced a shut down at about the same time and the city had set up a workers assistance center to facilitate their getting placed into job training programs as quickly as possible and get their unemployment processed quickly.

So the P&L workers were, 'Well, how come nobody's doing anything for us?' They came to CPA and asked us if we could help them figure this out.

So they started organizing and the more they organized, the more they were just being told, 'All you can do is study English. It will take you years before you can learn enough English to really get a job.'

And yes they really did need to study English, that's true, but the attitudes that they were getting from people were just really arrogant; they were really just being dismissed and disrespected.

And it was only after organizing and demonstrating that money was released and a RFP (Request for Proposal) was released and so on.

And throughout that process the workers were fighting for a voice in what kind of training they wanted.

And the agencies they were dealing with continued to refuse to allow them that voice and just implied — not even implied — but just said, 'That's not your job; professionals need to do that.'

They were basically telling these women, 'You don't have any role in this because you're not professionals; only professional training agencies can deal with these kinds of questions, so just go home.'

They also implied that the support committee must be putting them up to this. 'Because you guys don't have any ideas of your own.'

So it was really infuriating to the workers and also to the support committee because the more that we worked with the workers committee, the more we saw that these women had very clear ideas about what they wanted.

And it was a really transforming experience for them to see how important it was for them to speak up and to prove that this is our own idea and we want a say.

And it was also a real learning experience for supporters like myself to see how important it is to have that kind of grassroots organizing.

Through these two experiences I got much more involved in CPA. After the P&L garment workers were able to get their job training, the support committee and the workers committee decided to start an ongoing workers center.

We were talking about how we should get grant money and hire staff to do it. And people asked me if I wanted to work in the workers center, and I said yes, and I've been here ever since.

I think that Chinatown is really disenfranchised. It's been here for like 125 years but it's always been voiceless politically. As a result, it's lost more than half of its land and the people here have never had the clout to get their issues addressed for city services and jobs.

I think language is part of it, but I think it's a history of oppression of racial minorities too.

People who came from the Third World, from under-developed countries dominated by imperialism, came here and a similar kind of history occurred.

And even if you're here over generations and know English, you stand out more, so you're not as assimilate-able as European immigrants.

I think there is a whole history of laws and racial violence that went along with enforcing that.

And that legacy remains today. A lot of inequalities remain today. I mean the racism recently with this furor about the Chinese jet and the U.S. spy plane. It's just amazing!

There's a radio station in Texas calling for a boycott of all Chinese restaurants. Some of the people on our youth committee have also been complaining.

When one guy goes to school his classmates were all giving him a hard time, saying, "Give us back our plane."

Another woman went to the BRA (Boston Redevelopment Authority) to do some research and the BRA staff person said the same thing to her.

So I think it's just below the surface nowadays. There's still that clear connection that If you look Asian then you're never really an American, no matter if you've lived here for generations.

So I see it as an oppressed community which is part of its history and also part of how Boston politics works.

At the same time I also see that for the community to really be able to organize and fight for equality and fight for a stronger voice there has to be changes within the community as well.

I think that the dominant leadership within the community over the years has had a losing strategy to advance the community's interests.

I think it's the approach of the Chin brothers. I think that their strategy seems to be to turn out the vote, support the winning politicians, and try to get benefits from them, some good things for the community, some people placed in jobs (their people).

It's all part of a strategy to have those connections at City Hall, but I don't think they're just doing it for themselves.

I mean they certainly gain a lot for themselves because it's also in their financial interest, but I think they're also motivated by a concern for the community.

I think, for instance, that having Frank Chin as the city's purchasing agent was certainly a beneficial position if you want to run a small business.

So I think on the one hand there have been some gains. They have been able to get some things for Chinatown and they've also been able to get people into City Hall — their own people — but I think that it hasn't resulted in significant changes for the community as a whole.

I think the Parcel C garage issue was a good example of the problem with the dominant leadership strategy. It was like, just be cynical, get what you can, get whatever money you can that's being offered.

Let them do anything they want to us, even though it was clear the community didn't really want that garage.

That's why at CPA we're trying to organize people on a more grassroots level. The goal isn't just to get some individuals into more influential positions but to really get people on a broader level more involved in decision making and being able to exercise more political power.

Last night's hearing was a good example. We helped organize this City Council hearing on political access.

And one of the main things that we called for was multilingual access to all public meetings and hearings sponsored by the City, so that people could go to City Council meetings, school committee meetings, BRA hearings, zoning and licensing hearings, whatever, and the city would provide interpreting equipment and have a pool of interpreters you could order in advance. That way you could actually participate in the meeting.

And that's a small thing which actually wouldn't cost a lot of money but would give people much more access. One of the reasons that people a lot of times don't vote is because they don't know enough about what's going on in local politics.

This would allow people to actually have a voice when they're discussing housing or zoning or something that matters to them.

To us, that's an important approach to gaining community clout. It's saying that political power shouldn't just be about getting an individual Asian into office and turning out lots of voters and telling them how to vote, but it should be about the community really learning about who makes the decisions that affect their lives and having the means to go out and demand the things they want and the policies that they want and feel they can accomplish that.

It also involves electing officials or getting people into positions where they can push for things they want. I think it's a very different approach to building political clout.

Frank Chin came to last night's hearing and spoke at the end. He said, "I've been doing voter registration for 30 years," which is true, but he hasn't been doing voter education, which is a different thing.

We have opposing strategies but in a way we're working towards a similar goal.

Today everybody likes to say everything is fine with the institutions (Tufts University Medical School and the New England Medical Center) – the institutions are good neighbors, they're done expanding.

But I think even today they continue to have that kind of arrogant approach to the community. Like right now with Tufts' new (Jeharis) building. I think a lot of the community doesn't know what their rights are and how to deal with these things.

Building that giant building was approved because it's part of their (Tufts) master plan and had been approved by the Chinatown Neighborhood Council and the BRA.

But a lot of the ordinary residents and the building owners around there were not really part of that process.

It's a lot harder to fight fights like that within your own community. If it's not something that people see as really immediately hurting them, they're not really going to get up in arms about something and fight people in their community that they don't really want to go up against.

When restaurant workers didn't get paid, CPA was willing to picket Dynasty or fight the Lei Jing Restaurant or Grand China.

And there were even other people in the community that were willing to support us.

But a lot of people wouldn't take a side even though it was clearly outrageous and indecent that these people weren't paid.

And when we started the pledge for community labor standards, we actually got a lot of flack for that. Even a lot of workers on our committee started having questions about that, whether it was the best strategy.

They felt we shouldn't be targeting restaurants that haven't done anything wrong yet.

It's the workers committee that runs the workers center and makes the decisions, and the workers were torn about whether that was the right strategy.

Unless it's something that is really extreme and happening and hurting a known individual, then people are reluctant to take it up.

Generally CPA doesn't take up a fight that we don't think other people on a popular level are going to fight for.

We still believe in bringing the restaurants up to the standard and we're still doing a lot of workers rights education and helping workers fight those cases, but we haven't really aggressively pursued the pledge for community labor standards, which is more of a proactive pledge campaign.

People were calling the workers troublemakers and saying, 'What are you doing? These restaurants didn't do anything wrong.'

And then I said, 'Well, let's just publicize and reward those businesses that are doing the right thing by signing on.

And then businesses started saying, 'Oh, I signed that a year ago, but don't put my name out now.'

Because they were getting a lot of pressure from the Business Association and other business owners, who were saying, 'Why did you sign that pledge?'

They (the business owners) didn't directly talk to us, but the Chinatown Business Association met with us, and they are pretty tight with those owners.

They were really upset. They told us, 'If there's a problem, why don't you just come to us and we'll help you resolve it?

'But don't air our dirty laundry in public. Once you start opening this can of worms you're going to let out the fact that we paid people under the table.

'But everybody does it. Every restaurant does it. So why are you just targeting Chinatown?

'The suburban restaurants are worse? But just because we're visible and we're in Chinatown we have to be held to a higher standard.'

They were saying every Chinese restaurant does it but actually a lot of other restaurants do it (under-report wages) too.

They don't completely pay people under the table usually — usually they under-report the wages and don't pay full taxes.

I think most immigrants' goal is just to have a better life as a family and have a home and education for their kids. But I think that when they come here it doesn't meet their expectations a lot of times; life's a lot harder than they expected.

They and their kids get alienated from each other, the education isn't as good as they thought it would be, and their work is much harder. It tears their families apart. All these things happen when people come here."

OLD LOYALTIES

Celebrating Hong Kong's Return

TO CELEBRATE OR NOT TO CELEBRATE? It's a question some Boston Chinese are asking themselves as 150 years of British colonial rule in Hong Kong comes to a close on July 1, 1997.

Most local Chinese feel a sense of pride that Hong Kong will no longer be ruled by a Western colonial power, but many are wary at the prospect of having the territory ruled by the same Chinese Communist Party whose troops opened fire on pro-democracy demonstrators eight years ago in Beijing's Tiananmen Square.

In Boston, the Committee of New England Chinese will celebrate the end of Western colonialism and the return of Hong Kong to the People's Republic of China with a banquet at the Grand China Restaurant in Chinatown.

Some members of the Chinatown community say they will attend the event, but others vow to sit this one out. Local representatives of the Taiwan Government say they won't attend and won't encourage others to attend either.

Some Chinese say that promoting Chinese nationalism rather than human rights in China is a mistake and plays into the hands of a Chinese Communist Party, which denies its citizens democratic rule and freedom of speech, assembly and the press.

Although some people say a generational change is looming within the Communist Party that could lead to more freedoms for the Chinese people, the Party in 1997 continues to jail pro-democracy dissidents such as Wei Jing-Sheng and Wang Dan.

Some Chinese say the Chinese Government is mounting a propaganda campaign in overseas Chinese communities as the turnover draws near to focus attention on the end of British colonial rule and pride in "the motherland" in part to deflect criticism from its own flawed human rights record and autocratic rule.

Boston's Chinese generally fall into three camps when responding to the Hong Kong turnover.

The first group wants to celebrate the end of Colonialism, which they consider a "slap in the face for all Chinese people." It's an attitude shared by almost all Chinese — even those who won't be celebrating the turnover — though it's the primary focus of the organizers of the Chinatown celebration who tend to be sympathetic to the People's Republic of China.

Among these organizations is the Chinese Progressive Association, whose board chairperson and founder, Suzanne Lee, has been invited by the PRC government to attend the Hong Kong ceremony.

"The PRC is trying to use this for a propaganda advantage...they want to stress there's 1,000 people to celebrate this one thing," says one local observer who wanted to remain anonymous.

Supporters of Taiwan and promoters of a democratic China offer another perspective. Local Taiwan supporters believe the people celebrating the turnover are being "used as puppets" by the PRC government. They welcome the end of colonialism but they believe the turnover has been spoiled by the involvement of the PRC.

"They don't like it because it's going back to the PRC," says the same person. "This group doesn't want their friends to participate in the celebration."

If Hong Kong were being returned to a non-communist government they would be celebrating with other Chinese.

A third group includes people who are indifferent to Asian politics. Their reaction to the turnover is: "So what? We're US citizens. We want to be good American citizens."

This group is made up largely of American-born or -raised Chinese and includes a fair number of Chinatown merchants who don't want to get involved in politics.

One young Chinese American says she hasn't any strong feelings about the return or about Hong Kong in general but believes it would be better if the territory wasn't being handed over to the mainland's communist regime.

Most Chinese believe the end of the colonial era is cause for celebration, says Tao Kai, the principal of the Cambridge Chinese School and an organizer of the Chinatown Hong Kong celebration.

Tao, who originally came to the U.S. as a visiting scientist from Beijing, says the celebration's organizers are trying to focus on the wrong done to the Chinese people by the opium trade and the ceding of Hong Kong to Great Britain after the Opium War.

"This return is a really important thing for Chinese," she says. "If you are a Chinese person you must feel that way."

Tao says it shouldn't matter if you are a communist or a democrat. If "you are a Chinese person, you must feel proud."

She says her group hasn't received any support from the Chinese Consulate in New York or from the Taiwan government. The organizers of the banquet, she says, are trying to keep politics out of the celebration by prohibiting the display of PRC or Taiwan flags at the event. "I'm a scientist," she says. "I really don't care about political things."

But it's not as simple as that. Tao is a member of the Chinese School

Association of the United States, a group that has been invited to the upcoming ceremonies in Hong Kong.

The group was invited after composing a congratulatory message to be presented to the Chinese government during the ceremonies.

Tao says the 1989 crackdown on students in Beijing, which was vigourously protested on the streets of Chinatown, was wrong, but she believes that every government makes mistakes. "I think that now they have maybe started to recognize they're not right," she says.

She says people shouldn't oversimplify conditions in China by characterizing the PRC government as simply oppressive. Such a characterization isn't always accurate.

When she lived in China, she says, she never felt that the government imposed excessive controls on the people.

"I didn't feel I couldn't do this, I couldn't do that," she says. "I think China is better than before."

Tao and others are encouraging members of the Chinese community to celebrate the return, but Thomas Cheng, director general of Taiwan's Taipei Economic and Cultural office in Boston, sees the situation differently.

Cheng sees no reason to attend the celebration, though he says he understands the feelings of many Chinese regarding the return.

"Of course I think this turnover of Hong Kong is a major event in the Chinese community," he says. "Most people think this is a good thing. We also think that."

At the same time, Cheng believes "there's no particular reason to celebrate this turnover" and says he has "no particularly strong feeling toward this."

If anything, he says, the turnover should be an occasion to remind the PRC to keep its commitment to the Hong Kong people by maintaining a "one country, two systems" policy and Hong Kong's current capitalist system for the next 50 years.

He says the PRC has offered Taiwan a similar two-system option as a condition for reunification with the mainland.

Cheng believes Hong Kong residents' greatest worry is losing their freedoms and rights after the turnover. People shouldn't forget that many of today's Hong Kong residents fled to the British colony to escape the Chinese communists, he says.

If Hong Kong were being handed over to a democratic government, says Cheng, people would have more reason to celebrate.

Cheng says the Taiwan government is eager to see a smooth transition in Hong Kong and China's honoring of the one-country, two-system policy.

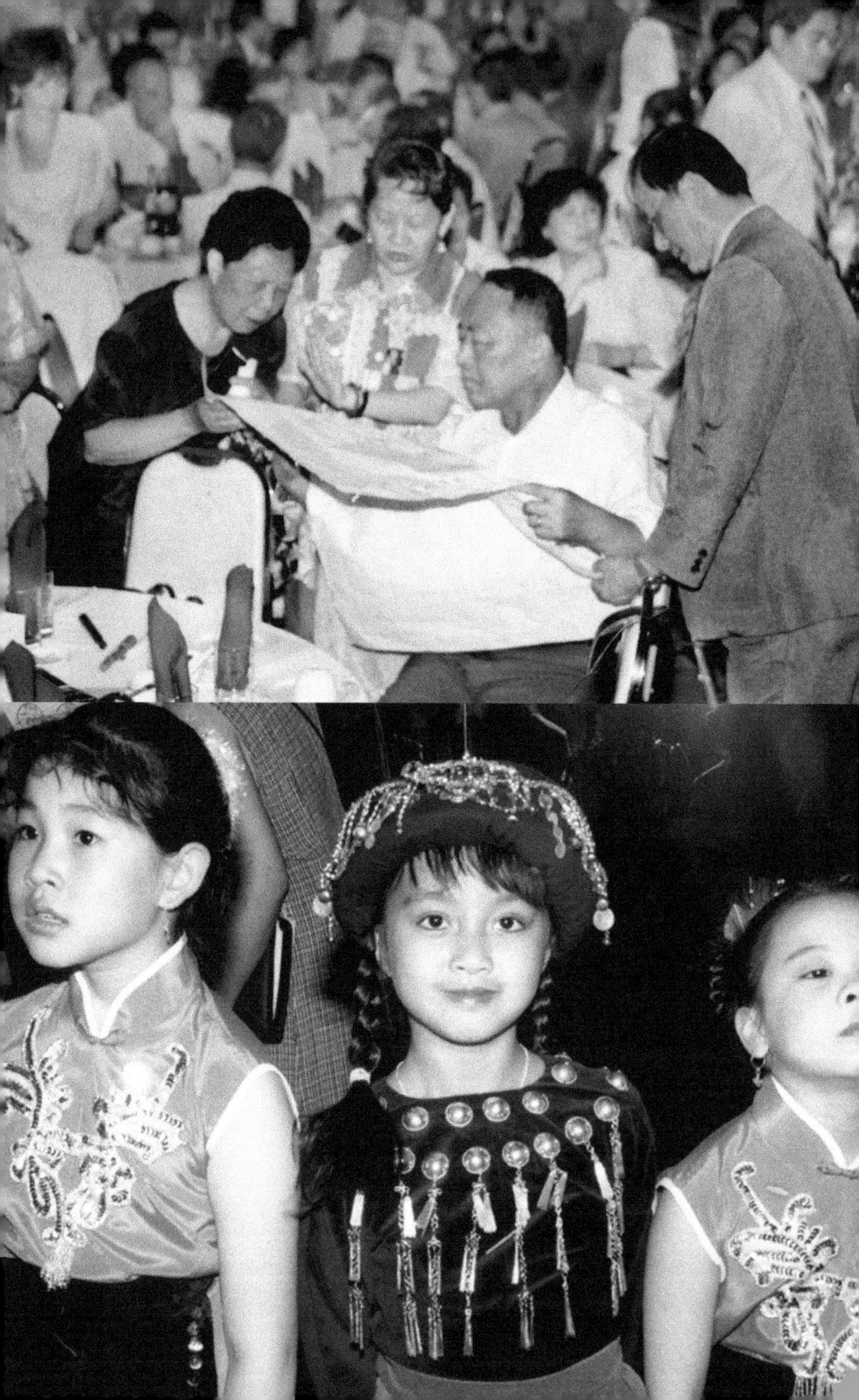

"I have mixed feelings about it because I lived there," says Yon Lee, whose family left China for Hong Kong when he was a child.

While the end of colonialism is cause for celebration, he says, his family fled to Hong Kong to escape communist rule. Now, he says, "those who escaped from China will be under the yoke again."

But he also understands the importance of celebrating the end of colonial rule. Under colonialism, Chinese were subjected to abuses by foreigners in their own country, he says. Older Chinese recall signs that read: "No dogs or Chinese allowed."

"There's no reason you can't celebrate the end of colonialism and still keep a watchful eye on things you believe should be changed in China," he says.

Lee says he isn't sure if he will attend the Chinatown celebration but realizes it may be hypocritical to take part in an event celebrating the return of Hong Kong to an autocratic regime, especially from the comfort of a democratic American city.

Shen Tong, who took part in the Tiananmen demonstrations of 1989 and escaped to the U.S. after the crackdown, believes the end of colonialism is a positive development but questions whether people should be celebrating turning Hong Kong over to the Chinese Communist Party. The turnover, he says, represents "the first time a free place is returned to a repressive regime."

Shen says true nationalism should be rooted in the belief that your country is providing a good life for its people. "I am not a nationalist," he says. "I would take individual human rights more seriously than national sovereignty."

He says the Chinese people shouldn't forget that the Communist Party still refuses to accept the free expression of opinion and criticism.

For years, many Chinese were eager to escape from China, preferring life in a British-controlled Hong Kong to life under the communist regime. Now many people are celebrating Hong Kong's return to China as an expression of patriotism.

"Even though it was under British rule, people thought it was safe and a better place to bring up their kids," says Wilson Lee, president of the Chinese Consolidated Benevolent Association.

But Lee says he isn't unduly concerned about the effect that Chinese rule will have on Hong Kong. "I was born in Hong Kong and I see it as a good thing," he says.

"Colonialism was shameful ... It's an embarrassment for all Chinese everywhere, but of course people have reservations."

"A lot of young people (including American-born Chinese) look at Hong Kong as an opportunity," he says.

Many Chinese are also hoping that ongoing economic development in China will eventually lead to a less autocratic government there and that Hong Kong's economic vitality will deter China's rulers from disrupting the territory's current way of life.

Still, Lee worries that China's takeover of Hong Kong will probably make the territory's residents more reluctant to demonstrate publicly against government policies.

"I don't think people who were willing to speak out in '89 will speak out now," he says. "Is that good? I don't think so."

The Taiwan-Mainland Divide in Chinatown

IT'S SEPTEMBER 1999, just days away from the Taiwan Government's Double Ten (October 10) national day celebration in Chinatown.

The Chinese Consolidated Benevolent Association has traditionally organized the national day events in Boston but this year a competing organization has taken over leadership of the festivities.

In the past, the CCBA organized the national day parade through the streets of Boston, which starts in Chinatown with an elaborate dragon dance and ends with a flag-raising ceremony at Boston City Hall.

Organizing the Double Ten events and Chinatown's Chinese New Year and August Moon (Mid-Autumn Festival) celebrations on the streets of Chinatown were symbols of the Benevolent Association's leadership role in the community.

But recent events have altered the Benevolent Association's standing in the community, while a growing number of immigrants from mainland China has led to growing support for the People's Republic of China in the overseas community.

This year's Double Ten celebration is being organized by the Double Ten Celebration Committee, whose members include Billy Chin, Bing Wong and Kai Lau.

Chin and Lau say the organizers of the events include people from the Chinatown and suburban Chinese communities. "This is the first time in a long long time it has been organized by another organization," says Lau.

Benevolent Association president Robert Leung says CCBA will hold its own celebration in Chinatown on Oct. 10, though the event this year will be called Chinese Heritage Day and make no specific reference to Taiwan's national day. At the top of a poster advertising the event is a picture of Dr. Sun Yet Sen — a figure revered by both the Taiwan and mainland governments.

In the past, says Leung, CCBA supported only Taiwan, but changing times requires the organization to be open now to the community's China and Taiwan supporters, he says.

It's rumored in Chinatown that Leung and CCBA aren't as loyal to the Republic of China as they once were because of pressures from PRC supporters.

In recent years, Chinatown's factional fighting has led to the emergence of the Chinatown Business Association to compete with the Benevolent Association. The Business Association has held competing Chinese New Year and August Moon festivals.

And while the Business Association isn't formally organizing the Double Ten events, some of its members are members of the Double Ten Celebration committee.

Chin says the Double Ten committee organized its own events this year because CCBA's current leadership isn't "open enough" to the broader Chinese community.

He also believes CCBA wasn't especially eager to hold the celebration. "I think the CCBA hesitated over whether they were going to do it," says Chin.

In addition to Chinatown factional disputes, long-standing tensions between supporters of the Republic of China on Taiwan and the People's Republic of China have also played a role in the Benevolent Association's absence from the traditional Double Ten events this year.

When Chinese Premier Zhu Rongji visited Boston and gave a speech at M.I.T. this year, Leung attended the event.

And when a picture of Leung and Zhu appeared in the Chinese newspapers, some members of the community concluded that "the CCBA president was leaning toward the People's Republic of China," says Lau.

Leung was also recently involved in another incident that sparked controversy in the Chinese community.

While it's customary for CCBA to invite the director general of the Taipei Economic and Cultural Office to the August Moon Festival in Chinatown, this year an invitation wasn't extended to the current director general, Thomas Cheng.

Cheng attended the event anyway and was invited up to the stage but ended up leaving in protest when Wilson Lee introduced a visiting official from the PRC consulate without extending the same courtesy to Cheng.

The PRC official had been invited to the event to accept a Red Cross check to aid flood victims in China.

Cheng says Leung told him he wasn't invited to the August Moon Festival because the organizing committee felt he favored the Chin-supported faction in Chinatown over his own group.

But Cheng believes he wasn't invited to the event because the organizers had already decided to invite the mainland officials.

"I left the stage to protest because I felt the organizing committee was not telling people the truth," says Cheng.

Cheng says that "traditionally CCBA has never invited the other side's officials" to these Chinatown events. "I had to tell the organizing committee where I stood," he says.

Cheng says he tries to avoid offending either group involved in the current Chinatown feuding. He says he attended the August Moon Festival to show his support for CCBA even though he hadn't been formally invited.

"We want to support CCBA and other groups as long as they're doing good things for the community," he says.

But Cheng says the current CCBA leadership hasn't been a productive force in Chinatown affairs.

"I'm sorry to say that CCBA has failed its duty and its mission," he says. "It's almost dysfunctional...The majority of the people in the community do not recognize CCBA as the leader of the community. It does not enjoy the leadership status anymore in this community."

Cheng says Robert Leung is no longer a recognized leader in many sectors of the local Chinese community. "I would say he may be the most controversial chairman in CCBA history," he says. "He has a dispute with almost every group in the community."

Cheng also believes that Leung has tried to develop closer relations with mainland China in part because of his business dealings there. Leung is the local distributor of Chung Hua Beer, which is imported from China.

Leung also angered many members of the community in the early 1990s when he invited the governor of Guangdong Province to Boston. At the time, Leung was chairman of the Guangdong Family Association

"He cannot separate his business and community affairs clearly," Cheng says. "So people feel he's more left leaning."

Cheng says many people "don't think he is the right person to preside over the Double Ten celebration."

The timing of CCBA's decision to present the flood-aid check at the August Moon Festival was also questioned. "Why didn't he give it sooner?" says Billy Chin. "One year later?"

Leung, meanwhile, has his own interpretation of recent events, saying he met earlier with local Taiwan officials and people such as Bing Wong and was told they didn't want CCBA to organize the Double Ten events this year. "They said they had a group to do the job," he says. "They don't want CCBA to do it."

Leung says Cheng was not invited to the Aug 15th August Moon festival because the Taiwan office didn't want CCBA to organize the celebration. "This is why CCBA didn't invite him," he says.

Leung contends that his opponents want to control Chinatown and that personal issues are at the center of the ongoing disputes.

He also says that Taiwan officials here have broken a community rule by favoring one group over another — a charge that Cheng has denied.

Leung rejects the charges that he is against Taiwan and that his business interests have motivated him to support China. "We're not against Taiwan," he says. "Taiwan still belongs to China. It's just a different government."

He says it's important for CCBA to remain open to Chinese from both China and Taiwan. "It's not the way it used to be," he says.

Leung says his business interests shouldn't be an issue because Bing Wong — who founded Biopure in Massachusetts — also does business in China now.

While overseas Chinese have traditionally been pro-Taiwan, Taiwan's influence in some sectors of the overseas community appears to be weakening for several reasons, according to Lau.

Economic and political changes in China have gradually increased the number of mainland Chinese living in Chinese communities here. These immigrants have come to the U.S. in part to seek freedom and the economic opportunities available in a capitalistic system — but many also remain loyal in spirit to the PRC.

On China's national day (Oct 1), the PRC flag was flying outside the Chinese Progressive Association in Chinatown while the Taiwan flag was flying from the building beside it, where the Taiwan government has a cultural center.

Lau says economics plays a role in determining people's allegiances now. Many local Chinese are doing business in China and are eager to show their support for it.

For example, many Chinese markets in the Boston area import foodstuffs from China, he says.

In the past mainland China's national day wasn't celebrated publicly by Chinese in the U.S., but for the last few years local groups have organized a flag-raising event at Boston City Hall.

Although mainland officials have a less visible presence in Chinatown than their Taiwanese counterparts, they tend to work behind the scenes with their supporters, who have arranged welcoming parties and events for visiting Chinese officials such as Zhu Rongji and Jiang Zemin.

The Chinese Progressive Association, the Shanghai Merchants Association, the Cambridge Center for Chinese Culture, and other groups were set to sponsor a China festival and flag-raising event at City Hall Plaza in September.

WHAT LASTS?

The Future of Chinese Culture in America

THE CHILDREN OF CHINATOWN'S Kwong Kow Chinese School repeat after the teacher in Cantonese:

We are overseas Chinese, we are overseas Chinese.

The exercise is meant to instill in the children a strong sense of Chinese identity.
The idea is that the children can be both Chinese and American simultaneously.
At home and in their hearts they are Chinese, but outside — in the society — they have their American experience, as one teacher put it.

Some Chinese have even started to use the term "American Chinese" instead of "Chinese American" to describe the Chinese in America.
The adults say they do this in part to offset the negative effects of Chinese children being taken for foreigners even if they're born here.
Some Americans see a Chinese face and assume that person isn't American. In their minds, Americans are either white or black.

Strengthening the children's Chinese identity gives them a stronger sense of self-worth when their American identity is called into question, the adults say.
But the children, says the school's principal, often reject the idea of being Chinese first. They say, "We are Americans."

The Chinese in America created Chinese schools to teach their children Chinese language and culture. Even some third or fourth generation Chinese Americans still send their children to the schools to expose them to their cultural roots.

After school and on weekends, the children spend part of their free time bent over desks scratching Chinese characters into notebooks.
The teacher's voice booms. The learning style is traditional Chinese. The teacher has an almost militaristic demeanor, ruling over a classroom filled with children who sit attentively at their desks.

The children are here to work and listen, to follow the orders of the teacher; they're here for serious business, they're not here to be entertained.

But while the first generation strives to preserve their root culture in America, American life has a way of diluting it over time.

When the Chinese community celebrates the Mid-Autumn Festival in Chinatown, they usually do it in the middle of August — but the moon festival falls much later in China.

According to tradition, the festival occurs on the fifteenth day of the eighth lunar month, and in 1996 that date is September 27.

In Boston, the festival is held during the eighth month of the solar calendar and has been renamed the August Moon Festival.

Chinatown businessmen decided to hold the festival on a Sunday in August so that more people would attend and visit their restaurants. Summer is a relatively slow time for the restaurant business and a summer street festival provides a much-needed jolt to business.

Such changes in old world traditions tend to be the norm in America. When traditions cross the ocean and take up residence in the United States, they often lose their deepest significance and become more decorative than authentic.

"I think the way Chinatown celebrates August Moon Festival is very misleading," says Renee Chen Lu, of the Greater Boston Chinese Cultural Association. "It's conducted like a flea market."

Lu says the true meaning of the festival tends to be lost in its American incarnation.

In China, the Mid-Autumn Festival is a time to remember the beauty of the night moon and hear the myths and storytelling associated with it. The roots of the festival are ancient and romantic, but in America the local businesses turn it into marketing, commercializing its mythical content.

Lu says Chinese culture in its purest form is slowly being eroded in the U.S. "It's probably an inevitable thing," she says.

Both of her children know how to speak Chinese, but their Chinese is not as good as their English, she says. They like eating Chinese food, but they don't want to eat it every day.

"After two or three generations, you cannot tell the difference" between Chinese Americans and other Americans, she says.

Lu says she doesn't expect her children to live as she did while growing up in a strictly Chinese environment in Taiwan. "They're living in a different society," she says.

Children may develop resentments if their parents demand they adhere too strictly to the traditional culture. "The parents should be careful not to put too much pressure on the children because that will have an adverse effect," she says.

At the same time, she says, it's important to give children a sense of their identity as Chinese so they won't be disheartened when people take them for foreigners or view them as less than full-fledged Americans.

Lu is optimistic that over time this "will become less of an issue." As Asians appear more frequently in the media and the arts and gain more prestigious positions in American society, the idea of what an American looks like will also change.

"Gradually they will accept that Asians are a part of American society as well and they will not treat Asians as foreigners or immigrants," she says.

Lu's organization — The Greater Boston Chinese Cultural Association — educates people about Chinese culture.

"We try to pass on those elements of culture we think are good for individuals and society," she says. "The hope is that American culture can "incorporate some of the valuable elements of other ethnic groups."

Children growing up in Chinatown tend to absorb more Chinese culture than their peers in the suburbs.

In Chinatown, traditional festivals continue to be celebrated. Lion dances are performed at most major events. The Chinese language is used daily in the shops.

Many Chinatown young people shuffle between using English and Chinese with their friends while speaking mostly Chinese at home with their parents.

Helen Luu, a high school student from the Chinatown area, says she speaks Chinese at home, eats Chinese food, and observes Chinese festivals with her family and friends.

But her favorite festival is Christmas because it allows her to exchange gifts with her friends.

She and her friends have also internalized another essential American idea: they "just want a little more freedom," she says.

Doris Chu, director of the Chinese Culture Institute in Chinatown, believes Chinese are facing fewer obstacles in the U.S. as American society becomes increasingly diverse and less Eurocentric.

"It is very natural for them (young Chinese-Americans) to be part of the country, the society," she says. "In fact, it's more difficult for them to be Chinese."

The trouble is that non-Chinese sometimes draw attention to their race. "Sometimes the other kids will remind them and that is the hard part for them," she says.

But Chu believes such incidents are becoming less of a problem as America becomes more racially and ethnically diverse.

She recently studied the history of Asian immigrants in the U.S. for a play she was writing. She says she was struck by how dramatically life for Chinese here has changed over the last 100 years.

When Chinese first came to the U.S., Americans were critical of Chinese food, but today it's available everywhere and admired for its healthful qualities.

"I have a great deal of hope for this society," says Chu. "I only see things changing for the better."

Free to Think about Who I am

YAHUI KU WORKS AS AN EDUCATIONAL coordinator at the Chinese Progressive Association in Chinatown.

The Taiwanese-born Ku came to the U.S. in the 1990s to attend graduate school at Simmons College.

She talks about her experience in America and her effort to balance the values of the two cultures in her daily life.

"I don't know if you'd call us middle class. My father was a policeman and my mother didn't work.

I'm the only child in my family who went to college in Taiwan, so maybe my parents love me the most. I'm the youngest one and the pride of my parents.

Chinese think education is the most important thing. I think I was lucky because it's hard to go to college in Taiwan. It's very competitive. You have to pass the examination.

I was the only person in my family who passed the exam and went to a very good college in Taiwan.

But my three sisters are still really good, even though they didn't pass the exam. Not passing the exam doesn't mean they are bad.

I think materially we have everything in Taiwan, but in terms of choices we don't have that many — especially the kids. Their future is set by the parents — by the whole society.

The Chinese believe the only way you can become an important person and make a lot of money and have a good life is through education. And if you don't have education you are nobody.

When I was in Taiwan I couldn't really think about what I wanted from my life. I just followed the path. I went to college.

It was only after I came to America that I began to think about what I really wanted and who I really am. In Taiwan no one really thinks about that.

Even though my sisters have their own families I'm sure they still don't know

what they want. Everybody just follows the path. The whole society sets the path.

I think maybe it's the culture. Chinese are supposed to have a good education. A person is supposed to do this and do that. In Taiwan I don't think you see many individualists.

When I was in children's literature I read a lot of books about teenagers and how they come of age and how they figure out who they are and what they want from their lives.

I began to think about myself in that way too. When I was in Taiwan I never thought like that; I never thought very much about who I am; I just followed the other people.

I figured out that people in Taiwan don't think about these things because they are in their homeland and they don't need to change their thinking.

But now I'm wondering if that is really good — maybe it's not. People just do things but they don't really think about what they're doing.

I also learned a lot from my relationships here. When I was with my boyfriend in Taiwan I acted like a traditional girlfriend, and when I came here I treated my ABC (American-born Chinese) boyfriend the same way.

But obviously they're different from the Taiwanese. I learned a lot from my relationship here. I realized that the relationship between the two sexes is different from what it is in Taiwan.

What the guy here expects from his girlfriend is different from what the Taiwanese guy expects. It's very subtle.

When you say to a guy in Taiwan, 'Drive carefully,' it means you're being thoughtful and you really care about that person. But if you say this to an ABC, he will think, 'Oh, you are not confident in my driving.'

Even though I meant well by saying it, he will think I said it because I don't believe him, I don't trust him. So I have to adjust myself in many ways here.

American culture, of course, has its own strengths and I want to learn more about them. I want to adjust what I have learned from Chinese culture — especially the idea that you follow others.

I want to have my own thinking. I want to be myself. The strength of American culture is its emphasis on individualism and having your own voice.

But its weakness is that people are too individualistic, too self-centered. This is what I cannot stand.

When I was in a relationship with a guy here, I thought, oh, this guy is too self-centered. I'm a very traditional Chinese who would be willing to do whatever for my boyfriend, even sacrifice myself.

But I don't think an ABC will do that. To them, they will always come first. A traditional Taiwanese woman will think her husband, the family comes first.

I'd like to find some combination of these two ways. I'm still thinking about it, though. I'm still adjusting myself; I'm still trying to decide which way I should go.

Education is also different here. In Taiwan the teacher is the authority. You can ask the teacher questions, but you cannot question the teacher.

But here you can question the teacher; here the teacher is more like someone who supports your education.

In Taiwan the teacher is high up there. A teacher may think: If you don't understand something that is your problem; you can ask me and I can answer you, but I'll think you're dumb for asking such a question. The result is you end up not understanding it.

But here the teachers are very friendly; they will support you in any way. You can ask them whatever dumb question you want and they won't look down on you.

I think the American way is better because students get closer to the teacher and are more willing to explore other fields.

When I was in Taiwan I never asked the teacher questions. If I didn't understand something I would just try to find the answer by myself, or I would ask my friends. But here teachers are more like your friend.

But I also think Americans need to have a more global view. They still think America is the most important place in the world. Their idea is that you guys have to learn things from us and we don't have to learn things from the other countries and other cultures.

Their idea is: everyone in the world has to learn English, but we don't have to learn Chinese.

In the media there's not even much news from around the world; most of the news is about local events. They're kind of isolated.

The people you meet on the street don't even know where Taiwan is or where Japan is. When I came here I realized they hardly talk about Asia. They probably pay more attention to Europe.

But the world is changing. I think Americans need to know more about what happens in other parts of the world. I think it's especially important in America, where there are racial problems.

I think it's important for Americans to learn more about South America and Asia because there are so many Hispanic and Asian people here.

If I decide to stay here I think I would be very careful about choosing a school for my kids. I think the most important thing is to give them more confidence in being Asian American.

I feel comfortable here because I grew up in Taiwan. I didn't feel any discrimination growing up.

But I know that a lot of ABC friends who grew up here don't feel comfortable because people discriminate against them. They are very sensitive about things like that.

But just because I feel pretty comfortable here doesn't mean the situation doesn't exist. If I stay here I would educate my kids about it.

I think the Chinese and Taiwanese are not satisfied with their governments. That's why the Chinese are all over the world. I think it's bad to be Chinese at this point.

Taiwan, Hong Kong, mainland China — none of these are really perfect places for people.

Look at Chinese history. There were so many wars, and the emperors were bad, and the people were poor and didn't have enough to eat.

The Taiwanese and the mainland Chinese have different reasons for being unhappy with their government.

The mainland Chinese don't have freedom, so of course they want to leave. I think they are not satisfied with communism, so they try to leave. Outside, they will have more opportunities to pursue their goals.

In Taiwan we have freedom, but we live under China's threat. The education system is bad and the country develops too slowly.

Taipei's traffic is so bad. The air pollution is so serious. People ride their motorcycles on the sidewalks. I personally think the government doesn't do a good job. That's why I want to stay here.

But I don't think Chinese culture is the problem. I think they (Chinese countries) will make it someday. I think Chinese culture has its own strengths. I really admire its emphasis on family values. I think it's the best.

Chinese value family a lot. That's why my father and my sisters put the money they earn back into the family; they never keep it for themselves; everyone works for their family; they are not selfish; the kids help each other out.

I have an American friend who doesn't have money to go to graduate school. Her sister has some money but she couldn't help her. I don't know why. My sister helped me, otherwise I couldn't be here. So I like the Chinese family concept.

But I also think the American people, the Western people, are more willing to follow the laws. They won't disobey the law, but the Chinese will.

Yes, there's a lot of crime in this country, but criminals are different. I'm talking about normal people.

Let's say you are riding in a car and you know you are required to use a seat belt. Most of the people here will wear the seat belt. But the Chinese — forget it. They will say, I don't care; if the police want to give me a ticket, I don't even care; I'll pay the fine.

Or take littering, for example. You are not supposed to throw your garbage on the street. If you do it the police will give you a ticket. But Chinese still do it. I don't know why. It's so weird.

I think the people in Chinatown are not that polite. They're rude. If they bump into you in Chinatown they won't say excuse me.

And if they want to buy something they don't even line up. If you go to a Chinese restaurant they throw the food at you; they are not friendly.

But if you go to an Italian restaurant or a French restaurant they're so nice, so friendly.

Chinese are taught to be polite. In Taiwan I was very polite. I would say thank you to a bus driver; I would say thank you to everybody.

But I guess people are different; it depends on how you are educated. They don't have that much education.

I may be wrong but I think some Chinese don't really respect their careers. If a waiter liked being a waiter he would probably have a better attitude. They make you feel like you owe them something. They can be very mean to the customers.

I think Chinese are more bureaucratic. They'll do a job even though they may not really like it. They use the power of their position to manipulate people. I worked in the public schools, and I heard a lot from the Chinese teachers. They manipulate their own people.

Confucius taught Chinese that they have to be polite, but we don't have that kind of spirit anymore. I think it's a shame. We are proud of being a polite country, but people are not polite anymore.

Maybe it's because we are changing — the social structure is changing.

Maybe it's because the Chinese were oppressed by the emperor for a long long time and are still almost enslaved by it. The emperor said: If you don't do this I'm going to kill you. So the people would obey.

But if you give people the freedom to do this or that, the people don't know how to control themselves — they don't know how to control their freedom.

That's why you see Taiwanese fighting in Congress. People are suddenly given freedom and they think they can do whatever they want. I think people really need to be re-educated.

Eight out of 10 times people cannot get what they really want. So you might ask, what's the point of your life?

I think I feel closer to Buddhism. In Buddhism, everything is based on suffering.

On Sunday I went to the Buddhist temple in Lexington. I went there to pray for my sister because she's going to have a baby. The position of the baby isn't right so I prayed for her.

I think Chinese society is Buddhist.

I believe in Buddhism but it doesn't control me. I won't go there every week to worship.

To me praying in a Buddhist temple is like having a lucky charm. I think maybe its true that everything is based on suffering.

But I'm still waiting - I'm waiting for a good relationship and a good paying job.

Working here (at CPA) is good but my eventual goal is to work in a school.

But nothing is perfect. Maybe Buddhists know that the world is based on suffering. They know that people can never satisfy their desires.

Many of the stories in "Neighborhood" originally appeared in a slightly different form in *Sampan*, a bilingual Chinese-English newspaper published in Boston's Chinatown since 1972.

RE O'Malley is a writer and photographer based in Massachusetts. He served as English editor of the *Sampan*, a bilingual Chinese-English newspaper in Boston, between 1989 and 1999. He is the author of *Dragon Bay: Stories from a Chinese Village*.

www.ingramcontent.com/pod-product-compliance
Ingram Content Group UK Ltd.
Pitfield, Milton Keynes, MK11 3LW, UK
UKHW020247240426
12048UKWH00027B/1653